AULD CAMPAIGNER
A Life of Alexander Scott

The publisher acknowledges support from the
Scottish Arts Council towards the publication of this title.

AULD CAMPAIGNER
A Life of Alexander Scott

Dr David Robb
Senior Lecturer, English, University of Dundee

DUNEDIN ACADEMIC PRESS
EDINBURGH

Published by
Dunedin Academic Press Ltd
Hudson House
8 Albany Street
Edinburgh EH1 3QB
Scotland

ISBN 978-1-903765-38-8

British Library Cataloguing in Publication Data
A catalogue record for this book is available from the British Library

Typeset in 10/13pt Sabon by Makar Publishing Production
Printed in Great Britain by Cromwell Press

To E, A and F ~ as always.

This time, however,
also to
D and B

Contents

Acknowledgements

My principal acknowledgement must be to my interviewees, who are listed elsewhere. Their careful consideration of my written queries and patient exploration of my face-to-face questions provided me with so much of whatever is worthwhile in this book. It was they who told me, between them, the story of Alexander Scott's life and helped me to understand his significance. In particular, it is surely not invidious to single out Catherine Scott and her son Crombie for their trusting honesty in recalling and commenting upon the husband and father who is still so much part of their lives. I hope that they recognise the man I describe, and that the account I give adds many positive things to their memories of him, and feelings for him. Cath Scott became one of my friends in the years after Alex asked me to help his family deal with his literary remains: to her I owe my basic understanding of the man, an understanding immensely deepened in comparison with my knowledge of him when he was alive. I also owe her gratitude for the access she provided to crucial documents before they were placed in the public domain. Gratitude, too, for many excellent lunches when I visited her in Kirklee Terrace. Friendship with Crombie came more recently, but he has been unfailing in his willingness to help both with his recollections and in practical matters such as the illustrations. It should be said, however, that this is in no way an 'official biography', by which I mean a telling of the story dictated by how the family would want the world to have it. Neither Cath nor Crombie wanted any such thing, and my other interviewees have seen to it that this account is as objective as I can make it, or at least as reflective of a variety of viewpoints as possible. The friendly co-operation of all these people has made this book simply the most enjoyable piece of academic research I have ever carried out.

There were many, too, whom I did not interview formally but with whom I had useful conversations, directly or by telephone, or with whom I corresponded by letter or email. Others, again, helped in a variety of ways. I wish to thank, in particular, James Aitchison, James Alison, Ian Begg, Jenny Brown, Bill Bruce, John Calder, the late Morven Cameron, Ian Campbell, John Corbett, Tom Craik, Robert Crawford, Nancy Davie, Joyce Dietz, Rita Edwards, Martin Garnett, the late Hazel Goodsir Smith, Rita Gordon, Penny Hartley, Douglas Kynoch, Mary-Catherine Lagan, Hilary Managh, Cate and Ken Newton, Donald and Brenda Rennie, Alan Riach, Michael Schmidt, Ally Shewan, Helen Watson and

Clara Young. John Blackie, Alan Dobson and Ken Newton read portions of the work at different stages of its development: I thank them particularly, knowing that I am myself responsible for any remaining inaccuracies or imperfections.

The other principal resource I have drawn upon has been the materials available in major libraries and archives. The National Library of Scotland has been my central resource (as ever) and I must thank, in particular, Robin Smith of the Manuscripts Division who first guided me towards the material I needed. The libraries of the four older Scottish universities, also, have been crucial. Above all, Glasgow University Archive Services, inevitably, contain much that I required and I must thank Moira Rankin and her colleagues for the able and friendly support they provided. The archive services of the universities of Edinburgh, Aberdeen and St Andrews also made me welcome with their full co-operation. It was a pleasure to make use of them. The same has to be said, also, of the staff and facilities of the BBC Written Archives Centre, Caversham Park, Reading and of the Public Record Office at Kew. Individuals, furthermore, have helped me get the best out of library resources. I must thank Maurice Lindsay for alerting me to the existence of the considerable archive of his papers in Edinburgh University Library, while Archie Duncan provided his invaluable knowledge of the official records of Glasgow University. Isobel Murray informed me of the richness of the BBC archives in Reading and Trevor Royle, as an expert military historian, prepared me for getting the best out of the material in the Public Record Office. My thanks, also, to John Calder for his kind permission to use the quotations from his book on pp. 163–4.

I am extremely grateful to the University of Dundee for granting me an extended period of study leave, which got the book off to a flying start. Equally important at that stage was a Small Research Grant from The British Academy, which enabled me to undertake the considerable amount of travel which proved necessary.

Dunedin Academic Press has been supportive from the beginning, even when the financial viability of the project was long in doubt. I am immensely grateful to Douglas Grant for all his help. I also wish to thank my copy editor Joanna Chisholm, and the book's indexer Alison Brown, both of whom substantially improved the text and were a pleasure to work with.

The author has attempted to trace the copyright holders of all material and illustrations reproduced in this volume and acknowledgements are given. In the event of any query, please contact the publisher.

And, finally, the apparently customary thanks to one's spouse is no mere matter of form. Elizabeth has allowed (as so often before) the needs of this book to dictate much of our day-to-day life during the past few years. I hope that she thinks the end result worth it.

Interviews

Donald Campbell	3 September 2004
Tom Crawford	30 September 2002
Alan and Jean Daiches	17 August 2004
Prof. Archibald A. M. Duncan	9 January 2003
Prof. Douglas Dunn	23 September 2003
Prof. T. Douglas Gifford	11 September 2003
Prof. Duncan Glen	20 September 2002
Dr John Herdman	13 January 2004
Prof. David Hewitt	16 June 2004
Prof. Philip Hobsbaum	31 August 2004
Prof. Ronald D. S. Jack	15 November 2002
Prof. Tom Leonard	17 December 2003
Dr Maurice Lindsay	10 September 2002
Dr Liz Lochhead	19 November 2004
Prof. Roderick Lyall	24 January 2003
Ellie MacDonald	8 September 2003
Robert MacDonald	15 November 2002
Prof. John MacQueen	9 October 2003
Prof. Edwin Morgan	5 September 2002
Prof. Isobel Murray	22 September 2003
Tessa Ransford	12 November 2004
Jack Rillie	28 June 2003
William B. Robertson	14 February 2003
Trevor Royle	8 January 2003
Catherine Scott	27 October, 15 and 29 November 2002, 18 September 2003
Crombie Scott	9 January 2003
Paul H. Scott	18 September 2002
Robert Tait	22 September 2003
Prof. Derick Thomson	7 November 2002

Syne there was brakkin o shields.
Drucken wi bluid, the fremmit men gaed breengan forrart.
But nou an auld campaigner shook his swurd
and stranglie spak til oor ain sodgers:
'Thocht maun be the harder, hert the keener,
smeddum the mair, for aa that oor micht is dwynan.'

Alexander Scott: 'Sang for a Flodden'

Most nationalist intelligentsias see themselves as the servants of a national *Geist*. They do not court metropolitan recognition; indeed, given their usual language loyalties, they cannot.

Christopher Harvie

Introduction

There are at least three reasons for a book on Alexander Scott. In the first place, he was for long one of Scotland's best-known and most popular poets, particularly during the 1950s, '60s and '70s, and so far there has been very little detailed discussion of him and his work. As well as being an invariable presence in the period's anthologies of Scottish verse and a regular and frequent contributor of poems to the literary journals then current in Scotland, he was also the author of seven books of verse in his lifetime. He wrote accessible, shapely, witty, heartfelt and entertaining verse in both English and (especially) Scots, and helped prolong into the 1960s and '70s the patriotic impulse in twentieth-century Scottish writing particularly associated with C. M. Grieve ('Hugh MacDiarmid') and his Renaissance movement of the 1920s. (When 'the Renaissance' is mentioned in this volume, it is almost invariably a reference to this twentieth-century movement.) Since his death in 1989, however, Scott and his poetry have largely slipped from public awareness, and where he had once been a notably kenspeckle presence in Scotland's literary life he is now becoming part of that immense company, the forgotten ones of Scotland's poetic past. (For example, his poetry is not mentioned in a recent study of modern Scottish poetry, though its author does claim that 'the omission of a poet should not be taken as a judgement on the value of his or her work'.)[1]

In Scott's case, the irony of falling victim to the oblivion of history is particularly marked for in life he never played the recluse; part of his concept of poetry was that it has a social role both in the sense that it deserves, and repays, a respected place in any healthy society and also in the sense that writing opens up to the writer a world of sympathetic friendships. Alex Scott, as he was universally known, placed himself (especially during the 1950s to 1970s) at or near the centre of Scotland's literary and cultural life, and his prominence in the generation which connected MacDiarmid's renaissance with our present vibrant Scottish literary scene arose from his own need to construct a framework of literary companionship. For him, to be a writer was to be engaged in a communal activity and the necessary solitariness of the act of poetic creation spilled over into a range of shared literary endeavours. In his heyday he was a tireless—and at times seemingly omnipresent—promoter of Scottish writing past and present, putting his considerable gifts as journalist, reviewer, editor and anthologist at its service. Committed above all to the encouragement of contemporary writing, he strove to improve the means by which writers in Scotland could find their way into print, laboured to keep alive Scottish traditions and precedents so that new Scottish writing might shape itself in their light, and strove to satisfy and indeed enlarge the readership for Scottish literature, which he was convinced existed. If no bookshop in Scotland now lacks a prominent 'Scottish' section, part of the credit for that demand is due to the promotional and educational efforts of people such as Alexander Scott.

Finally, he was the first head of what was (and remains) the world's only university department of Scottish literature. Although Scottish writers and performers would naturally claim to have won their current popularity and esteem on their own account, the development of the academic study of Scottish literature and the widespread provision of increasingly popular undergraduate courses in the subject (with the consequent encouragement of the use of Scottish texts in schools by teachers enabled to teach the subject with a degree of knowledge, confidence and enthusiasm, which their predecessors largely lacked) have made their own crucial contribution to the vitality of Scotland's cultural liveliness in the new millennium. And along with the provision of new courses has come provision of the means to teach them. Undergraduates (and readers generally) can now obtain good, inexpensive, modern editions of much of the writing which constitutes Scotland's cultural heritage, where their predecessors (such as the present writer) had to delve after dusty copies of ancient editions in the depths of university libraries. The explosion of publishing, teaching and researching in Scottish literature has been one of the decisive and most influential trends in Scottish education since the 1960s. It is a trend, too, from which many outside the universities have also benefited. Writers and readers alike now live in an ethos in which Scottish writing is no longer regarded as a weak and provincial adjunct to English or World literature; rather it is perceived as a notably vibrant contemporary literary environment with a distinctive and valuable history. Alexander Scott was a prominent part of this revolution and to tell his story is to explore the development of some of the best of the Scotland we currently inhabit.

His life and work, then, touch on important elements in the creation of contemporary Scotland. And beyond all this he was in himself a strong, memorable and paradoxical personality, a man of immense energy, ability and ambition who nevertheless failed, in some ways, to achieve what he might have been expected to attain. Once met, never forgotten; he combined a bluff aggressiveness of manner with real charm. Whether encountered in person or simply on the page, he confronted the world with a persona of great vigour, of strongly held (and expressed) opinions, and at times of unhesitating combativeness. As all agree who knew him, he always spoke his mind without fear, either for himself or for the feelings of others. His tall and striking appearance was a good introduction to a man who always dominated any group in which he found himself. Behind what Trevor Royle calls his 'roughy-toughy' demeanour, however, he was extraordinarily sensitive—insecure, even—and capable of surprising gentleness and thoughtfulness.[2] His bluntness was legendary, but so was the warmth of his praise, especially when he discovered writing which corresponded to his sense of what literature is all about (at least in Scotland). He must have been, too, the most highly decorated Scottish poet to have fought in the Second World War. He deserves a book.

Although Scott used both of the principal languages available to him, English and Scots, he was particularly associated with the latter, using it for the poems which common consensus views as his best. In that post-war generation of (in Douglas Dunn's words) '*cognoscenti*, adepts and coteries', he was a central member of that highly committed group (which included Douglas Young and Sydney Goodsir Smith) who took up MacDiarmid's linguistic renaissance and promoted Lallans as an essential means of expression for Scottish poets.[3] His wartime discovery of what MacDiarmid and William Soutar had been doing seems to have been decisive in bringing him to his own maturity as a poet, after many years of juvenilia. From the end of the war in 1945, he began to write in the still controversial 'aggrandised Scots', and was capable of producing poems which would rank with his best.

The makars who met in Rose Street, Edinburgh, immediately after the war could regard themselves as a new Scottish avant-garde; quarter of a century later those same writers were an increasingly beleaguered old guard defending their beliefs and practice against younger generations for whom MacDiarmid's notion of a literary Scots poetic language held little appeal. Scott always had his finger on the pulse of the Scottish literary world of his time—indeed, his strong journalistic instincts and his ever-ready judgemental response to everything going on in Scottish letters made him one of the least 'ivory tower' poets of his generation. At the same time, however, he had a day job teaching in the potentially ivory tower environment of Glasgow University, and the competing demands of these distinct, though related, spheres of activity took their mutual toll. It is probable that he did not regard these activities as separate and saw everything he did as conducive to one grand end—the encouragement of a healthy and distinctively Scottish literary life. But in reality the demands of academia and the demands of the muse would appear to be in potential conflict, as poets currently working in universities are increasingly willing to admit. When Scott started his university career in 1947, the demands of university teaching could occasionally be punishing but were at least fairly straightforward. If classes were not too large, a bright lecturer could rely on a fair amount of spare time. As university life has developed in recent decades, however, the expectations placed upon lecturers have increased in number and complexity: the profession has become, one might say, much more professional and its demands immensely more precise. Where, in the 1940s and 1950s, the lecturer was largely free of well-defined expectations arising outwith his (almost always 'his' then) conscience and commitment, his successors have to work within an ever-developing regime of centralised demands, which can sometimes feel tyrannous. Established in his ways during the immediate post-war years, Scott had an academic career which spanned a period of crucial transition and which paralleled the changes occurring in Scottish literary life. In both spheres, his increasingly old-fashioned approach caused him personal difficulties, which brought occasional disappointment and pain. Equally, however, both spheres contain lasting achievements. He was central to the bringing into being of Glasgow University's department of Scottish Literature, a development which gave huge impetus and legitimacy to Scottish literature as an academic subject. And he created a body of poems with their own distinctive place in the corpus of twentieth-century Scottish verse.

I first encountered Alexander Scott at the Sir Walter Scott Bicentenary Conference held in the University of Edinburgh in August 1971. We were both delegates to the conference, I a postgraduate student still in the early stages of research, he (a fact unknown to me at the time) within weeks of embarking upon his first academic year as head of the new department of Scottish Literature. We had no conversation at that time, though I remember noticing the tall and magnetic man cramming himself into the space-saving desks of Edinburgh's seminar rooms. I knew his name, for I had started exploring contemporary Scottish poetry and his excellent anthology, edited jointly with Norman MacCaig, *Contemporary Scottish Verse 1959–1969*, was well thumbed. In retrospect, it is clear that his new wave of enthusiasm for his academic career was signalled at the conference by the fact that he was the only speaker to deliver two papers at it (on poetry by Scott, and by Hogg).

We were next in the same room two years later. By this time I was beginning to teach in the English department of the University of Dundee, and had been sent as the department's representative to the Universities Committee on Scottish Literature, a gathering of Scottish literature scholars from all of the Scottish universities, seeking ways to develop the subject and its literature both inside and outside the universities. Not only was I welcomed as Dundee's new representative but I was also immediately co-opted on to the Council of the fledgling Association for Scottish Literary Studies (ASLS), which had grown out of the Universities Committee a few years previously as a mechanism for actually bringing about the desired developments. Scott was then secretary of ASLS. In a year or two he would become its president. In the course of meetings four or five times a year (with their near-invariable drinking sessions afterwards), we grew to be on friendly terms, I as a junior member of this cross-university community, Alex as a very senior member indeed. But the gap lessened at least a little when I became secretary of ASLS in my turn, for much of the 1980s. It was a period of continuing development for ASLS, which was widely seen as having an important and innovative role to play, especially in the provision of publishing outlets both for academic work in the field and also for creative work, with the establishment in 1983 of *New Writing Scotland*, still an important annual vehicle for Scottish verse and short fiction. We asked Alexander Scott to be one of the two founding editors, given his decades of experience in editing literary magazines and his ability to spot worthwhile new work. The journal's success is testament to the good work he then did.

For much of the 1980s we could all see that Scott's health was not ideal; as the decade wore on, he began to be a less frequent presence at meetings—something which would have been impossible in the 1970s. Towards the end of my period as secretary, early in 1989, I was asked by Council to write offering him honorary life membership of the association, as a mark of appreciation for all he had done both for ASLS and for Scottish literature as a whole. It was some time before I received a reply. When it came, dated 11 August 1989, I was taken aback.

> Dear David,
> Sorry to be so long in acknowledging your kind letter about the honorary membership, but I've been ill for the past three months, and at present I'm recuperating after hospitalisation and treatment for a tumour on the left lung.
>
> A major illness certainly concentrates the mind upon essentials, and I realise that, after I shuffle off this mortal coil, my literary executors (wife and/or sons) will need the help of a scholar who knows his way about books in dealing with what I may call my literary remains. Would you be prepared to take this on? I should be most grateful.
>
> Forgive brevity of scrawl, but breathlessness affects even control of the fingers.
>
> Best wishes,
> As ever,
> Alex

I had scarcely a notion of what might be involved in this, but naturally wrote back immediately, in the affirmative. Nor did I realise how short his time now was, and had a further shock a month later when I saw his obituary in *The Scotsman*.

It was at his funeral that I introduced myself to Mrs Catherine Scott and her sons Crombie and Ewan. I had not known them at all previous to this, but they were clearly pleased to be able to put a face to the name which Alex had passed to them of someone willing to help deal with the mass of material he was leaving. Visiting Cath Scott in Glasgow a few weeks later, I began a friendship which has grown steadily with the years and for which I am very grateful. I found a widow not only grieving (as she has done ever since) but also terribly aware of the comparative earliness of her husband's death (he had not reached his sixty-ninth birthday) and determined to see to it that as much as possible of the work on which he was engaged should be completed and published. That determination remained with her over the years, to a remarkable extent.

It soon emerged that two projects in particular needed attention. Scott had been preparing the outline of a major new anthology of Scottish poetry of all periods, intended to rival the twenty-year-old *Oxford Book of Scottish Verse*. Negotiations were needed with the prospective publisher to carry the task forward; in particular, I was asked to suggest a possible new editor which I did, proposing that Roderick Watson of the University of Stirling be approached. The volume, when it eventually appeared, had become his book rather than Alexander Scott's, as I knew it would be and ought to be, but I was glad that he dedicated it to Alex.

The other project was a large final collection of poems, which Scott had named *Incantations*. It consisted of many new poems, as well as a very large number from earlier phases of his career. How were we to bring this into the light of day? Discussions with Scott's friends and colleagues soon suggested that *Incantations* should be incorporated into a Collected Poems, which eventually appeared in 1994. Interested readers should consult the introduction to that volume for a more detailed account of its contents and rationale.

This unexpected direction into which a dying man had diverted my academic endeavours proceeded to yield much more material. In addition to many letters, manuscripts and typescripts, Scott had left behind two unusual documents of great importance. One was a collection of notebooks in which he had recorded a completed version of (apparently) every poem he had written since his schooldays. The immediately obvious, and somewhat mysterious, absence from these notebooks was his fine poem on Aberdeen, 'Heart of Stone'. As time has gone by, however, I have encountered one or two more poems that he did not record there. These invaluable notebooks are now in the National Library of Scotland, a precious resource for future scholars but, for a few years, my own private preserve. A large proportion of their poems had either only ever appeared once in obscure periodicals or had never reached print at all. The other document was a hand-written autobiography, written between 1939 and 1941 before he was conscripted, and telling of his life in Aberdeen as a schoolboy and undergraduate. Having explored this material, I began to publish more about Scott's writings until the opportunity of an extended period of university study leave coincided with the sense that, were a biography of Scott to be written, 'twere better that it be done while enough of those who knew him and worked with him could still be interviewed. A long series of interviews with family, friends and colleagues began, while archives in the National Library of Scotland, a number of Scottish university libraries, the Public Record Office in Kew and the BBC Written Archives Centre in Caversham yielded copious material. Even so, it has not been possible to interview all who remember him.

The present volume is the result. It is primarily an account of the man and his life, and especially of his contribution to the educational and cultural life of Scotland in the post-war era. Had Scott been granted a longer life, it would have been possible for him to write his own autobiography, which would have been revealing not only of himself but also of the Scotland he had lived in—not that I have detected any indications that he had been thinking along those lines. That a personalised account of the post-war period of Scotland's literary and public life, focused through the experience of an individual writer, can tell us much about the history of that writer's times is shown by John Herdman in an essay that is one of the many reminiscences, in many forms, which have proved helpful here.[4] It is a period that invites much further study. While it is envisaged that the present volume will be of interest primarily to those concerned with Scott himself on the basis of his poetic legacy, it may be that other readers, curious about the transition from the post-war years to what we habitually think of as 'modern Scotland', will also find it of use. Consequently, readers will find more than a few pages here which offer more historical 'background' than might be thought strictly necessary in a straightforward biography. Yet it remains a very personal book.

It was not possible, at this point, to include a full study of Scott's writings, although brief discussions of his poems, plays and academic writings are provided. I hope, however, that this will prove a useful basis for future work on this pivotal figure. I hope, too, that those who knew him, whether I interviewed them or not, recognise here something of the Alexander Scott they remember.

Chapter 1

Aberdeen

There is a hint of the myth of the 'lad o' pairts' in the opening of Scott's brief account of himself in the 1979 autobiographical essay, 'Growing up with granite': 'I was born poor, in a two-roomed but-and-ben cottage in the working-class suburb of Woodside on the northern boundary of Aberdeen, and I grew up in that northernmost of Scottish cities, unaware either of my poverty or of the richness of my inheritance.'[1] It is a note absent from the student autobiography (1939–41) upon which the essay was based: its war-obsessed opening pages were written in the summer of 1939.[2] Scott describes himself as 'a post-war baby' and instantly falls to describing experiences of his parents during the First World War. He was writing this account of his schooldays (and, in its latter pages, of his first year as an undergraduate at Aberdeen) knowing that he would soon be called up to fight. The later essay, on the other hand, is the work of a senior Scottish poet and academic who had long been associated (by this time) with the literary nationalism of MacDiarmid's Scottish Renaissance movement: the Scottish literary tradition had become everything to him. The school-leaver, by contrast, impelled to record his brief life in extremely troubled times, had possibly never heard of MacDiarmid, had not yet begun to read Scottish writing seriously and had certainly not yet done enough to justify thinking of himself as a 'lad o' pairts'.

The two autobiographies share at least one strong quality in common, however: a palpable pleasure and self-confidence in their writing. Scott always wrote about his own past with boyish enthusiasm. Partly, it was just that he was his own most accessible subject. Partly, the backward look was habitual to him—as we shall see, many of his most characteristic poems look backwards, juxtaposing past and present. Above all, however, both accounts are about his growth as a writer, and so they reflect in their different ways, the one prolix and unstructured, the other witty, shapely and concentrated, his deepest sense of himself. While the later essay is one of a collection of such accounts by well-established writers, the earlier one has no conventional published achievement behind it. Nevertheless, on one of its earliest pages[3] he bluntly proclaims, 'I am a writer' and it is clear that, by the time he came to write it, he already regarded himself as a very experienced and fairly mature (if unpublished) author. In it he sees himself as a sophisticated literary man-about-town, as when he expatiates upon 'that reminiscent mood that comes after a good supper when the first cigarette has been lighted'.[4]

Both accounts provide the conventional early statement of family background: the brief, later one goes into considerable detail about the country origins of the family on both sides.

> On my father's side I came of a long line of craftsmen and musicians. My great-grandfather, the soutar (cobbler) in the nearby village of Bucksburn, was also conductor of the community band; my grandfather, a ship's cook who had become a master-baker, played the organ; my father, the first of the family to be born in town, was a power-loom tuner in the Grandholm textile-mill on the other side of the River Don from our house, and a soloist with the works choir. Everyone else, on both sides of the family tree, was sprung from the land, my father's mother the daughter of a grieve (foreman) from Huntly, in the far north-west of Aberdeenshire, my mother's parents both from farming folk in the lee of the Mormond Braes in the far north-east. My mother, too, had been a singer, meeting my father as members of the choir of the Free Kirk which both families attended. Like him, again, she belonged to the first generation of her family to be city-born.[5]

In Scott, the family tradition of practical music-making seems to have petered out, though the notion of poetry as a kind of song was habitual to him. The dominant note in the opening pages of 'Growing up with granite', however, is the rural influence on his makeup. In addition to emphasising the country origins of his family, he portrays the Aberdeen of his childhood as a place where town met country and his earliest years as a time of outdoor adventures in a natural landscape. In this account, city streets and street games are absent.

> Even after we moved away from Woodside when I was three, and lived in the top flat of a granite tenement a mile nearer the centre of the town, the sea-links on the one hand and the open fields on the other were within easy walking distance, even for a child. All our early holidays, too, were spent on a farm near the tiny hamlet of Gartly, on the river Bogie of folk-song fame, and other early memories are all of country adventures, herding kye (cattle), hunting the half-wild bubblyjocks (turkeys) in the bushes round the steading, digging peat in the local moss and travelling back to the farm among the cart-load of peats, a tarpaulin over our heads as protection against a torrential thunder-storm.[6]

This is particularly true of his adventures on the extensive open ground in the immediate vicinity of Aberdeen's Cattofield Place—open ground that was steadily covered in housing during his time there in the 1930s. But as his rural wilderness vanished, a new landscape of words and mental images began to take its place.

There is no reason to doubt his picture of a semi-rural boyhood spent among rocks, stones and trees. Yet the absence of the city's granite from his account of 'growing up with granite' is striking. Until he starts recounting his move to Aberdeen Central School, there is little sense, in either version, of a city boy's existence. Indeed, in the 1979 account the city is absent until he discovered the act of writing poetry, when he was apparently in his eighteenth year. His first serious attempts at poetry seem to have enlivened his sense of his surroundings.

> As if my eyes had been newly-washed in some magical elixir, I realised that I lived in a city of surpassing beauty, glittering in granite, arched by a dizzying width of ever-changing skies, the stone-grey sea walling the eastern horizon, the hills swelling darkly-green in all the other airts, the rivers trenching the bounds to north and south, glistening silver or brimming brown—and after dark, in the cutting clarity of the northern night, the steel-bright onset of the stars.[7]

By this account, it was not so much the granite city which helped make him a poet; rather, writing poetry created the city round about him, just as the act of writing in a sudden poetic flood of lyricism and alliteration creates here the union of poet and place.

To the student writing at the end of 1939, building gang huts on waste ground, or risking death in a flooded quarry, or enjoying holidays in Gartly, or starting to smoke (which he seems to have done around the age of nine or ten) were simply the most colourful and entertaining parts of a city-based boyhood. The implication of the writer in his late fifties, on the other hand, that city streets did not mould him seems more wilful. The later narrative bestows on him a rather literary notion of 'boyhood' ('The place was a paradise for boys ...' etc.) and distances him from the mundane aspects of being brought up in the city. The implication is that it was the Scottish countryside that helped form him as a poet, rather than the city. While his poem 'Heart of Stone' would associate him irrevocably with Aberdeen city, his mature concept of the appropriate style for a poet in Scots leant away from anything based upon a distinctive city speech—'thi langwij a thi guhtr', as Tom Leonard puts it in his poem sequence 'Unrelated incidents'. In contrast to the rural emphasis of 'Growing up with granite', the student autobiography portrays the countryside as an influence on him only in its last pages, where he explains how his summer as a forestry worker in 1940 blew away (for the first time) his Romantic notions about Nature, and about country people and their ways. If anything, the close encounter with the reality of country life merely confirmed his city origins.

Throughout his writing, Scott derived inspiration from the backward look, from contemplating the relationship between past and present; the conjunction of the two prompted him to many a creative act. Equally, while the two major autobiographical statements contain a wealth of useful information for the biographer, they were primarily deeply exultant acts of writing, immensely congenial opportunities to write. He wrote them as he wrote everything, to be a writer in the act of writing. For Scott, simply being a writer was central to his sense of himself. Everything else he did, as academic and man of letters, was peripheral to this. In his battalion, there was a joke that Lt. Scott was the only man in the British army to list his occupation, in his pay-book, as 'poet'.[8] Whether or not the rumour was true, the soldiers around him clearly knew him well.

ALEX SCOTT SHARED HIS NAME with his father, Alexander Mackie Scott (1894–1976). Scott senior had been in the Gordon Highlanders during the First World War, soldiering throughout that conflict till he was demobbed in 1919, by which time he had risen to be sergeant-major but was permanently affected by gas encountered at Ypres. It was his mother whose maiden name was Mackie. Alex Scott's father's father (the ship's cook and master-baker), for whom in November 1948 Scott wrote his fine elegy 'Deathsang for an Auld Man Young', was 'quite a character', according to Cath Scott. She describes him as a thrifty but extremely likeable and 'passionate' man, emotional like his son and grandson. Eighty years old but still handsome, he would wink at his grandson's young wife and say, 'Aye, Cath, I wish I was twenty years younger.' He still enjoyed, in the last years of his life, going out to the pub at weekends. He would play the harmonium to accompany family evening sing-songs.

His son, Alex Scott's father, had been a boxer and a footballer in his youth and even in his sixties would run home to Hilton from his work at Crombie Mills by the river Don—a long, unremitting climb. He is described by his son[9] as possessing 'a gift of physical co-ordination which made him a first-class athlete, a wizard outside-left at soccer, a demon left-arm bowler at cricket'. Crombie Scott, Alex's elder son, recalls how his grandfather was greatly loved by his apprentice, a feeling he clearly shared, admitting that, as a child, he sometimes found his grandfather more approachable than his father. Alexander Scott senior kept up some of the country ways which his son describes in his account of his family background: his garden was assiduously cultivated for vegetables. Cath Scott regarded him as 'a very attractive man' and as someone who could have gone much further than he did, only his wife was unwilling to leave Aberdeen. He was a keen and fine singer with a lovely baritone voice. He took solo parts in performances of *Messiah*, and at least once sang on the radio.

Alex Scott's mother, Magdalena Cheyne Adams (1895–1988), was also a powerful presence, a 'big, strapping woman', according to Cath Scott, who got on very well with her. She was much less emotional than her husband, and had a strong sense of responsibility. When Scott was nine years old, he and his parents moved in with his father's parents in their comfortable new bungalow recently built at 55 Cattofield Place, Aberdeen: his grandmother had had a serious illness, which left her unequal to the running of a house. Scott's mother became the principal housekeeper, and cared for her in-laws for the rest of their lives—the escape from a small tenement flat at 22 Jamaica Street, at the top of Aberdeen's George Street, to the comfortable bungalow providing whatever compensation was required for this new responsibility. Cath Scott describes her in-laws as 'sensible people', but not given to socialising. Mrs Scott ran the household on a tight rein: her husband and father-in-law would go out to the pub on Saturday nights (after the war, Alex Scott would join them), but they had to be back for a meal at 9.00. The men-folk enjoyed a drink, but Scott's mother controlled their drinking and discouraged it, though alcohol was allowed in the house. Crombie Scott says that there was some feeling, in the family, that men-folk were rather wild and that it was the female role to rein them in. It was his mother who disciplined Alex, not his father who was not strict with him at all. Father and son were very close: Scott senior opened up to his son about his experiences in the First World War and, later, his father was one of the few people to whom Alex Scott described his experiences in the Second. He was an 'ardent socialist' but never joined the Labour Party. He and his wife were church-goers, meeting in the drama society of Mounthooly Church, a Free Kirk congregation, where Alex Scott was sent to Sunday school. Yet the father's church-going ceased after the First World War. (Scott's own religious belief apparently fell away with adolescence, despite a few schoolboy and undergraduate poems which employ the rhetoric of religion.) Neither parent was bookish: the student autobiographer is rather blunt about their lack of book-learning, and about his mother's devotion to the *Women's Weekly.* (The student autobiographer is rather blunt about a whole lot of things, especially the many young ladies he had encountered in his short life.) The elder Scotts were, says Cath Scott, working parents who wanted a good education for their child. Both were quite tall: there was no mystery as to where Alex Scott's height came from. Crombie Scott remembers his grandparents as, simply, 'lovely, lovely people'.[10]

Their only son was born on 28 November 1920 in the but-and-ben he describes: its address was 13 Western Road, Woodside, Aberdeen. That part of the city still has a leafy, rural character. The area is overlooked by a high ridge to the east crowned by a distinctive line of trees. In 'Heart of Stone' Scott writes of:

> ... the trees whas line alang the lift
> Aince gart a bairn believe the mairch o the warld
> Fand endin thonder ...'

His mother had a difficult pregnancy and turned her face against any further ones. Despite his recollections of countryside and seaside, the move to the George Street tenement flat provided him with a taste of a more urban childhood. His student autobiography contains memories of solitary games on the 'very long and very shiny staircase', and of playing with friends in the basement wash-house and cellar. The image of a striking, red, stained-glass window stuck with him, also. Nor were his journeys outside the house always towards fields or sea: once a week his mother would take him to visit her father, then janitor in the Aberdeen Central School on Schoolhill, where he would eventually go himself as a pupil. The janitor lived on the premises, and Scott was familiar with the playground at the Central School by the time he was four.

The move to Cattofield Place had obvious benefits for the whole family: a substantial house offered more space and greater respectability. It is clear that, while living in George Street and also during his first years with his grandparents, Scott participated in games and adventures with the other children of the streets—he was a normal, active, sociable boy. By the time he became known to Rita Edward, a younger girl who lived at No. 35 Cattofield Place and whose aunt, uncle and cousin lived at No. 57 next door to the Scotts, a change had set in. (Rita Edward was born six years after Scott, went to the Central School just after he left, and eventually became a maths teacher there.) Scott had committed himself to writing.

On 5 January 1926, he entered Kittybrewster Primary School: his student account of his early years there, containing the usual amusing anecdotes of an infant settling in to school routine, clearly exhibits the sheer pleasure of writing. That pleasure began in the later years of primary school: 'I cannot remember exactly how old I was when I first started writing, but I must have been nine or ten.'[11] Success and satisfaction in writing 'compositions' in class led to efforts at home at summarising the stories in a boys' paper, *The Rover*: this 'literature' stimulated in him (as he later wrote about it) both superiority and continuing affection. (A fascination with popular culture never left him.) Nevertheless, the decisive moment came a little later, thanks to his senior teacher at Kittybrewster, Miss Anderson. There seems to have been a hint of Jean Brodie in Miss Anderson.

> Miss Anderson, I think, believed it her mission in life to guide her pupils into the paths of beauty ... In the spring evenings, or during week-ends, she would take those of us who cared to go for rambles in the country round Aberdeen, where she would point out the different varieties of trees and wild flowers. At other times she conducted us round the Art Gallery—which, sad to relate, I had never entered ... But, above all, Miss Anderson had a consuming passion for literature—a passion which she did her best to foster in our breasts.[12]

She had encouraged previous pupils to produce their own little handwritten magazines, containing stories they had invented themselves—a discovery which sparked in young Scott the desire to do the same. In his writing, précis gave way to original invention, in tales both of the *Rover* kind (pirates, westerns, etc.) and also others imitative of the English boarding-school worlds of Frank

Richards and Edwy Searles Brooks, as found in *The Gem* and *The Magnet*. Before he left primary school, Scott had embarked on a series of handwritten replicas of complete magazines for boys, manufactured with the schoolboy equipment of pages from jotters, and pen and ink. These imitation periodicals were complete with fictitious advertisements, editorial columns, illustrations and stories—both serial and one-off. He called his magazine *Schoolboys' Own*, and it first appeared:

> on a Monday early in January 1932, some six weeks after my eleventh birthday, and it went on to appear at more or less weekly intervals for the next three years and a quarter, until April 1935.[13]

Each 'issue' was three inches across by eight inches high, and varied in length between thirty-two and thirty-six pages. They were produced with great regularity over a sustained period, and are an astonishing product from such a young pen: the junior schoolboy's commitment to them takes one's breath away.[14]

Scott was writing purely for his own satisfaction, and if the endeavour was solitary it may also have been a response to solitariness. There was surely much honest self-awareness when he made the hero of an unfinished and untitled short story, found in his papers, follow closely his own school-age experiences: 'Almost as soon as I learned to write, it seems, I began to put pen to paper for the pleasure of telling myself stories, the only son's consolation for the lack of siblings.' No one else read what he was producing, at least not until he spent a couple of terms at Hilton Intermediate School during the first half of 1933 before transferring to the Central School, for which he had passed the entrance examination. At the time, 'the Central' was the only free secondary school in Aberdeen. At Hilton, he befriended another boy, Danny Shepherd, who was attracted to what Scott was doing and who began to co-operate with him by producing his own fortnightly effort entitled *Every Boy's Paper*. Each 'advertised' the companion magazine in his own, though even now no one else was reading them. The pair inhabited this Brontë-like creative world for their first two years at secondary school, despite Danny proceeding to Robert Gordon's College rather than to the Central.

When creating each issue, Scott clearly desired to capture as much of the detail, and the spirit, of 'the real thing' as possible. So, once the pages had been folded to form a standard format, he devised for each issue all the features then found in papers of this type: a cheerful editor's page, 'In the Editor's Office!', in which the non-existent readership is addressed and enthused; a taster page for the following week's issue, complete with the next cover illustration; a page puffing the stable-mate periodical, Dan Shepherd's *Every Boy's Paper*; even, for a while, a page of cricket or football league statistics for the various fictional schools about which he wrote. This done, he would insert the titles for each of the issue's stories, spreading them out at intervals of two, three or four pages. Finally, he would begin writing his stories, stopping (and sometimes winding up in great haste) when the allotted number of pages had been filled up. As time went on and he matured as a writer, he began to devote whole issues to single stories. And when after a break he took up the series once more during a few months in 1937, he began to use larger jotters with pages allowing more realistic double columns. He clearly wanted to write at ever greater length: these final efforts contain an immense amount of school-yarn dialogue, which he clearly loves imitating, and the stories have become substantial short stories indeed.

The time and effort that young Scott put into this enterprise was staggering, and its products were carefully treasured by him for the rest of his life. (His own sons were allowed to see them as a periodic treat, but with dire warnings about the need to be careful with them.) They were still overwhelmingly important when, years after he created them, he wrote about them in his student autobiography. (And in that document, there are corrections and amplifications in the handwriting of an even older Alex Scott: at some later time he cared sufficiently to make the 'history' of this part of his creative life as full and accurate as he possibly could.) The account of these magazines covers pages 57 to 73 of the student autobiography, most of it detailed description of the contents of each 'issue'. He writes of them as living things, recounting the emerging conflict for space and priority between the different stories and types of stories, particularly the tales of the different fictional schools and the characters inhabiting them, starting with No. 4, where Harry Richards and Co. of Blackfriars School first appear. The Blackfriars adventures eventually took over the magazine, though at the outset they were only half a dozen pages long. 'Writing these stories week in, week out, for three years, I grew to know and love every character, until Blackfriars School became a real place to me.'[15] Other 'schools' emerged in other stories, however—St James' and St Tony's in particular. Scott writes of the development of these tales as if each school and its characters were real but locked in combat with its so-similar rivals in a competition for supremacy within the inky sheets. He describes the conflict between them with all the attention to detail of a regimental historian. It is as if each of these school worlds had a life of its own.

By the time he became a student, these stories, and the whole creative effort of which they were part, had clearly become central to his sense of himself—and that meant, by then, his sense that he was nothing more nor less than a writer. (On 20 November 1940, when a second-year undergraduate, he would return to the unfinished last 'issue' of 23 August 1937 and complete it so as to round off properly the series of Blackfriars stories.) Looking back at his first undertaking, the *Schoolboys' Own*, he saw it as 'a new era' in his life. 'This new era—of which I am just as proud as the French Revolutionists of 1789—began when I moved up from Miss S's class into Miss Anderson's.'[16] It was a development, however, which complicated his relationships with his peers. The commitment to writing had the effect of isolating him from friends and classmates. He describes himself as he was before he met Danny Shepherd:

> Till this time, I had been a solitary figure. Though I had entered into all the activities of the boys in the street where I lived, I had never found anyone who shared my delight in this wonderful pastime of setting words on paper and weaving them into phrases and sentences and story.[17]

This solitariness is what Rita Edward recalls, also.[18] She describes him as a 'reserved kind of boy' who stood out as not being involved in street games. By the time she was aware of him in the early and mid-1930s, he already had a bookish air, and he certainly 'wasn't the life and soul of the party'. His commitment to writing partly explains his manner, but Miss Edward sees him as also taking after his parents. They too were 'reserved', though seen as very nice people. The family had a tendency to keep itself to itself. And she recalls that they did not speak the local dialect; rather, they were a 'nicely spoken family'. That 'nicely spoken' air may help explain the immense appeal the fictions of Frank Richards and the others had for Scott. Making his way, a Scottish working-class boy, through the middle years of the Aberdeen municipal school system, his imagination was caught by the conventions and atmosphere of that very different, and very English, world. It had a permanent imaginative appeal: during his brief retirement, he was actively working towards a book on Frank Richards. One also notices at this early stage, however, that his literary creativity already existed for him in a world separate from more everyday affairs. It is a pattern which would become more significant later, in the army and also in his life as a Glasgow academic. For him, being a poet often seems to have been at odds with the other demands of life: he had great difficulty in negotiating a *rapprochement* between them. The conflict arguably hampered his academic career, and one wonders if his poetry might have been even better had he seen things differently. Certainly, the loneliness of 'being a writer', first experienced in his last months at primary school, can be glimpsed later in his life.

Being 'nicely spoken' largely means, in this context, 'English- (not Scots dialect-) speaking'. In 'Growing up with granite', Scott touched on the issue of how he spoke as a child:

> All of us, and all our friends and neighbours and acquaintances, spoke the Scots of Aberdeen, and I was scarcely aware of any other language until I went to the local primary school, Kittybrewster, at the age of five. There the language of our alphabet-book was English, but the incongruity of using English in the classroom and Scots everywhere else scarcely impinged on me.[19]

On every occasion, he would insist that his 'native tongue' had been Scots. In a complex linguistic situation such as Scotland's, however, there can be all sorts of gradations in speech usages. His account of the sudden onset of English has something of the air of the standard nationalist cultural critique: Scottish children, we are told, speak Scots at their mother's knee, until school imposes the alien English upon them, thus condemning them to a crippling duality of speech and consciousness. One wonders how much the reality, in this case, actually conformed to the stereotype. Certainly, by the time Rita Edward encountered the Scotts in the early 1930s, they were not to be heard speaking the local dialect, so far as she remembers. On the other hand, in the student autobiography, Scott renders conversation between schoolboys in fairly broad Aberdeen Scots. And on the many pages in which he describes his 'boorish' adolescent behaviour (towards classmates and in his dealings with girls, especially) he presents himself as speaking in as 'broad' and foul-mouthed a way as any of his rougher chums. This was particularly true of his middle years at the Central. In his last couple of years there his 'aesthetic' side won out, partly thanks to the influence of a new friend, Hamish Lawrie. In describing his schooldays, Scott projects himself as a Jekyll and Hyde personality: the thoughtful and artistic intellectual would give way, at weekends, to a foul-mouthed womaniser. Describing this latter self, he stresses his verbal crudeness as one of the habits from which he eventually turned away. These inner tensions, and the language-choice they involved, may be relevant to the attitudes he eventually brought to the matter of poetic language.

As regards the Scott household, Crombie Scott, recalling family practice about twenty years later, paints a somewhat complex picture.[20] He says that his grandparents spoke Scots to one another, but spoke 'properly' (i.e. Scots-English) before the children. There can be no doubt that Alex Scott was familiar with Aberdeen-city dialect heard both in the street and at home, but the domestic environment seems to have been biased towards a more Anglified usage. Perhaps one can extrapolate backwards from the next generation: Crombie insists that, at home, his father spoke English, a reflection in part of his sense of himself as 'an officer and a gentleman'. Scott's parents were committed to helping their son 'get on' and like him had a strong social sense of language difference. Crombie is in no way surprised to hear that a contemporary from the same street believes that his father did not, in adolescence, speak like the other children. One has the impression that when Alex Scott was in or near his home he spoke in the approved 'nice' way; in the playground and when out on the town, he would speak in as rough a version of Aberdeen Scots as his persona demanded. As time went by, however, roughness of behaviour and speech was rejected in favour of a life of culture and aesthetics—his sense of the writer's role combined with elements in his upbringing to make his schoolboy coarseness something to be abhorred.

His domain as a schoolboy writer was the Cattofield bungalow's attic, which was given over to him. His parents were aware and proud of his special gifts and tastes, as is clear from the encouragement they gave him to enter, at age fourteen, an unlikely competition. His grandmother spotted, in one of D. C. Thomson's publications, an advertisement for a boy's story competition. 'The advertisement was so worded that my father and mother thought the competition was for stories by boys. I argued in vain. They were adamant that I should enter for the competition. The first prize was £50.'[21] Already by this stage (second year at secondary school) he had a typewriter, and he eventually sent in:

> a yarn called 'The message from Mars', which combined my old interest in school-stories and my new interest in science-fiction, with an English public-schoolboy who won £100 in a crossword competition and invested it in a radio designed to measure rays from space.[22]

He was not placed in the competition, but the publishers were sufficiently impressed to send the editor of *The Hotspur*, William Blain (as Scott points out, later the author of *Witch's Blood*, an important local Dundee novel), to meet him. Blain was not expecting to meet a fourteen-year-old schoolboy and his mum, but took the story for £5 and advised Scott to stay on at school to sit his Highers. This persuaded the parents to keep their son at school, despite the financial sacrifice involved. Like many other families in the 1930s, the Scotts were having great difficulty making ends meet, but this encouragement chimed with their strong sense of ambition for their son. The £5 was Scott's more immediate reward: it was spent on a bicycle.

The story eventually appeared in *The Hotspur* No. 98, on 13 July 1935, under the title, 'The red planet calling red circle'. (At Blain's request, Scott had adapted it to form part of a series about the curiously named Red Circle School.) The ending had been much altered, but the rest was essentially Scott's. It is a tale of around five thousand words, utterly within the conventions of the boarding-school story, with Third Form feasts, bullying prefects, postal orders from rich uncles, a stream of 'japes' and much physical violence. The science-fiction element is slight—no more than the basic idea of communicating with Mars by radio. Although it has been tidied up by Thomson editors, it graphically demonstrates the proficiency young Scott had achieved. He treasured it as his first publication, carefully preserving the copy of *The Hotspur*, which is now in the National Library of Scotland.[23]

This episode is the single most curious event in his schooldays. The student autobiography focuses on the ups and downs of his academic performance, on his social life and on his writing. In his second year, he emerged as an essentially strong performer in most subjects, though he always had trouble with languages. He dropped Latin after three years, and was plagued by the demands of French throughout school, though it was eventually one of the subjects in which he gained a Higher Leaving Certificate pass. He was always good at English. He was unsure whether he would do sufficiently well to gain a fifth-year Higher Leaving Certificate, and elected to aim at the minimum group which could be attempted then, namely two Higher subjects and two Lower. Higher English was compulsory and included History. Along with this he sat Higher French, Lower Maths and Lower Science. In the event, he failed the Science, but achieved sufficiently high marks in the other three to gain the Certificate at his first attempt and the strength of his English result encouraged the family decision that he should stay for a sixth year. Nevertheless, these results were insufficient to win him university entrance, so in his sixth year he sat Higher Maths and re-sat Lower Science, both of which he passed.

His approach to Highers revealed, he claimed, his 'laziness of temperament'[24]—at each stage he would take on only the minimum academic challenge. He may have been, in part, insecure about his general abilities, but this approach foreshadows a pattern that would mark his career as a whole: an apparently 'lazy' and minimal commitment to formal academic demands, coupled with an extraordinary commitment of time and effort to his private literary interests. Throughout, the autobiography implies that his schoolwork was a diversion from his main concern—his personal life and his writing. It is a portrait of the artist as a young man, in the form of a school story: his early imitations of the stories of Bunter and the others pave the way for his own personal school yarn. But just as in Frank Richards' tales school life seems to consist of everything outside the work of the classroom, so here, too, the emphasis is on what life contained beyond the next exam or ink exercise. Juvenile passion and literary precocity make far more interesting reading than the classroom routine, and no doubt made for far more interesting living, as well.

Luckily he was clever enough to be able to coast through most of his academic work, though he could put in some real effort when absolutely necessary, as when he overcame his difficulties with French so that it became one of his strongest subjects in his fifth year. More often, he would estimate the minimum necessary to obtain the desired result, and confine himself to that. His final year revision for Higher Maths, for example, occupied only the day before the exam:

> I sat at home before a roaring fire, a glass of port at my side and a cigarette between my lips, swotting the year's work in Arithmetic, Trigonometry, Algebra, and Geometry. I went hard at it all day and rose early next morning for a final glance over the work.[25]

In the upper school, he was put in the 'B' class with those regarded as less academically ambitious and capable, thus escaping the pressure to attain the highest academic results, which students in 'A' were expected to achieve.

> For which I was, and always have been, profoundly grateful ... In this way one was free to spend more of one's life on things which one felt were ultimately of more importance than a Higher in Latin or Maths—political science, comparative religion, modern poetry, world—as distinct from British Imperial—history, or on any other subject in which one's extra-school interest lay.[26]

During the months leading up to his fifth-year Highers Scott was primarily focused on the class magazine he was creating with Hamish Lawrie, and even in the week of the exams he was writing an ambitious historical novel-fragment, *Troy Falls*, rather than revising. It seems remarkable that this extraordinarily intelligent and well-read young man seems to have had little or no leaning towards academic success for its own sake, priding himself instead on his lack of academic commitment. Admittedly, his career goal while at school was journalistic rather than academic, while as a student he assured his parents he was going to be a teacher, knowing full well that he intended to be a writer instead. Even in English, his 'studies' increasingly avoided pathways mapped out by teachers: he was usually left alone to sit at the back of the class to get on with his private reading. Writing about this from his undergraduate perspective, he states bluntly that: 'I have never had a great opinion of the academic point of view. It attains a serenity and an old-world clarity which are deceitful because they are almost completely divorced from ordinary life.'[27] At university, he chose not to revise properly for his first-year exams: 'The weather was too beautiful for me to stay indoors and work. My revision was confined to feverish last minute attempts on the evenings before each Degree.'[28] Indeed, the bulk of the autobiography was written during his second undergraduate year, a huge investment of time and energy. Admittedly he describes his literary output, during his first undergraduate winter, as considerably depleted compared with the three previous winters, but not as a result of a new commitment to the library: 'In the course of the year I attended hundreds of meetings—dramatic, discussion and pacifist—and I found myself with less and less opportunity to sit down quietly and write.'[29] Indeed, at his first meeting with his university Advisor of Studies, he 'quite flummoxed the poor man by stating blandly that I could not possibly get through all the work, and asking him what was the minimum amount necessary to enable me to get through the Degree Examinations next June'.[30]

The young Scott was not being idle but was focusing, rather, on different priorities—an attitude that continued into his mature years. His account of his school and pre-army university days is not the story of someone who is disengaged—quite the opposite. It depicts, rather, an already passionate writer, a self-aware intellectual and a seeker after the personal relationships and the environments his peculiar priorities required. As regards personal relationships, the autobiography gives lively and often brutally honest accounts of his youthful dealings with girls, as well as recollections of his various male friendships. The brutal honesty is applied both to the numerous young women in his life (he spares neither person nor character) and also to himself and his behaviour with them. One of those about whom he speaks his mind is Catherine Goodall, who had been a year above him at school and whom he encountered again when he went up to university in 1939. In 1944, he married her. As she now says cheerfully: 'He doesn't seem to have been too impressed at first!'

He, too, was cheerful as he recounted these liaisons, especially those of his girl-obsessed fourth year at school. By his fifth year, he was quite the weekend man-about-town:

> Every Saturday evening we patrolled Union Street, meeting and conversing with cronies, trying to 'get off' with every good-looking girl we saw. We were men of the world, then, with our hats pulled over one eye and a cigarette drooping from one corner of our mouths.[31]

In the autobiography, we already find him aware of the gap, upon which various later poems are built, between the glamour of sex appeal and the mundane reality behind it. Scott was very tall and strikingly good-looking, and was seldom short of girls with whom to amuse himself. By his own account, he could have gone 'all the way' with at least one young lady but the fear of early fatherhood (with consequent inevitable marriage) held him back and he reformed his ways 'for my soul's salvation, for the salvation of my artistic sensibilities'.[32] The excitement of dalliance, and of the girls with whom he dallied, gave way to boredom: 'The glamour was revealed as nothing more or less than lip-stick, rouge and powder.'[33] On the whole, his amorousness lent his youth gaiety rather than intensity, although he had his share of rapture and hurt. More important, in a way, were his male friendships because they fed his self-perceived status of writer and intellectual. The creation of his imitation boys' magazines was shared with Danny Shepherd. In his fifth year at the Central, Scott started an ambitious class magazine with Hamish Lawrie, his closest friend by the time he left school. In their sixth year, the pair embarked on an anti-war book of satirical essays and short stories, *Down With the Pacifists*. And the autobiography peters out just as he was entering the Junior Honours English class in October 1941, where he struck up a friendship with Derick Thomson, whom he credits with first arousing his interest in Scottish writing as a whole.[34]

His ideal of companionship, however, was not confined to the intensities of one-to-one friendships. It was just as important for him to be at the centre of a lively, coherent group and also to feel strongly part of and supported by the institution—school or university—to which he belonged. The Central School provided him with three such groupings: his class, 'the Lit'—the school's Literary, Dramatic and Musical Society—and the Lit's 'Dramatic Section'. What he looked for from these groups is summed up in his response to the Lit: 'Here was enthusiasm, laughter, and good-fellowship.'[35] His allegiance also to his 'B' stream, in the Upper School, is clear from the detailed and loving description of its people and events, especially in his fourth year. He was greatly troubled by the loss of camaraderie, however, in 5B:

> It was with dismay that I regarded the disintegration of the class as a corporate body which the Fifth heralded. I worried over it. I racked my brains for a solution, for a means, not only of checking the disintegration, but of giving the class a greater coherence than it had ever had before. The solution which my brains offered to me was a Class Magazine.[36]

This would not be the last occasion when he would set about improving an unsatisfactory situation by initiating a shared literary enterprise—with himself as editor-in-chief! He and Hamish Lawrie put much energy into the first issue, and succeeded in bringing out a second by the end of the year. His joy in shared literary activity is clear in his account, as is the fact that his work on it took precedence over any preparation for the looming Higher exam. Equally characteristic of his future endeavours was his stated policy for the magazine:

> Our main idea in producing *Fanfare* is to correct the general impression in the Upper School that 5B is a backward class ... it is the object of *Fanfare, the Official Magazine of Class 5B*, to put 5B on the map.[37]

Years of later striving on behalf of Scottish writing, then regarded by most readers as so 'backward' as to be almost beyond help, would be fuelled by the same spirit.

His account of the Lit presents it as one of the key elements in his school experience. Essentially a debating society for the Upper School, it met for an hour on Friday evenings, forming an important focus for the burgeoning social lives of many of the senior pupils. For Scott, however, its social function in his fourth year was overtaken by its intellectual opportunities during his fifth. In that year, Class 5A organised a takeover of all the office-bearers' posts, and also of the formal speaking in the scheduled debates: Scott and Lawrie realised that sleight-of-hand had excluded everyone from 5B, and decided to fight back by dominating the speaking after the set speeches. They apparently succeeded, even after the initial flush of antagonism had passed. Their weapons were 'whips of epigrammatic scorn' and the fact that 'no matter what the subject of the debate, we always assumed that we knew everything there was to know about it'. They also discovered the rhetorical value of humour: 'Like bullfighters we hurled our darts of invective at our opponents, goaded them to fury, and then slew them with one thrust of the sword of scornful epigrams while the spectators roared their applause.'[38] At the end of the year, he was elected vice-president of the Lit for 1938–9.

In addition to aggressive debating, Scott and Lawrie joined the Lit's dramatic section, which traditionally staged an evening of three short dramatic pieces in May of each year. The autobiography tells not only of Scott as Mark Antony in the great scene from *Julius Caesar* (Cath Scott remembers his 'Friends, Romans, countrymen ...' making a considerable impact), but also of the fun generated by the rehearsals of all three items. This was Scott's first taste of anything theatrical since he 'dramatised and produced' a classroom version of *Treasure Island* while at primary school. His joining the Lit's drama section, however, was to be the beginning of a lengthy involvement with the writing and performance of plays, which lasted until the early 1960s.

To such activities, schoolwork formed merely a background distraction. He loved his school years, the autobiographical impulse clearly demonstrating his desire to revisit and preserve them. He was quite clear about what he found most helpful in them:

> The Central gave me what was more valuable than formal education, it gave me an environment which was in the main eminently sympathetic ... And at Central I was safe; all through my life there I had my position in the society of its commonwealth.[39]

It is a note which returns when he proceeds to describe his first year at Aberdeen University's King's College. Like everyone moving from school to university, he felt that he had returned to the bottom of the heap and that a university is a very impersonal environment. Nevertheless, in summarising his feelings about this (by this time well into his second undergraduate year), he does not simply recall how he had felt on first entering King's College. Rather, he makes general statements which he still regards as true: 'Universities are notorious for their clique spirit, and it is not easy to make friends there, at least not at first.'[40] He uses the word again a few pages later: he and three other ex-Central students 'formed a clique of four in a clique-ridden society'.[41] In his first year, he says,[42] he was more in sympathy with science students than with Arts ones. One wonders how much of this perception of cliquishness he continued to hold in later life.

His initial strangeness was overcome by joining the student drama society, and by participating in the students' campaign of 1939 to choose a rector, in which he (like other arts students) supported the actress Sybil Thorndike. By the end of the first term he felt he had found his feet, but his way of expressing this is striking: 'I no longer jarred against my environment.'[43] Scott and his environments would continue to be something of an issue. He valued the sense of participation, and of being part of a unity—this is what he had found at school, and he found it again as an undergraduate. Knowing that he must soon be called up, he addressed the founder of the university, thanking him for the companionship his university was providing:

> Guid Maister Bishop Elphinstone, morituri te salutant. On the continent of Europe nations are striving to destroy one another, to grind one another into the dust. But this shining citadel you have given us, that links us together with chains stronger than iron, this badge of unity we wear in our hearts, is permanent in a world of transience, can never be destroyed.[44]

For years after the war, Aberdeen University and Aberdeen in general remained for him ideals of safety and of happiness—environments against which he had in no way jarred. During the early war years, however, he felt at times that his academic haven was insufficiently substantial in the face of the challenges of the moment:

But with the storm howling about my ears
With threat to hurl me over the precipice,
How does the 'long view' help me? How can I stem
The hail that flies in showers, or break the frost
Binding my life in ice, with knowledge of Beowulf? ...
('Long View')[45]

In his senior years at school, Scott had become so wrapped up in literature and aesthetics that the possibility of close friendship depended on his finding someone who could at least sympathise with these tastes. He had been lucky to encounter Hamish Lawrie who hailed from Hamilton and joined the class in Scott's fourth year. A year older than Alex Scott and his chums, far less boorish and generally more mature than them, he rather took against Scott until he heard about the story published in the *Hotspur*. This prompted a spell of friendship in the fourth year, but their association really took off with their joint 5B campaign at the Lit and their work on the class magazine. Lawrie was an artist. (He would later specialise in landscapes and outdoor scenes, particularly of Scotland and Venice.) The pair of them would cycle into the country, where Lawrie painted while Scott lay and read. Lawrie's soft-spoken, south-western accent always appealed to Scott, and for several years he seems to have had a strong influence on the Aberdonian, developing his artistic and intellectual perceptions, and involving him in at least two idealistic and high-flown extra-curricular endeavours. One of these was the Peace Pledge Union (PPU), the pacifist organisation begun by the Rev. Dick Shepherd in 1934. It had a distinctly intellectual, idealistic tone which appealed to Lawrie, who persuaded Scott to come along. The pair had been strongly pacifist since the Munich Crisis of September 1938: Lawrie joined the PPU while still at school but Scott, although he attended its meetings during his sixth year, swithered until August 1939. Their involvement with the PPU generated a further social-intellectual focus, a study circle. Imbued with the pacifism of the parent body, this diverse and earnest group held discussions:

> on all sorts of subjects—on education, on politics—Fascism, Communism, democracy—on poetry, on the drama, on philosophy—there were a series of papers in which each of us gave 'My Philosophy of Life'—on religion, on science, on sex, on dietetics, on sociology, on economics. We discussed spiritualism and atheism, marriage and birth-control, Christianity and Buddhism, vegetarianism and malnutrition, war and peace, the pictorial and plastic arts. At the Study Circle I made the important discovery that the practice of masturbation is widely distributed over the population: until then I had thought of it as a behaviour-pattern peculiar to myself. We wrote and acted short plays ...[46]

At this stage, he claims[47] to have had an instinctive dislike of nationalisms, including Scottish nationalism. One notes, too, that although in 'Growing up with granite' he portrays a summer job in Durris (1940) as significant for his new exploration of Burns[48] he makes no mention of this while describing the summer in the autobiography: writing in 1941, his cultural nationalism had still not been ignited.

Weighty as the study circle's discussions sound, the bulk of Scott's account of it is given over to its social and amorous undercurrents. One particular new friend made within its ranks was George Main, 'a young man with a bold, impudent, Byronic cast of face',[49] with whom Scott got on especially well. (Main would eventually be a memorable teacher of languages at Portobello High School.) This group provided support for Hamish Lawrie when he had to appear before an exemption tribunal once war broke out. Lawrie then did war-work in forestry, at Durris to the west of Aberdeen where Scott joined him for vacation employment in 1940. (For the previous two summers, Scott had been employed at Aberdeen's Joint Station, ticketing train seats.) Lawrie's friendship was not merely pleasurable: thanks to him and the intellectual activity he stimulated, he helped Scott reconcile his outward style of life with that inner belief that he was, in essence, a writer.

Although liable for military service, Scott was exempted for his first two undergraduate years and managed to complete a couple of months in the Junior Honours English class before his call-up papers arrived on his birthday at the end of November 1941. It was during these months that he became particularly friendly with Derick Thomson, though they had joined the university at the same time and had known each other the previous year. In 'Growing up with granite', Scott credits Thomson's Scottish nationalism and awareness of what had been happening in twentieth-century Scottish writing with sparking his own lifelong commitment to the subject. His first step, apparently, was to purchase MacDiarmid's anthology *The Golden Treasury of Scottish Poetry*. Thomson recalls many conversations with Scott about Scottish literature, and also about politics, although Thomson remembers him as 'a moderate leftie' rather than a fully committed party man.[50] The relationship only fully ripened after the war when they were completing their degree. It is surprising, however, that in an autobiographical letter to Alan Bold written in the same year that 'Growing up with granite' appeared, he makes no mention of Thomson's influence in 1941:

> [The *North-East Review*], to which I started contributing poems in English in December '41, was also instrumental in turning my attention to Scots, in 1942, when it published the prize-winning entries in a competition for poems and short stories in Scots organised by a local organisation devoted to the survival of the language. At first, rather like Chris [Grieve] twenty years earlier, I was opposed to this aim (for similar pseudo-'internationalist' and anti-'parochial' reasons), publishing in

> *NER* a hostile article entitled 'Emptiness in Alba', but I became interested almost in spite of myself and began to write short stories in Scots which started to appear in the paper during 1943. My first encounter with the contemporary makars was through Maurice Lindsay's *Poetry Scotland* [1943–9] anthologies, which led on in the autumn of '44 (while I was recuperating from wounds at the Gordons barracks in Aberdeen) to my purchasing Soutar's *Poems in Scots* and Chris's *Selected Poems* and to my writing a first poem in Scots, 'Untrue Tammas', a satirical sequel to the Thomas Rhymer ballad.[51]

The two versions are not necessarily incompatible: it sounds as if Scott became interested in Scottish literature as a whole in 1941 (having begun to explore Burns in 1940) but only focused on the language issue later in the war.

The *North-East Review* (*NER*), first issued on 16 February 1940, became a central concern in his life during most of the 1940s. It had been started by a group of Aberdeen intellectuals who desired a more stimulating local periodical than anything being produced by the dominant Kemsley newspaper press. The group consisted of R. F. Mackenzie (later to be well known as the controversial headmaster of Aberdeen's Summerhill Academy), his friend Hunter Diack (who became a leading educational psychologist), John Foster, John Mackintosh and Vincent Park. All were variously associated with Robert Gordon's College in Aberdeen, either as ex-pupils or as teachers. Scott's first published poem, 'At Summer's End', was also his first contribution to *NER*: it appeared in the week between his call-up papers arriving and his departure for the army. His lifelong instinct to keep his writer's life going, whatever the demands of 'the day job', is shown by nothing so clearly as the stream of writing for *NER* he maintained throughout the war.

HITLER'S WAR DISRUPTED SCOTT'S undergraduate education, but it seems sensible to complete this account of the latter before returning to his time in uniform. When he rejoined his university English class after the war, coursework was performed with his by-now-familiar ease, for his Honours years were concluded in 1947 with a good First-Class degree, despite the fact that he had also thrown himself into his favourite literary activities with an intensity all the greater for his years in uniform. For Honours he focused on English, although before entering the army he had been aiming (Cath Scott believes) at a joint English–History degree. A further indication, however, of the direction in which his literary interests were turning was his winning the Sir G. A. Smith (D. M. Cowan) essay prize in 1946, with an essay entitled 'Scottish poetry between 1918 and 1937'. This was especially unusual as the normal emphasis in Honours English courses at the time allowed for little or no coverage of Modernist or contemporary writing. Scott was fortunate, however, to encounter a young teacher with Scottish interests who had also just newly returned from the war. This was Matthew P. MacDiarmid, who was Scott's tutor for a special paper on Dunbar and who gave ten lectures to the Honours class on Scottish poetry from Barbour to Burns. He also gave a lecture on Sir Walter Scott.[52] (After a period teaching in Belfast, MacDiarmid would return to Aberdeen in the 1960s to join with Scott and others in playing a significant part in the development of the academic study of Scottish writing. See Chapter 4.) Derick Thomson recalls that Scott would also have had to do a 'reasonable amount' of Old English as part of his course but that he was never really 'enticed' by it, so that when he began writing Scots versions of some of the great poems 'from the West Saxon' he was probably using modern English versions. (Similarly, when Scott produced several Scots poems 'frae the Gaelic o Derick Thomson', he was drawing on Thomson's English versions of his own poems in his first collection of 1951: Scott had no real knowledge of Gaelic. Nevertheless, he was genuinely interested in Thomson's poetry.)[53]

Scott threw himself once more into every available literary activity, instinctively letting coursework look after itself. In particular, he took over the editing of *NER*. As he put it himself in one of his earliest letters to Maurice Lindsay (1 January 1946), 'I'm reading English at the University here, and spending most of my time editing the *North-East Review*, of which you may have heard.'[54] He was warned by the University Principal himself that he was risking the quality of his degree. With both his wife and his mother preaching the same message at home, he behaved sensibly for once and reduced the extra-curricular activity in order to prepare properly for Finals. In the end he sailed through, graduating on the same day as Thomson, and also as Walter A. S. Keir, who had become another close friend and who, like M. P. MacDiarmid, would make a distinctive contribution to the teaching of literature at Aberdeen University. Yet another friend, Vincent Park, graduated in 1949 with an Upper Second; when Park asked why he had received only a 2.1 while Scott had got a First, he was told: 'Everything Alex Scott wrote was a work of art.'[55]

Clearly, Scott was still successfully negotiating the claims of his academic work and his other literary involvements. Thomson remembers that he was mad keen to write and to publish everywhere he could. He was writing a lot of poetry, he was involved once more with student drama, and was running the university Literature Society. It was at a meeting of this last that Maurice Lindsay first met him: Lindsay was invited to speak to the society and recalls encountering Scott in the company of George Main, Walter Keir and Matthew MacDiarmid.[56] Lindsay recalls 'a talented, agreeable group' but Scott stood out. He and Lindsay had corresponded as soon as Scott was demobilised: Scott was by this time known to Douglas Young, who had suggested Lindsay's *Poetry: Scotland* anthologies as an outlet for Scott's work. Perhaps of even greater significance to Scott himself than the successful completion of his degree was the fact that he had won the university's Grierson Verse Prize with a long poem in English, originally called 'Snow' but eventually named 'The White Devil'. This success involved him in an exchange of letters with Grierson himself, in which he expatiates on his current opinions on heroism, and on poetry.[57] At one level, the poem reflects some of his wartime experiences, to which we should now turn.

Chapter 2

War and Poetry

Despite the autobiographical impulse of the student memoir, Scott kept no wartime diary. (Doing so while on active service in Europe was a court-martial offence, though occasionally soldiers did.) Notes in his poetry notebooks, however, indicate where and when he wrote his few campaign poems.[1] This sequence provides a ghostly outline of his journey during those months. Apart from this, the material on which any account of his war must be based consists of less immediate, less personal evidence. His army record is available,[2] as is the war diary of his unit, the 5/7th battalion, Gordon Highlanders,[3] in which, however, he is mentioned by name only twice. Beyond that are two tiny personal accounts: the first a brief newspaper article (see p. 24), the other a letter sent to Alan Bold.[4] For facts that might particularise his experiences, one must rely on the recollections of his family as to what he let slip. Cath Scott believes that it was to his father that he opened up most, but once his elder son Crombie grew up he told him also a good deal of what he had experienced, and I am grateful to Crombie for sharing some of those recollections with me.[5] I have been fortunate, also, in being able to speak to William (Bill) Robertson, then a nineteen-year-old private who, like Scott, fought in 'C' Company and was commanded by him, for a month or so, in 13 Platoon.[6] Nevertheless, in the account that follows I have had to base much on the general record of his battalion. Un-attributed quotations come from the battalion war diary.

Scott enlisted on 4 December 1941 at Marske-by-the-Sea, Yorkshire—an unlikely-seeming location, which always amused him in later life. There, as Squad Lance-Bombardier Scott, he joined a training regiment of the Royal Artillery before being stationed, in April 1942, at Watford. His father had advised him that he stood a slightly better chance by joining the artillery. A motor-cycle accident hospitalised him for several months but he was back by December when he applied for a commission. We glimpse him in the note appended to the army paperwork:

> He is an able gunner and specialist and handles a squad well. He shows keenness in his work and is at his best while taking part in discussion, having a wide knowledge of, and interest in, current affairs.

(Against these compliments, there is a family tradition which has another report describing him as highly intelligent but with zero interest in gunnery.)

We have some poems written on leave in Aberdeen on 31 January and 6 February 1943.[7] A few months later he was home again under less happy circumstances. Cath Scott recalls encountering him at a university dance on Saturday 17 April. Mutual interest was apparently beginning to grow ('we were hotting up!') but she was nevertheless surprised to see him at the next dance exactly one week later by which time he should have been back with his unit. He had indeed returned south but was in Aberdeen again on compassionate leave, the bungalow in Cattofield Place having been destroyed on the night of Wednesday 21 April during Aberdeen's worst raid of the war. His parents and grandparents had only just made it into the air-raid shelter in the garden. Their next-door neighbours were killed and their own house rendered uninhabitable with the attic (where Scott had been sleeping only a few nights before) damaged beyond repair. The family was re-housed in a council flat at 64 Hilton Terrace, his parents' home for the rest of their lives.

Scott became a Second Lieutenant in September 1943 but like many other young officers in regiments such as the Royal Artillery during the build-up to the invasion of Europe he was transferred in January 1944 to a rifle regiment, in his case 5/7th Gordon Highlanders, stationed at Chalfont St Giles. As in the First World War, casualties among junior officers were expected to be high, and the invasion required as many subalterns as could be found for the attack units. Together with the other regiments forming the 51st Highland Division, the Gordon Highlanders had been fighting in the desert and in Italy before being brought back to the UK for the invasion. When Scott joined them they were training intensively: familiarising themselves with the latest weaponry and practising street fighting and river crossings. A couple of months later, another Scott, Lt. T. Scott, also joined the battalion.

However, in this unpropitious period, Scott's personal life took a huge turn for the better. He bumped into Catherine Goodall once more, in Edinburgh. She had recently graduated and taken a teaching post there; he was stationed for a period in Dunbar. Dinner at the North British Hotel was soon followed by a proposal of marriage. Alex urgently wanted to marry before he left for the invasion. The fears and pressures of the time doubtless contributed to this hastiness, but it was a love match. And it was one which lasted, as all who knew them could see. They were married in King's College Chapel, Aberdeen, on 10 May 1944. The new bride remained in Aberdeen, living in her parental home of Woodside House, the hotel which the Goodall family owned near Scott's birthplace.

The war allowed them only the briefest time together, of course. On 16 May the battalion began to move to its pre-invasion marshalling area and on the 26th the camp was sealed. On 3 June, at Tilbury, the battalion embarked in its landing crafts and set off down the Thames. Next morning, minutes before they sailed from Southend, came the news of the invasion's postponement for twenty-four hours. By 5 June they were sailing along the south coast (and discovering, for the first time, that their destination was Normandy) and on the afternoon of D-Day itself (6 June) they approached Juno Beach (the Canadian objective) with Courseulles at its centre. The 51st was one of the follow-up divisions, though most of its units landed farther along the coast near Ouistreham, at Sword Beach. The 5/7th Gordons were all ashore by eight in the evening. Ten years later, Scott provided his own account of D-Day, writing up his memories for *The Bulletin*, a Glasgow newspaper which printed the piece on 5 June 1954. Here is his article.

> It was all very odd. The sunlight dazzled on the water, the beach shone golden, the countryside of France beyond it was hazed in a green dream. And all around me on the deck as our landing-craft nosed into the shore were men cluttered and bundled and bowed by equipment and weapons. Each man's back was humped by pack and blankets, and from their webbing spades and entrenching tools, Bren gun barrels and rifle stocks, thrust out like additional ungainly arms. The scene before us was beautiful; and we seemed extremely out of place in it.
>
> The ship grounded on a sandbank 100 yards from the beach and, according to plan, I led the way down the ramp into the glittering waves. I stepped off the bottom of the ramp into 9ft of water. The next few moments were very unpleasant indeed.
>
> I still remember the sudden thought that battlefields were places where people got shot, not drowned, and that this kind of thing ought not to happen. Fortunately the beach shelved steeply, and after a little I was able to get my feet on the bottom and my nose above surface, but my sergeant, a much smaller man, would have drowned if a corporal and I hadn't reached him. The three of us were the only men in the ship who got ashore at that point; the rest were held back while the vessel was taken off and brought in elsewhere, closer to the beach. We three made our way to the battalion rendezvous on our own. The beach here was deserted, and the minefields beyond had been conveniently marked with warning signs by the Germans themselves.
>
> At the corner of the first village we came on death—a Canadian soldier lying on the grassy verge, a tricolour spread over his waxen face. Again, very odd, almost melodramatic, in a street that dozed in the afternoon sunlight. And the smashed gliders in the fields seemed like broken bits of stage scenery. Then German prisoners, shuffling back from the front somewhere just ahead, dusty, dishevelled, disheartened men with that strange, anonymous look which all prisoners have. They hardly seemed adequate to embody that abstract term, 'the enemy'.
>
> After the rest of the company had joined us—and we had impatiently

scrounged cigarettes, our own having been ruined in the sea—we dug in for the night among the trees of a cherry orchard. As darkness fell and the world quietened, the guns of the Canadian battery in the next meadow roared more deafeningly than in daylight. About midnight, while I was attempting to doze as deeply as the soddenness of my clothes and the stoniness of my slit trench would allow, a message came to investigate a German patrol which the Canadians suspected to be on the outskirts of their battery position. There followed a tense hour's hunt in the darkness before the area could be declared clear of intruders; then back to our holes in the ground to wait for the dawn.

That whole day had an air of unreality about it, almost a theatrical atmosphere, as if we had stumbled into a play in which our own parts had not yet been written. The war was all round us, bellowing from the nearby artillery and chattering from the machine-guns up the road, and yet it seemed remote, not yet our own personal affair. It became our own personal affair at dawn, and stayed that way until the end of the campaign. For those of us who lived to see the end.

This last note is understandable, especially since, as he himself put it to Alan Bold: 'Of all the fifteen subalterns in our battalion who landed in Normandy on D-Day, I was the only one still there in Germany on VE-Day eleven months later.' As Bill Robertson recalls, there was an especially high casualty rate in the 51st Highland Division. Replacements were scarce and there was a general dearth of officers. The 5/7th Gordons eventually had a considerable number of Canadian officers transferred to them, but platoons were often commanded by sergeants.

According to the battalion war diary, it was on 9 June 1944, just south of Hermanville, that they were first seriously engaged. 'Here for the first time those of the Bn. who had not seen action before came under shell fire.' This must have included Alexander Scott. They were in considerable danger from anti-aircraft fire directed against low-flying German aircraft by the navy and by land-based anti-aircraft units. From here they moved to a point just east of the canal bridge across the River Orne, the famous 'Pegasus Bridge', corpses still evidence of the recent heavy fighting by Allied paratroopers. Here, too, snipers began to make their presence felt. On the 11th, they entered Touffreville, to the east of Caen, without a fight, where they remained for several days, confidently beating off various attacks but suffering considerably from lack of sleep. On the 13th, they received a couple of replacement officers including Lt. T. McN. Scott. Three days later, a more serious attack, with tanks, was mounted by the Germans. Once again these were beaten off but the newly arrived Lt. Scott was listed as missing.

It is understandable that under these circumstances confusion could arise. Nevertheless, it was clearly unfortunate that Cath Scott was informed that it was her husband of five weeks who was missing in action. She went to tell her new parents-in-law, and it is still an unhappy memory for her that the old couple were lost together in their shared despair, entirely ignoring the woe of their daughter-in-law. It was twenty-four hours before the army's mistake was corrected.

Alex Scott had survived, however, and spent the following weeks with the battalion in various locations to the east of Caen while the breakout from the beachhead stalled. They were involved in no major actions but lived in constant danger from the deadly local skirmishing all around them. At the beginning of August, however, they found themselves caught up in the decisive phase of the Normandy campaign, as the battle of the Falaise Gap unfolded. But as the Gap was closing, Scott was being returned to Britain, wounded.

On 14 August, the battalion moved south to St Sylvain, taken by Polish units on the 9th. From here they were to attack enemy positions in woods to the south-east of the village, their first major action of the campaign. Here is how the war diary puts it.

> The attack on the woods MR 157536 was very successful indeed and a large number of prisoners were taken. Our casualities were comparatively light in comparison but the difficulty in evacuating the wounded was considerable owing to M.G. [machine-gun] and Mortar fire. The stretcher bearers did magnificent work and worked ceaselessly all day. Pte Hutchinson did particularly good work. Some very fine Officers and men were lost, but the morale of the Battalion was terrific and it was just such an action as this that was needed to give the Battalion the 'punch' it required. Casualties—Major Glennie, Capt. Inglis, Lieut. Aston, Lieut. Taylor, Lieut. Birse, and Lieut. Scott wounded.

The war diary dates the whole action as occurring on 14 August. On Scott's personal army record, however, the date of his wounding is given as 17 August—the '7' is unambiguous. Similarly, the diary suggests a daytime attack ('the stretcher bearers . . . worked ceaselessly all day'). On the other hand, Crombie Scott remembers being told by his father that he was wounded at night. Whichever way it was, Scott was apparently crawling behind a roadside hedge when a grenade wounded him in both thighs. He bore the marks for the rest of his life. He always insisted that his very first action on being wounded was to check that it was still possible for the Scott name to continue into another generation. He seems to have waited a considerable time before being stretchered out on the bonnet of a jeep—that, at least, fits with the diary account.

Just over a week later, on 25 August, Scott was in Bruntswood EMS Hospital, Lichfield, where he stayed till 25 September. There, he managed at least one poem, 'Winter Season', on 7 September. There, too, Cath Scott was able to visit him. He had a spell back in Aberdeen, being posted to the Gordon Barracks on 4 October for almost a fortnight, then to the 4th Black Watch, probably at Haywards Heath, where another couple of poems are recorded.

Alex's family can recall various details he mentioned:

Before his first action, an experienced soldier took Scott under his wing and told him, 'Watch me. When I fall down, you fall down. When I get up, etc. . . .' Within a few weeks, Scott was saying the same thing to replacements newly arrived from the UK. (When Bill Robertson arrived in France in the autumn of 1944, he found that he would be taking part in an attack the following day. His fatherly platoon sergeant gave him immeasurable reassurance, saying 'Watch me. When I fall down, you fall down. . . .' In the attack next day, the sergeant was nearly cut in two by a burst of spandau fire.)

Early in the Normandy campaign, Scott and his platoon were suddenly confronted by German tanks crashing unexpectedly through the undergrowth at them. The result was a less than dignified retreat by the entire platoon, including its officer. When they regrouped they found that one man was missing. He was never seen again, and Scott never knew whether he had been killed or captured, or what had happened to him. Scott blamed himself bitterly for this, knowing that it had been his responsibility to ensure that all his men had properly received the order to retreat and feeling that he had failed to handle the situation properly.

Scott lay in a slit trench in Normandy, being mortared with the rest of his platoon. While this was going on, there was a mail delivery from home, which included a tin of that Aberdeen favourite, sweet and buttery Swiss-milk toffee. As it was being passed to him, a nearby soldier was killed by a direct hit; the tin, like everything and everyone in the vicinity, was coated with blood, etc. Nevertheless, it was opened and the contents shared out amongst the platoon. As Scott was consuming his portion, he opened his other item of mail. It turned out to be a demand for his annual subscription to the Aberdeen branch of the Peace Pledge Union.

When he returned to his unit on 10 December 1944, they were in Holland undergoing a spell of rest and training. The German offensive in the Ardennes, however, soon sucked them (and so many others) into sudden movement and action just as Europe's worst winter weather for many years was taking hold. On 3 January 1945, the 5/7th Gordons were committed with the rest of the 51st in Montgomery's counterattack. Slit trenches could not be dug in the normal way; instead, soldiers had to look for shell holes, or German trenches, or had to break up the ground with a grenade. In one incident, the crew of a disabled tank froze to death. Nor were all units equally equipped for these conditions: the Black Watch had been issued with white overalls as camouflage, whereas the Gordons had nothing of the sort. They were very conscious of their prominence as they advanced through the wooded and hilly terrain south of Liege. On the 12th, they moved at night into La Roche, liberated the day before by the Black Watch, who had linked up there with American units from the south. That night, says the diary, there was thirty-five degrees of frost. When the Gordons entered it, the whole town was still ablaze: not only was it currently being shelled by the Germans but it had also been the target of heavy Allied shelling and bombing raids before the 51st arrived. La Roche is the meeting point for a number of roads and a communications centre for the area. It was therefore a major staging point for many units of the division, and from there the final operations to capture a number of further villages were mounted. A few days later, on 16 January, the 51st division was withdrawn to prepare for the assault on the Rhineland: the 5/7th Gordons returned to an area twenty miles east of Antwerp.

In the battalion war diary for 1 February, there is the first mention of Operation VERITABLE, the northern thrust of Montgomery's two-front attack on the remaining German armies west of the Rhine. VERITABLE was a Canadian and British operation launched from the area of Nijmegen, while the Americans attacked much further south. The first major task for the British and Canadian forces was the clearing of one of Germany's state forests, the Reichswald, a densely wooded area about five miles by eight, located just east of the river Maas about ten miles south-east of Nijmegen. The intention was to mount a quick assault, taking advantage of surprise and of the German belief that no major attack with armour was possible by that route. In the event, the operation turned into a slow and costly advance lasting thirty-one days. A principal contributor to Allied difficulties was once again the weather, for the bitter temperatures of the Ardennes campaign did not last far into February. Rock-hard frozen ground gave way to rain and mud, turning terrain that would have been favourable to armour into near-impossible going. Eventually, of course, the operation was a success, but it proved a very different experience from what had been planned.

At 0500 hrs on 8 February, the Allied barrage started: the troops had been told that it would outdo the legendary barrage that initiated the Battle of El Alamein, and the war diary states: 'The fire support was truly colossal—one thousand guns of all types, rocket batteries, M.G.s and tanks. The morale of the troops was very high.' At 0800 hrs, the Gordons moved to their concentration area. The Black Watch made the initial assault, then 5/7th Gordons passed through up to Negenasud 'on the edge of the forbidding Reichswald Forest'. In the Gordons' attack, 'C' Company was the leading company and Scott's platoon the lead unit, his objective a German regimental HQ at the south-western corner of the forest. This area was a wooded plateau and the objective a 'known enemy observation post'.[8] 'C' Company 'reached its objective just before dark. Opposition was stiff and the company suffered a number of casualities'. By 0300 hrs on the 9th, 'C' Company still confronted enemy troops offering considerable resistance. They fought all night without food until more movement was achieved elsewhere in the sector and resistance in front of 'C' Company lessened. By the time Scott and his men had their first food for twenty-four hours, he had earned himself the Military Cross.

The Military Cross is an award 'for gallant and distinguished services in action'. Instituted in 1915, it is a gallantry award of lesser status than the VC or the DSO available to junior officers—captains or below. The citation for Scott's award is as follows:

> On 8th February, 1945, the Battalion was carrying out the initial attack on the Reichswald Forest. 'C' Company was one of the leading companies.
>
> Lieut. Scott was commanding the leading Platoon. On the approach march, the company had been heavily shelled and sniped at from the flanks. Disregarding these dangers, Lieut. Scott exposed himself for long periods in the open exhorting his men forward and finally he had his platoon ready for the final assault on to his objective on the edge of the wood. The spandau and rifle fire was now very heavy covering the last open stretch of 300 yards on to the objective.
>
> Undismayed, Lieut. Scott showing a high degree of courage, led on his platoon. Such was the confidence they had in their leader, the whole platoon responded magnificently and the objective was taken. Had it not been for Lieut. Scott's fine example and inspiring leadership, the platoon would have been cut to ribbons by the heavy fire before reaching their objective.
>
> Once on their objective, disregarding the continual spandau fire and sniping from the flanks and heights above, Lieut. Scott organised his platoon defences. He stood in full view of the enemy so as to be in a better position to direct 2" mortar and Piat fire on to the enemy positions. By this exceedingly brave act, he silenced several enemy posts.
>
> The enemy counter-attacked, fighting was heavy, but Lieut. Scott went round section after section cheering on his men to even greater efforts and the attack was repulsed. He was an inspiration to all around him by his coolness in the face of well directed enemy spandau fire.
>
> During the whole night amidst heavy rain and mud, he continued going round his men personally directing harassing fire wherever the enemy tried to form up for a counter-attack. Lieut. Scott all through this action displayed gallantry and a devotion to duty of the highest order. There is little doubt that the very fine example he set his men so inspired them that they carried on all night firing back at the enemy and kept a firm hold on the strong enemy position they had captured.

Ever afterwards, while drinking with friends, Scott would joke about having been awarded the MC 'for exposing himself to the enemy'. Yet he seldom talked seriously about the experience: Donald Campbell, for example, found him 'touchy' about his medal.[9]

The further line of assault for the 51st was not so much into the heart of the Reichswald as along its south-western edge. As Bill Robertson says, it was all 'close-quarter stuff' in the dense woodland. All accounts of the battle stress what a peculiarly difficult place it was to fight in even without the steady rain making near-impossible conditions for men and vehicles alike: the muddy ruts could be two feet deep. There was a lot of night-fighting. Furthermore, they had been briefed that the defending Germans would be poor-quality troops—a battalion of over-forties. In fact, at the last minute, some of their best units had been transferred in. Once the initial objectives in the forest had been captured, the battalion was directed to help take the towns and villages lying a few miles to the south of the woodland. These proved just as difficult as the forest, particularly Goch, which the Gordon Highlanders now regard as one of their major actions of the war. It was a forty-eight-hour struggle of intense street fighting. As Bill Robertson says: 'Goch was a nightmare, an absolute nightmare.'

At some point during hostilities, Scott was threatened by one of his own men, who reminded him darkly that after a battle no one would be able to tell the difference between a wound caused by a British round, or by a German one. Scott did not take action against him.

Bill Robertson remembers that when Scott was awarded the MC he said to his men: 'This medal really belongs to all of you.' Someone piped up: 'Does that mean we all get a shot at wearing it, sir?'

Just before Goch, Mick MacAndrew, the Glaswegian sergeant saved from drowning at Juno Beach, and Corporal 'Big John' Wood dug slit trenches in the wet, sandy soil by the side of the road and fell asleep. A column of armour passed up the road and dislodged the soil, burying the two men. Others realised what was happening and fought to save them, but it was too late. His troops woke Scott with the news of what had happened to MacAndrew (who, of course, had been with him since the beginning). All Scott could do was to cover his head in a blanket, and burst into tears. The news travelled through the whole battalion and many soldiers were badly affected by it.

Each soldier had, no doubt, at least one memory which caused lingering upset. Bill Robertson mentions the sight of the corpse of a young German woman, unclothed, lying by the road as they advanced into Goch. Scott occasionally mentioned to his wife his discovery—he did not say where—of an elderly couple lying dead together on a bed.

Both Cath and Crombie Scott mention, independently, Alex Scott's loss, at some point, of his second-in-command, who was standing just by Scott's shoulder and who was struck by a bullet in the face. Scott told his son that such a wound did not necessarily mean a swift and merciful death.

The battalion fought in this area until 27 February, when they were withdrawn to rehearse the crossing of the Rhine itself. This took place on the evening of 23 March, with the 51st again in the lead. Their objective was the town of Rees, but 5/7th Gordons never actually entered the town: they had been assigned the task of clearing a large spit of land, almost an island, a little to the south and east of the town, separated from the far bank proper by a subsidiary channel of the river. They took this 'island' (a process which, says Bill Robertson, was 'quite violent') but could not get across to the far bank and were pinned down for three days. They and their comrades in Rees had encountered the stiffest resistance met by Allied troops, other than airborne forces, anywhere during the Rhine crossing.

The following weeks brought swifter movement, however, as the Allies drove deeper into Germany. The 51st advanced in a north-easterly direction, engaging with small groups of enemy in a series of frequent and dangerous encounters. They were still meeting stiff resistance on 3 May at Ebersdorf, eighteen miles east of Bremerhaven, where 'C' Company was again the lead company. This was their last fight of the war. At 0800 hrs on the 5th, all enemy opposition ceased, though the battalion was nervous when given the task of being first into Bremerhaven, still occupied by a German corps. The Germans in the town outnumbered the Jocks nine to one.

In the last weeks of the war, Scott and his men killed or captured many extremely young Hitler Youth, sometimes fourteen or fifteen years old but quite often very drunk. They were capable of putting up a ferocious fight, but once captured they would frequently revert to a state appropriate for their age, weeping and crying for their mothers.

The battalion had to adapt swiftly to the role of army of occupation, a particularly difficult (and sometimes dangerous) task in the first chaotic days and weeks. However, they swiftly established their presence and participated in a victory parade on 12 May when the entire 51st Highland Division marched past the commander of 30 Corps, General Brian Horrocks. They handed over the town to the Americans at another parade on the 20th, after which they immediately drove south to Stolzenau on the river Weser, their permanent location while part of the army of occupation. During the immediate post-war period, Scott spent some time acting as officer for the defence in the courts-martial of deserters. According to Crombie, he found that there were only really two possible defences. Either the soldier was 'an auld campaigner' too experienced in war, with his nerves in tatters and no longer up to bearing the sustained terror. Or the soldier was a raw arrival, too inexperienced in war, his nerves never having been capable of bearing the sustained terror. Once more, debating society experience seems to have been helpful.

I asked Bill Robertson if he had known that his officer was a poet. Yes, somehow this was known, although no one saw him sitting scribbling poetry. Nevertheless, the joke was circulating about him writing 'poet' in his pay book. Officers normally had separate quarters during rest periods, and Scott would have had some privacy for writing.

Scott did not fall into the 'fatherly' mould of officer; he 'kept himself rather aloof', says Robertson. Cath Scott recalls that her husband was particularly friendly with the battalion padre, often in animated discussion with him. Robertson understands how Scott might have come across as abrasive, or aggressive, and would not always endear himself to lower ranks. He was not arrogant, however. Robertson agrees with Scott's own analysis that it was probably the lengthy period out of battle following his wounding in Normandy which enabled him to survive the war. Scarcely any junior officers could have survived the whole eleven months after D-Day had wounds not given them spells of withdrawal from front-line duties. As Scott himself well knew, the kind of bravery he showed when he won his medal was far from unique. This didn't mean that he was any less deserving of the award; it was simply that others were equally deserving. 'If you led a platoon, you were medal material', says Bill Robertson. I asked both Robertson and Crombie Scott what weaponry Scott usually employed: both agreed on the officer's pistol, but while Robertson recalled Scott with a Sten gun Crombie insisted that his father had followed the frequent practice of officers who carried rifles like ordinary squaddies least they stood out for German snipers, and that Scott had furthermore worn a leather jacket to hide the officer's insignia on his uniform. The rifle was also more reliable. In an attack, Scott was always the first to rise and go forward: as he said to Crombie: 'If I hadn't stood up first, none of the other buggers would have!' Paradoxically, his habit of leading from the front may have tilted the odds a little in his favour, as the Germans had apparently been told that, in an attack, it was the platoon section in the middle (i.e. immediate follow-up) which usually contained the officer: the middle sections were frequently shot up particularly badly.

After receiving his award, Scott undoubtedly meant it when he told his men that the medal really belonged to all of them, but there can be no doubt that he had been a particularly meritorious and effective officer, well deserving peculiar distinction. As Max Hastings has written recently: 'the greatest challenge for an officer was to keep his men going forward'—something Scott achieved time and time again. And Hastings points to the difficulty of keeping effective operational control 'in wooded country or at night'—Scott had to contend with both these conditions during the action for which he was decorated.[10]

The first officer to leave 5/7th Gordons went in August 1945. Scott was fortunate in also leaving early. He was given Class B release, the scheme that allowed for the early release of men with skills needed for post-war reconstruction: support from a university helped get one out swiftly. He was struck off the unit strength on 11 November 1945, being finally released from the army, after a period of 'release leave', on 2 December. By then, however, he had been back in the UK for several months. He had been granted UK leave during the first half of June, finally returning to Britain (posted to a BAOR holding battalion) on 24 September. Between that date and the beginning of December, he seems to have seen quite a lot of Aberdeen, spending at least part of this period helping to blow up and clear beach defences at the Bridge of Don. It was not until December that he could return to the life which had been disrupted in 1941, when he re-entered the Junior Honours English class.

SCOTT WOULD NOT HAVE thanked us for studying his earliest poetry in any great detail, if his dismissive comments in 'Growing up with granite' are anything to go by: 'The poetry I continued to keep on spouting like a gusher was still redolent of nineteenth-century romanticism.' That romanticism was banished when a fellow first-year student, Tom Kennedy, at last got him reading the poetry of contemporaries such as Auden, Spender and C. Day Lewis.[11] The poetry notebooks for the early war years show the sudden emergence of a different approach in his writing: around the middle of 1940 the romantic rhetoric and imagery begin to fall away, and his writing becomes more colloquial, direct and conversational. He also starts to write many more short poems.

The first poem we have from him is 'Sonnet—Our Passing', written sometime in 1937 when he was, at most, in his fifth year at the Central School:

There was a boy; his name it matters not,
But he was young, and life before him lay;
The cares of earth were all by him forgot,
And ever he was merry, bright, and gay.

While he was young, there to that boy did come
A grisly visitor—his name was Death;
He said the boy's few years had reached their sum,
And breathed on him his hungry, fetid breath.

He died, that boy, and all his comrades wept,
And mourned his fruitless passing; only he
Returnèd not; heedless of all, he slept;
He did not hear the wind, the rain, the sea.

And, as this boy, soon must our race of men
Forever pass from out of mortal ken.

This is the first of many poems focused on the idea of death. The moody, adolescent gloom and self-pity had (for once) considerable justification in the perils of the time: the sense of being part of a doomed generation marks these poems from the beginning. In fact, their reflection of the unsettled times is one of their main sources of interest. They are the emotional diary of a young man confronting the impending challenge of peculiarly challenging times. He realises that a happy and secure existence is about to be torn apart. These adolescent poems reveal what it was like to live one's youth through that world crisis: schoolboy gloom, youthful pacifism, patriotism, the belief that the doomed world is fatally corrupt, the sense of injustice that one's golden years should be so threatened and truncated, the fear of the realities of war, the slowly strengthening resolve to stand up to dictatorship, the life of the conscript, the experience of combat and danger, the immediate post-war drabness and depression—all are reflected in Scott's poems up to 1945. And those few poems about the war from yet later years continue the psychology of the story: they suggest the resurgence of unwelcome memories into a determinedly different life. These memories, indeed, were still surfacing only seven years before his death when, in 'Grace Ungraced', he grasped the horrors of the 1982 massacre in the camps of West Beirut with a vividness born of his own experience of machine-gun fire.

Few young men just going up to university, however, are likely to remain for long in a state of gloom, even at such a time. The group of 'war poems' (as he was calling them in his autobiography) ended: 'For at this point I happened to fall in love, and my emotional life ceased to be occupied solely by world-wide issues, while the lips and eyes and breasts of a young woman became very important indeed.'[12] The result was verse like the following—'Amazèd Moon':

> Swift as a grey goose-shaft the moon of harvest
> Sped o'er a sky spumed silver, held in his hand
> A fiery cross far-flaming: but yet he checked,
> Paused in his panting race, and gazed entranced
> To see your deep dark eyes wake wide to wonder,
> And jealous was that I with trembling hands
> Heart-close should hold you, and should trembling kiss
> The velvet petals soft of your tender lips.

One cannot be certain, however, that all the love poems in these volumes reflect immediate emotions and relationships. In part, he was writing for the sake of writing, desiring to cover as many pages with as many lines as possible. His most frequent resort was to nature imagery—these poems enjoy a superabundance of flowers—and the glories of the natural scene could be pressed into service whichever of his stock themes was uppermost. Whoever the young lady of the moment, or whatever his gloomy thoughts, his real muse at this time was Beauty.

Stylistic transition began in 1940, as he himself indicates. At the beginning of that year, he was projecting himself as Pan, to his own later amusement,[13] in 'No One Is Making Music':

> I have searched everywhere, and cannot find
> The goat-hooved Pan: I cannot hear his pipes:
> Never the oldest satyr, the smallest faun
> Is in this city: no one is making music:
> So I have put vines about my head, and come
> Down to the river, and cut these slender reeds.

The vines soon fell away, however. By 22 May 1940, one can sense a tougher approach emerging in this treatment of the contrast between the war and his own private world:

> Once they meant almost nothing to us, names
> In headlines, faces on the newsreels, voices
> Over the wireless—foreigners to life.
> Now they have stolen blood, humanity,
> They walk the streets with us, sit at our tables,
> Drink beer in pubs, sweat in the factories,
> No longer political articles, fragments from speeches.
> To-day within the lecture room, that hall
> As cool and dim as old Venetian glass,
> While the professor theorised on life,
> I saw in one corner the worried politicians
> Arguing round their tables, in the other
> The generals crouched across map-littered desks.

Soon after this, a somewhat different Pan appears:

> Twentieth-century Pan, in tennis-shirt and flannels,
> Sat on a hill-top, seeing on one side the smoke
> Of the city, upon the other the country's pleasant downs,
> While he jazzed out syncopations upon his harmonica.

'Pan à la vingtième siècle' is a poem about the stylistic transition which is under way, and several other poems show the same self-awareness.[14] Moving from his earlier, lush and copious style to a more 'modern' one, Scott writes many much shorter poems, and develops a more cynical persona with new satiric purpose. His own account sketches a move from 'aestheticism' to 'a sardonic austerity'.[15]

And more radical stylistic experiments occur. 'The Gutter's The Place For Me', from early 1941, is his first attempt at a poem in the mode of popular song:

The gutter's the place for me.
    When coupons are done and the rich must walk
    And along the pavement they roll or stalk
    With prowl of jackal or strut of cock
The gutter's the place for me, heigh-ho!
The gutter's the place for me ...

'Facts Of Life—A Shocking Ballad', with its sexually explicit account of the Fall, is a radical shift from his swooning earlier treatments of love: Eve falls for Satan in a big way and gets more than an apple ('she'd learnt quite a lot'), Adam can't hold off long enough for her to fall into his post-lapsarian arms ('And there he was, quietly masturbating'), and Scott refuses to fall back on his earlier aestheticism:

And if this poem you find to be shocking
What should you do here? What should you do?
You're hypocrite, fool, or silly blue-stocking
And I'll tell you what you should do.

The decade which ended with his return to undergraduate study was a long poetic apprenticeship. The transformation of his style in 1940–1 was not followed by much further development while the war lasted, as he himself indicated in a letter to Cath Scott (10 April 1945) in the latter part of the war:

> Not that I have very many illusions about my poetry. Since I joined the Army it has not progressed; I have not had the leisure for the necessary study. Much of what I write now is careless, slack, muddled and wordy. It could not be otherwise, since I haven't the time to pay it the attention required for the achievement of true excellence. But I do go on writing, simply because I must, because there is something which compels me to go on, something which tells me that if I turn a deaf ear to the muse now she may desert me altogether!

He underwent, nevertheless, not one but two stylistic revolutions. The plunge into 'modernity' was followed, later in the war, by his adoption of Scots as a poetic medium. In 1938, there had been one mysterious effort at a poem in Scots, called 'In Manus Tuas, Domine', and sometime in the early war years he wrote an extensive poem in the language, 'Frae Steel A Sang: A Scots Rhapsody'.[16] By his own account,[17] he began exploring the richness of Scots poetry, Burns and the makars etc., in 1940. Nevertheless, it was only later in the war that he fully engaged with the modern movement in Scottish writing. A brief curriculum vitae found in his papers says:

> Discovered contemporary verse in Scots in the war-time annuals, *Poetry Scotland* and *Scottish Art & Letters*. At first hostile, but personal

experimentation in Scots quickly led to increasing involvement with the medium.

These journals first appeared well after 1940–1: *Poetry Scotland* in 1943 and *Scottish Art & Letters* in 1944. The letter of 19 February 1979, to Alan Bold (quoted on pp. 18–9), however, puts yet another twist on the story, pointing to the *North-East Review* as having made him think about contemporary poetry in Scots a year before he saw *Poetry Scotland*.

Even before he took up Scots, however, he had been expressing resistance to the current poetic fashions in English verse. On leave in Aberdeen during July 1942, for example, Scott wrote 'Letter to a Literary Review':

> I would be free of the oligarchic schools,
> Pylon's starkness, muddled Apocalypse,
> Free of Auden's censoring shadow, rules
> Scratched up from Spender's practice, dogma and tips
> Ridden by White Horsemen …
> I desire my first slim volume to stand alone,
> No other name on its pages but this my own.
>
> Alexander Scott[18]

A few months later, in November, he had apparently been reading and enjoying Joyce's *Ulysses* and in 'After *Ulysses*'[19] he saw in it a treatment of the conflict between two sides of himself, the intellectual and the sensualist (his word), which had troubled him since his schooldays. The poem sees the two combining to form a successful human being. But if Joyce spoke to him, Eliot antagonised. 'O God! O T. S. Eliot!', written in December 1942,[20] shows how the religiosity of Eliot's more recent work repelled him. It concludes:

> For Eliot loved his ruins so
> He chose the oldest wreck of all
> And clad it crimson like a throne
> But could not check the winds that blow
> Through the Church's broken wall
> Standing bleak and all alone.

A question which naturally occurs to anyone knowing of Scott's military involvement is 'Where are his war poems?', for his verse collections (and the *Collected Poems*) contain extremely few poems that reflect that profound aspect of his experience. It was a theme to which he scarcely ever returned in his mature years as a poet. Indeed, those years seem to embody his vigorous determination to put the past behind him and to press on with all aspects of his life, after the disruption of war. Just as he never wished to return in person to the scenes of his combat experiences, so he had little desire to return to a theme of undoubted pain which, to some extent, he had covered exhaustively while living through it. A response to Alan Bold, who had posed the question, confirms this:

> The reason why I have written so little about the war since it ended is that I wrote and published innumerable poems, articles and stories about it while it was still going on. However, none of this work has been collected.[21]

From the poems of his years in uniform, two strands might usefully be picked out. One is his verse response to army life itself; the other is his developing awareness of Aberdeen, the vision of which became ever more important to him. In his post-war career he would further develop these strands. His later poetry of war produced poems of adjustment, poems in which he accommodated wartime recollections with the privileged life of a survivor and man of letters. At least one exceptional poem resulted: 'Coronach'. The Aberdeen strand eventually produced 'Heart of Stone'.

Even in the few poems written while on active service, there are scarcely any glimpses of actual combat. When Scott comes close to describing battle, it is fleetingly, with pained eyes already beginning to turn away. One senses that in addition to the sheer awfulness of the material, poetry was still, for him, an alternative domain, an activity at odds with war, so that the latter could never nourish his writing. One can observe the aversion of his gaze from the physical realities of the campaign in one of the last poems written while the shooting was going on, 'One More River To Cross'.[22] Its penultimate line suggests that writing verse, and maintaining a sense of himself as an artist, was a means by which he dealt with the fears and stresses of the campaign: 'Here I must build a song against my own terror.' Poetry was a brief escape from the war he was fighting, not a means of confronting it more directly. Poem after poem, written in the quiet spells between actions, evokes the thoughts and observations focused by those lulls; perhaps they were a way of inhabiting those lulls ever more intensely.

'One More River To Cross' is both the last of the seventeen poems he recorded between D-Day and the cessation of hostilities and also one of the longest. As the title hints, the river is the Rhine and the poem was written under the immediate shadow of the British army's last major challenge of the war. It is dated 16 March, two days after a rehearsal for the Rhine crossing in which the Highland Division would play a leading part, and exactly a week before the crossing itself. The landscapes described in the poem are clearly war-torn, but the work modulates into a visionary mode with Scott's refusal to describe in realistic terms his combat experiences up to this point. Rather, he treats his progress across northern Europe almost as a dream: he sketches a strange trek through a lonely landscape, with no hint of fighting and, indeed, no acknowledgement of his being part of an army. It seems a visionary, solitary quest: his longed-for goal is a glimpse of a peopled, peacetime city. And yet the immediate military challenge of the Rhine is there in the poem as well, in the strong sense of its being a final, possibly fatal, destination. In part, this is the river of Death. Like so many of these poems, this one is finally unachieved, yet in its very rawness it is moving in its humane response to dire circumstances. Its mode is significant, however: Scott paints out all combat experience including the Rhineland battles in which, five weeks earlier, he had won the Military Cross. Nor does he depict the dreaded crossing as an explicitly military venture. Only the combat-transformed landscape, and the fears and longings deep inside himself, are left. It is a poem that embodies, as well as any, his unwillingness to write about combat, an unwillingness that never really left him.

We do not know the exact circumstances in which these war-time poems were written. Perhaps some were actually composed in slit trenches. More likely, rest periods out of the line were eagerly grasped opportunities for privateness. Several of the seventeen were written while he was back in Britain recovering from his Normandy wounding. His commitment to his vocation as poet was undimmed, as can be seen from the letter to his wife, of 10 April 1945.

> In my present circumstances I'm afraid that being an artist forces me to be a very bad friend. In the little spare time I have I find it impossible to write both poetry and letters, and up till now that infrequent leisure has been claimed by my giddy-pated muddled muse. Except for bulletins to my people and business communications to the *North-East Review*, which publishes some of my stuff, this is the first letter I have written for a month and more. Nothing—not even love, or affection, or friendship, or duty, or patriotism, or any other of the recognised as praiseworthy emotions—matters to the artist in the same way as his art matters; and when it comes to a tussle between his art and his emotions, the latter lose every time, and very decidedly.

He explains one reason for his poetic tenacity: he is worried that inspiration may finally leave him:

> Poetry may be a natural flower, but it must be cultivated if it is to thrive. At present I am just able to keep mine alive, only just. If I were to neglect it altogether, it would die completely and beyond resurrection. And to me, at least, it is supremely important that that poetry, my own personal expression, the only justification I can find for my existence on the earth, should not die. All of which may sound very high-falutin but at least pays you the compliment of sincerity.

He was committed to the Scottish Renaissance movement even before he was demobbed. This is suggested by a poem he wrote in Stolzenau, during the period of post-war occupation. In 'Darkness and Light'[23] he describes himself reading MacDiarmid's poems in bed by lamp light—until matters take a strange turn: a moth startles him as it strives to get to the light within the light bulb and he angrily kills it by snapping the book shut upon it. Suddenly filled with horror and revulsion, he flicks it on to the floor, but the sight of its crushed body continues to horrify him and in something of a funk he switches the light out, abandoning his reading. The poem labours to develop a portentous symbolism of darkness and light, apparently one of his attempts to conjure verse out of a real if entirely trivial incident, and perhaps to handle the topic of killing—until one encounters a very similar poem published by Douglas Young in his volume *Auntran Blads* (1943). There, in 'August Night', Young describes how, in a fright, he had killed a bat which had got into his bedroom: he kills it with a towel and it lands on 'Farnéli's Pindar,/volume III'. Calming down, he sees himself as a criminal, 'and was shocked at my own terror'. Scott has clearly modelled his poem on Young's, an indication that by this time he was exploring Scottish Renaissance poetry beyond the MacDiarmid and Soutar volumes he had obtained in Aberdeen the previous autumn while recovering from wounds.

The first poem from that commitment was 'Untrue Tammas'.[24] Its first readers, in Aberdeen University's nationalist journal *Alba Mater* (February 1946), no doubt read it merely as an amusingly irreverent and wittily original revision of the familiar legend: as we have seen, Scott himself, writing to Alan Bold, called it simply 'a satirical sequel to the Thomas Rhymer ballad'. Readers of a certain ingenuity may also find in it an image of the isolation and incomprehension to which creative artists can fall victim. Furthermore, once the circumstances of the poem's origins are known, it is hard to avoid a yet further layer of meaning. It was recorded in December 1944, in Louvain in Belgium and so was written when he had just returned to his unit after his recuperation in Britain. Consequently, it is hard not to read it as a poem about the juxtaposition of 'worlds' he is experiencing. We know, of course, that soldiers returned from the front often cannot make the folk back home comprehend what it is like 'over there'. But if Scott is writing about that problem here, then the poem is not simply a cheerful jest at the legend's expense but a deeply, even bitterly ironic utterance. Seen thus, the reality behind the implausibly wonderful domain Tammas describes is (we know) a realm of horror, death and destruction. The poem's cheerfulness and witty literariness emerge as distancing alternatives to the gloomy reality to which Scott has returned. Once alerted, one can sense bitter irony in Tam's description:

> 'I've been,' said Tam, 'whaur yirth's a wonder,
> It never needs the graip or plou,
> There's hairst the haill year roun out yonder.'

(Mortars plough this earth; there is an ongoing harvest of lives.)

> 'But yon's a place there's gowd aplenty
> Jist liggan lowse, nae fash to howk it,
> The chiels retire afore they're twenty.'

(The vast financial implications of the war is a topic to which he returned several times in these campaign poems and the expenditure of lives involved many under twenty—most of those under Scott's command were eighteen or nineteen years old.)

The last stanza, written as he returns to the dangers of war-torn Europe, appears inescapably ironic, and the responses of 'the neibours' suddenly sound like the voice of sanity:

> 'I'm aff mysel to the easy wey o't
> Whar life is leisure, sweet and saft,
> And milk-and-hinney's never dry o't.'
> 'Awa ye go, ye sumph, ye're daft!'

The idyllic vision of the land of easy living reflects, while it conceals, a bitter reality, in something of the manner of the American hobo song 'The Big Rock Candy Mountain'. If this reading is correct, 'Untrue Tammas' is one of Scott's most ingenious treatments of active service.

The journey in 'One More River To Cross' leads the poet to the bank of 'a very broad river' with the opposite shore shrouded in mist, through which he occasionally attains:

> A glimpse through a swirl in the fog of a great city
> Whose walls rise up unruined out of a golden earth,
> And people strolling easily along unbroken streets,
> A great unruined city and people walking.

A visionary city is an ancient symbol of life's goal; however, by the time he wrote this Scott had already produced a number of poems in which Aberdeen, specifically, was the focus of his hopes and desires.[25] The earliest of them had been little more than descriptions of the Aberdeen townscape. In 'The River', however, which must date from 1939, he produced a long poem on the history of Aberdeen.[26] He describes how, over the centuries, waves of incomers have impinged on the place, culminating in the German bombers of the First World War. Describing the city's emergence and growth, he sees it as a place of defence against a dangerous world. Old Aberdeen emerges from history as a sanctuary and place of safety, where a wall 'very thick and very high, / And built of granite' protects against marauding Highlanders. The poem, in fact, is steeped in a sense of Aberdeen as a place safe from the world's threats.

Even once in uniform, he is able for a while to keep picturing Aberdeen as a fortress, effective against nature at least:

> The splendour of her granite steadfastness,
> Outfacing ocean's anger, stands alone;
> Though flanked by rivers, though the hills buttress,
> She is more surely bastioned in her stone;
> Man's fortress, built against a miser nature's …

In a letter to Alan Bold (11 June 1979) he singles out this poem—'Homage to Grey Granite'—as the first in a series of attempts to write the poem that eventually emerged, quarter of a century later, as 'Heart of Stone'.[27]

Against war and Man's cruelty, however, Aberdeen was not so reliable. In 'Leave's End' (4 November 1942)[28]—the title explains the poem—he wrote:

almost ended, all this week of wonder
Crumbles towards the crowded dusty past;
As wrought in sand, these walls of granite sunder.

And in 'Citizen Soldier' (6 February 1943)[29] he saw Aberdeen no longer as a safe haven; furthermore, he had realised how he was now separated irrevocably from the life he had known there.

Listen! The granite, gaunt and void of pity,
Speaks to an exile, back so brief a season:
'O once my son, now stranger in this city,
Logic of time destroys your dreaming's reason,
Others possess your peace, your best-loved places,
Others have built their lives where you projected
Memory's architecture, other faces
Laugh where your laughter's youth, by time infected,
Dies without an echo, unprotected.

'You have no city now except that storied
Township far across the bleeding river,
Spur of serfs and flame of freedom, gloried
Borough that all mankind have sought forever –
Capital of content whose cherished-charters,
Written upon the hearts of men, have made
How many heroes, O how many martyrs?
Thus were your city's strong foundations laid:
Go out and claim its freedom, unafraid.'

The sensation of alienation from the Aberdeen he had known is even more directly expressed a few months later, in 'I Seek A City' (9 May 1943).[30] In the period between the two poems, his home had been bombed and the sense of dispossession is even stronger:

For to me there was a magic in the singular myth of my own youth, and O a spell about the memory of my city …

Till the bombs fell, loud with death and splintered of destruction, and I went back and found my city mine no longer.

There was my house in ruins, and there my people homeless; there was my mother pale with tears, my father white with unavailing anger; and there my childhood lay in dust and fragments; and there the bitter wind blew upon the ashes of my adolescence.

> Strangers were in the streets, whose unfamiliar mouths were full of laughter, and their pointing fingers did not know me; the girls my love once magnified to queens had dwindled into women; the friends I had were battle-distant exiles …
>
> Others possess my peace; others say of my city, 'This is mine'; others have built their lives where I projected the dreaming architecture of memory; and I am left with dust, with dust and ruins.

A sense of the mythic quality of his own life lingered with him for some time, and can still be seen in 'The River'. However, as 'the singular myth of my own youth' faded in the world's upheaval, he tried to substitute a universal myth of the future for the personal myth of his past. As the months of war go by, however, he can also be seen reaching after a more objective vision of the city. One begins to encounter images and phrases which will find their place in 'Heart of Stone', the great poem that would be his eventual statement about Aberdeen. For a detailed account of this process, readers should consult my article 'Granite's secret beauty'.[31] Here, what must be stressed is the way in which, during this period, the city of Aberdeen appears to have become bound up with his sense of his essential self, a self most visible in those golden years (as they seemed in his imagination) at school and at university, before he was snatched away by the war. The sudden loss of security hit him hard. Looking back sadly to his naïve Aberdonian self, in 'Portrait and History' (October 1944), he wrote: 'I lived unaware terror and pain could ever reach me there.'[32]

His personal and poetic development, during the war, saw him slough off naivety and escapism. Personal friendship with Tom Kennedy no doubt influenced him to explore the more astringent verse of contemporary writers, but behind Kennedy's influence the whole world crisis bore down upon him. Aestheticism and Beauty had to go; brutal reality could not be ignored. Looking back in 1954, in 'Words for the Warld', at his prolonged development as a youthful poet, he put it this way:

> 'Find words for the warld,' they tellt me—sae
> I left no a chuckie unturned i the stanie limits,
> In aa the avenues roun I splored exploran,
> Convened wi hither, confabbed wi yon, conferred
> Wi beuks-o-the-month (and beuks) frae Hugh til Homer
> (And aa gey Greek), yet fient a word for the ferlie —
>
> Til the warld itsel gaed grab at the scruff o my life,
> Shuke me intil a shennachie, skailed frae my ain
> New-opened makar's mou the wale o words.

The events of the 1940s 'shuke me intil a shennachie'. Nevertheless, the war did not 'grow' his poetry because it was so at variance with his conception of how one might develop as a poet and man of letters. Perhaps it came at the wrong time for him (if there is ever a 'right time' for a war to come along): had he reached adulthood as a poet before the war then perhaps he might have been able to incorporate its experience into mature verse. While the war years shattered his 'egotism' as a poet and made his youthful poetic modes impossible, they did not, in the event, result in a major body of war poetry. It was primarily a question of timing: the war coincided with his immaturity as a writer, prolonging it rather than hastening its end. When he resumed his 'real life' in 1945 he was ready to move into new poetic pastures.

Chapter 3

An Academic Career Begins

When Scott returned to Aberdeen in October 1945 he wished to be clear of the army and to return to his studies as quickly as possible. Class B release placed him in the vanguard for demobilisation but nevertheless he and Cath found it frustrating when the university session started without him. It took a special trip to Edinburgh, to the Army High Command, to finally push the process through, before he was able to join the Junior Honours class in December.

They started married life living with Cath's mother in her hotel, Woodside House, on the northern outskirts of Aberdeen: Cath had stayed with her mother since the wedding and was teaching at Hilton School. Despite their poverty, Scott was impatient to get on with both his literary life and the starting of a family. Crombie Scott was born in 1946, his brother Ewan in 1948. In later years, Cath Scott would look back and wonder about the financial wisdom of this eagerness, but Alex always insisted that he had desired, above all, the earliest possible resumption of the life the war had delayed.

Cath Scott feels that war, however, changed her husband. In addition to the new intensity with which he addressed his various literary activities (his studies, his writing, his journalism), he had become more thoughtful and sad. Harder, too—capable of an impatience and roughness of manner which she had not seen in him before. She remembers him, for example, dragging her to shelter through a downpour of rain, all the loving kindness of his war-time letters replaced by a 'coorseness' (to use a North-East expression) which she found upsetting. At times, she felt that she did not recognise the man who had come back. He was smoking and drinking more, too.

In Woodside House Hotel they had a self-contained flat, small but viable. However, in March 1946 Scott fell out with his mother-in-law over a trivial matter (he objected to the pregnant Cath being asked to help out by serving some hotel guests): Cath feels that he was intent on 'showing who was boss'. The upshot was that the couple moved in with Scott's parents who were already sharing the Hilton Terrace flat with his grandparents. His grandmother, whose illness in 1929 had occasioned their move to the now-destroyed bungalow, was still alive but merely sat in a corner all day. The small house was terribly overcrowded and the young couple had no privacy. This contributed, no doubt, to the stress Cath Scott was noticing in her husband, as did financial pressures. Scott's annual grant during his two last student years was only £100, and he was beginning to write for the BBC to earn extra money. It must have been now that he first met the poet George Bruce, who joined the BBC as general programmes editor in Aberdeen in December 1946. Scott's poems began to be broadcast in 1946 and from that year Scott dated, in one of his CVs, the beginning of his spell (1946–50) as a radio actor. He also took over the editorship of *North-East Review* in November 1945, for the last year of its existence.

His social life at this time centred on his drinking companions in Aberdeen's post-war intellectual circles. Walter Keir and Vincent Park were particularly close friends: with them, Scott would often talk far into the night. Cath Scott chose to accompany him on many of his evenings out, partly with a view to looking after him and partly to have more time in the company of a husband so powerfully drawn to literary companionship outside the home. Scott could drink quite a lot at this time, once even passing out in the lavatory of his parents' flat.

Other friends included the future novelist Jessie Kesson and the librarian W. Lindsay Simpson. Isobel Murray has written about the relationship between Kesson and Simpson, describing a kind of platonic love affair.[1] And at least to some extent, Alex Scott was also an object of Simpson's affections. In the war-time absence of all his other close friends, Scott had asked Simpson to be best man at his wedding. As he said afterwards to Cath: 'I realise now that that was the cruellest thing I could have done.' Simpson's affection for Scott can be sensed in the booklet he brought out, *Apollo's Apprentice: Poet's Progress* (n.d.), an intensely lyrical, privately printed essay with the sub-heading 'Pioneer Appreciation of Alexander M. Scott', in which he reprints two of the poems of the war years, 'Homage to Grey Granite' and 'Leave's End'. (Cath Scott rightly describes the production as 'a bit over the top'.) Kesson remained a good friend of the Scotts throughout her life and they always had lots of fun together. Also prominent in their lives at this time was Vincent Park, who was slightly younger than Scott. They had met in the university drama society and Park directed the annual student show in 1948, in which one of Scott's first attempts at drama was presented, as discussed in a later chapter. Both Simpson and Park responded strongly to the youthful Scott who, in turn, clearly relished their companionship and appreciation.

For the two years immediately after the war, while he was completing his degree, Scott lived intensely, immersing himself in love, in family life, in learning and in literary activities of all kinds. He immersed himself in Aberdeen, in fact, and in everything that the city had come to mean for him. Survival made him appreciate the things that mattered to him, especially while his time in uniform deprived him of them. But the war's brake on his progress had also given him, as we have seen, an opportunity to re-orientate his whole literary direction. When it began he was a schoolboy poet confined to anachronistic Romantic pastiche;

when it ended he was committed to the world of contemporary Scottish verse. The world crisis had forced upon Scott the need for a contemporary approach; however, he had required a modernism other than that on offer from the current British poetic establishment. The big names of the 1920s and ’30s had never really appealed to him, but the experience of living (and surviving) furth of Scotland, in the most inhuman circumstances, had awakened his perception of his own country, and of its language and literature. In the poetry of MacDiarmid, Soutar and Young he had discovered a modernism in which he could participate, and a group he could join.

His letters to Grierson are helpful here (see Chapter 1). They were written on 6 June and 3 July 1946. (The former date was the same day that he wrote ‘Sir Patrick Spens: The True Tale’, ‘Sang for a Flodden’ and ‘Coronach’.) His comments include this on the writer’s isolation (already, long familiar to him):

> It is inevitable, I expect, that the writer should feel himself isolated to a greater or less degree, and, Scotland being what it is, I’m afraid that the isolation here is in the ‘greater’ class.

And when he turns to discussing heroism—knowing, obviously, that in the eyes of most people he himself had been a hero—he denies that heroic action really sets one apart from the majority. He had met in the war many heroes of the type ‘who disdains danger and snaps his fingers in the face of death’. Others ‘had no desire to die’, ‘realised that every breath they drew was in pawn to annihilation’ and ‘were fully aware of the flaw in fortune which had led them to their present situation’. They showed ‘a type of endurance which, far from being stoical, was very much aware of the cursed spite which compelled them to repair the ruins of the times’. Clearly he ranked himself with these much more numerous and commonplace heroes. And his view of contemporary poetry, as outlined to Grierson, closes ranks with the majority against the kind of poet who strives for privateness of utterance:

> I agree entirely that meaning is one of the essentials, though not the only essential, of any poem. I have no time for the mumbo-jumbo merchants who would make poetry pure music or pure incantation. Such gentlemen should cease using words in their verse and employ meaningless combinations of vowels and consonants instead, for all words have meaning as well as sound, and it is impossible for the reader to dissociate the two. George Campbell Hay has an excellent essay on the subject, ‘Poetry—in the World or out of it?’ in the spring number of *Scottish Art and Letters*, flaying André Gide and other supporters of the mumbo-jumbo position.

He then defends his use of the occasional North-East spelling (and pronunciation) in his own Lallans poems. Clearly, the Lallans movement held for him no danger of isolation, or of failure to communicate. Rather, in its assertion of Scottishness and the closeness of its language to the world in which he had grown up, it implied community.

Derick Thomson remembers discussing Scottish literature very often with Scott during their two final years as undergraduates.[2] Furthermore, Scott had begun to make the personal acquaintance of prominent members of the Scottish Renaissance movement. Maurice Lindsay was a guest of the university literary society in spring 1946,[3] and by then Douglas Young and Scott had been in contact with each other: Scott mentions Young (in a letter to Lindsay of 1 January 1946)[4] as having suggested Lindsay's *Poetry Scotland* anthologies as a possible outlet for Scott's poetry. It is not clear when Scott and Young first met: it could have been as early as 1939–41, when Young was teaching Greek at Aberdeen University. (The student autobiography makes no mention of him, but then it makes no mention of any university teachers, his unfortunate adviser of studies apart.) However, Scott's complete social assimilation into the Renaissance group came about only in the year following his graduation. His success in Finals led to him being offered a chance to study at Oxford (other bright students, such as Edwin Morgan, were being offered the same chance at this time)[5] but his circumstances were such that he had to get a job instead. He was appointed to an assistant lectureship in the English department of the University of Edinburgh, a post he held for the academic session 1947–8. There was little, if any, opportunity to teach Scottish material, but Scott immediately fitted into the department. He and his family moved to a flat at 22 Pitt Street (now Dundas Street), near the Water of Leith.

Scott loved Edinburgh, and during this year he established some of the friendships and relationships that would be central to him for decades afterwards. (It was now, for example, that Cath Scott recalls seeing Douglas Young a great deal—she does not associate him with the Aberdeen years.) In particular, he met Sydney Goodsir Smith and his wife, who became close friends of the Scotts. It is likely, too, that it was during this year that Scott made the personal acquaintance of C. M. Grieve ('Hugh MacDiarmid'). Evidence for this is pictorial rather than verbal. In his illustrated biography of MacDiarmid, Gordon Wright publishes a photograph of Scott with Sorley MacLean, Sydney Goodsir Smith and MacDiarmid on 10 February 1948 heading up North St David Street (making for Rose Street?) after recording a poetry reading for the BBC.[6]

And it is to the late Hazel Goodsir Smith that I am indebted for information regarding a far more obscure set of pictures which suggest how rapidly Scott had become one of the Renaissance literati. In the early 1990s, she accompanied her friend Isobel Nicolson to the Scottish National Portrait Gallery to deposit there a collection of drawings that had been in the possession of Mrs Nicolson and her husband Torquil since 1948. They are portraits of various friends, members of the Edinburgh cultural scene, including Sorley MacLean, Sydney Goodsir Smith, Norman MacCaig, Denis Peploe, Wilfred Taylor, C. M. Grieve and Alexander Scott. They were drawn by Gregoire Michonze, a visiting artist, French but of Russian origin, who stayed with the Nicolsons for a few weeks, probably during the 1948 Festival, and drew the people he encountered in their circle. The appealing portrait of the young Scott projects his sensitive and vulnerable side.[7] There is, however, a more tantalising image still. Hazel Smith's friend, the architect Ian Begg, recalls seeing, in the very early 1950s, a large drawing (about ten feet by four) also by Michonze adorning the French Institute in Edinburgh. When he went back to see it again, many years later, it had disappeared. By chance, in 1997, he was able to obtain a poor composite photograph of this drawing. It depicts a fanciful Parisian street scene, and in one section, sitting drinking at a street café, are (unmistakably) Norman MacCaig, Douglas Young, Sorley MacLean, Chris Grieve, Goodsir Smith and (once more) Alexander Scott. As Ian Begg says: 'Alexander Scott was obviously weel kent in Edinburgh and there were a lot of interesting people around.'[8]

Nevertheless, he was in Edinburgh for one year only. He was appointed, in 1948, as lecturer in Scottish literature in the University of Glasgow's department of Scottish History and Literature. From the Scotts' point of view, there were substantial reasons for the change. The year in Edinburgh entailed considerable financial difficulty—for one thing (as Cath Scott recalls), at that time Edinburgh University paid on a six-monthly basis and they required financial help to see them through. The Edinburgh post was an assistant lectureship, whereas Glasgow offered a full lectureship. And Scott must have been attracted by the prospect of teaching Scottish literature by itself. Nevertheless, he was never sure, afterwards, that the move to Glasgow had not been a mistake, and even in his last illness he was wondering, to his wife, whether he should have stayed in Edinburgh. There is a hint of Thomas Hardy in the circumstances: Scott told no one in the Edinburgh department that he was applying for the Glasgow job, and the professor, W. L. Renwick, was extremely displeased (according to Professor John MacQueen)[9] when he eventually found out. When Scott finally told him that he would be leaving, Renwick (apparently) said that he had intended to ask him to begin teaching Scottish literature from 1948 onwards. Cath Scott believes that had her husband known this, he would not have applied for the Glasgow position but would have gladly stayed in Edinburgh. The reticence of the two men had produced an outcome that one of them, at least, came partially to regret. As Cath Scott is sometimes inclined to think: 'That is where Alex's life went wrong.'

Scott went to Glasgow to start the university session while his wife took the boys (Ewan had recently been born) to stay in Aberdeen. He lodged first of all with Maurice Lindsay's brother at 10 Jedburgh Gardens but then with Lindsay himself and his wife Joyce in Southpark Avenue. His energies were entirely focused on the preparation of new lectures: Scott felt overwhelmed. The first year of teaching a university literature course, especially a lecture course, is always a frantic experience. Furthermore, Scott would have had no previous teaching material to fall back upon. His undergraduate course at Aberdeen would have had little Scottish coverage in it, though M. P. MacDiarmid's introductory teaching of early Scottish poetry will have helped considerably. His year of teaching at Edinburgh probably did not contain much Scottish material, if any. A claim, in a letter to Douglas Young (see p. 104) that he was 'ploughing through the whole of Scot. Lit. and trying to cut it up into lectures' was probably accurate.[10] It is not surprising that he concentrated on this to the exclusion of almost all else.

The Lindsays made him welcome and comfortable—perhaps too much so, because he made little effort to move on. In the end, Lindsay himself suggested that Cath and the boys come down from Aberdeen and move in, realising that only once she was in Glasgow would house-hunting begin in earnest. Cath Scott recalls that Alex made little effort to see if university accommodation might be available and it seems to have been largely due to her energy that in June 1949 they were able to move into a flat at 7 Lothian Gardens, where they would remain for ten years. The Lindsays found Scott a little thoughtless as a house-guest: for example, he would knock out the pipe he was currently smoking against the enamel of a brand new stove, to its detriment. Joyce Lindsay was also faintly shocked by his attitude to the lectures he was frantically writing: it was clear that once a lecture had been written, Scott did not envisage ever revising or replacing it later in his teaching career.

Glasgow University created its department of Scottish History and Literature in 1913. The first move in this direction was in 1909, when an anonymous donor provided funds for annual public lectures in Scottish history and Scottish literature. University calendars state that separate courses of lectures in these subjects had been given in each of the three academic years starting in 1909. In the calendars actually covering 1909–12, however, only two such courses in each subject are specified. The lecturers on Scottish literature were Sir George B. Douglas (in 1910–11) and Prof. J. H. Millar (in 1911–12). Lectures in 1912–13 are mentioned but no lecturers named. Meanwhile, local enthusiasts, hoping to endow chairs in both Scottish history and Scottish literature, had organised a major civic exhibition, the 'Scottish Exhibition of History, Art and Industry', which had raised around twenty thousand pounds. Of this, fifteen thousand pounds were donated to the university, supplemented by contributions from The Merchants' House, a local charity, and also from funds collected by a committee of Glasgow citizens.[11] All this effort, however, raised enough for only one chair, though it might have been sufficient to employ two lecturers. It was decided to go for a single chair to cover both subjects and the university was fortunate to appoint Robert Sangster Rait in 1913. The new chair, however, did not enjoy wholehearted support within the university, and strong denials of the merit and importance of Scottish studies could be heard both then and for many decades afterwards. The Professor of History, for example, was notoriously opposed to the development, insisting that the half-lecture per year he was in the habit of devoting to Scotland was quite sufficient.[12] These attitudes within the university would persist during the eventual emergence of the independent department of Scottish Literature.

Rait proved an excellent scholar and a distinguished professor. Indeed, he was made principal of the university in 1929, although his record in that post is usually held to have been less successful. Furthermore, he seems to have been peculiarly well fitted to occupy the joint chair: although primarily a historian, he had published a number of works of a literary kind, including editions of poems of James VI and I, and also selected poems of Marvell and Montrose. He had lectured on Andrew Lang—admittedly on Lang the historian—had edited an edition of Scott's *Rob Roy* and published a book entitled *'The Kingis Quair' and the New Criticism* (1898). The university calendar for 1913–14 states the following:

> The lectures will deal with selected topics in Scottish history and literature from the earliest times to the present day. No attempt will be made to treat Scottish literature from the standpoint of philology, but stress will be laid upon the connexion between history and literature. For the degree examinations a knowledge of the outlines of Scottish history and of the history of Scottish literature will be required.

Recommended reading for the literary aspect of the course comprised J. H. Millar's *A Literary History of Scotland* (1903) and L. M. Watt's *Scottish Life and Poetry* (1912), while the 'chapters dealing with Scotland' in the *Cambridge History of English Literature* 'will also be found useful'. Watt was later dropped as a recommendation in favour of T. F. Henderson's even older *Scottish Vernacular Literature: A Succinct History* (1898). Even from the early years, however, Scottish history was the primary discipline in the pairing. When he arrived in 1948, Scott had to lecture to all three classes (Ordinary, Higher Ordinary and Honours). Nevertheless, the calendars suggest that the focus of the Honours classes in particular was solidly historical (e.g. 'The Development of the kingdom of Scotland' in 1914–15; 'Scottish history, 1603–1707, with special reference to the Parliament and the General Assembly of the Church' in 1925–6). It would appear that the two subjects were never married; Scottish literature was at risk of being the handmaiden to Scottish history. Hints of literary content occasionally emerge: in the Higher Ordinary class in 1928–9, on 'Scottish history 1513–1612', students used 'literary histories, diaries, memoirs, etc.'; Sir David Lindsay's *Poetical Works* appear in the work of the Honours class of 1939–40. On the other hand, Phyllis McCloskey, in a letter to the *Scots Independent* of 20 July 1968, pointed out to Alexander Scott that Rait, in the 1920s, gave as much weight in his lectures to the literature of Scotland as to its history.

As the department grew, the emphasis on history would appear to have become stronger. Rait was joined by George S. Pryde as an assistant in 1928. A year later, when Rait became Principal and Vice-chancellor, Pryde became a full lecturer in 'Scottish history', with no hint of literary responsibilities in his title. Rait was replaced as professor by J. D. Mackie in 1930. Mackie's publications contain none of the literary colouring that Rait's had done, nor does his *A History of Scotland* (1964) contain any marked account of Scotland's literature, beyond the usual, which might have suggested that he had been giving it any special emphasis in his teaching. Nor do the names of other members of staff in the 1940s and '50s suggest literary expertise. By the early 1960s, the calendar entry for Scottish literature had changed little from what it had been in 1913. Even more astonishing, nor had the recommended reading: it was still Millar, Henderson and the *Cambridge History*. This trio would not change until 1963, on the institution of the new Ordinary class in Scottish literature, when the *Cambridge History* was at long last replaced by James Kinsley's collection of essays *Scottish Poetry: A Critical Survey* (1955).

To Mackie, however, must go the credit of persuading the university that a separate lecturer in Scottish literature was now necessary in the post-war period, though it is not clear whether this was due to his own pressure of work or to some other circumstance. It seems most likely that Mackie was taking advantage of the strong post-war spirit of innovation gripping the university as a whole, despite the conservatism which particularly characterised powerful elements in the Arts Faculty.[13] Despite opposition from traditionalists, the university was developing African studies, and also Slavonic and East European studies. There was a new consciousness, too, of the university's obligations to the local community. When Scott was appointed in 1948, the university had been looking for such a lecturer for some little time. When Douglas Young applied unsuccessfully to Glasgow, in 1946 and 1947, for a chair then for a lectureship in Greek, he was offered a lectureship in Scottish literature instead. He refused, and went to teach Classics in Dundee. According to Young's daughter, however, he it was who was 'instrumental in getting Alexander Scott the Scottish literature job in Glasgow',[14] though I have not been able to confirm this from any other source. What can be confirmed from letters in the National Library of Scotland is Young's arranging, very soon afterwards, for Scott to be involved in work on the diaries of William Soutar.[15]

If the idea of a chair of Scottish history and literature had originally been controversial, it was as a result of its Scottishness rather than because of its linkage of history and literature. As Andrew Hook and Robert Crawford have shown, a Scottish tradition saw the studies of history and literature as closely interlinked at least since the Victorian John Nichol, who had been 'the first professor at Glasgow to have the words "English literature" attached to his professorship'.[16] The enthusiasm behind the Glasgow exhibition of 1911, an attempt to propagate both Scottish history and literature, further reflected this national bias. Nevertheless, despite Rait's versatility, it should not be assumed that the existence of the Glasgow chair, or the fact of Scott's appointment thirty-seven years later, implied that the university teaching of Scottish literature there had become a mature discipline strengthened by an interdisciplinary pedagogic tradition. The reality seems to have been much more mundane. As we have seen, the occupants of the chair were always historians, rather than being qualified (at least in the modern sense) to teach literature. And the department Scott joined in 1948 was scarcely interdisciplinary in practice.

Undergraduate teaching in Arts subjects at Glasgow, in the 1940s and 1950s, was almost entirely lecture-based. Scott lectured to the first year Ordinary class once a week, on Mondays, coming in after an initial six-week course of lectures on Roman Scotland. A similar pattern, moreover, was applied to the more advanced classes also, and there can be no denying that his first year, during which he usually gave either two or three new lectures per week, would have been very hard for him. For the undergraduates, however, his subject must have seemed subsidiary fare since their principal study was history. They could not ignore it, however: the Scottish literature question in their examination papers was compulsory. Essay marking must have been fairly heavy: in Scott's first session at Glasgow, the Ordinary class had eighty-four students, and the Higher class forty-nine.

Because he was the sole teacher of a very different subject from that with which his fellow lecturers were concerned, Scott seems from the start to have been isolated, both intellectually and maybe to some extent socially, although at the level of daily interaction he seems to have got on with his colleagues well enough. It was a department of four: Mackie (professor), Pryde (lecturer in Scottish history), Margaret Burnett (assistant in Scottish history) and Scott (lecturer in Scottish literature). Everyone with any knowledge of the department of Scottish History and Literature in the days before Scottish Literature became a separate department agrees that there was no attempt to take advantage of the proximity of the two disciplines. The undergraduates experienced Scottish literature as a separate subject, heavily overshadowed by Scottish history. There was no synergy.

Perhaps other attitudes also played their part. Jack Rillie recalls that:

> there was a kind of air about the history departments (medieval, modern, Scottish) that in Arts THEY were about REAL academic scholarship. (Raleigh, our Regius [professor] after Bradley, confessed some shame in concentrating on literature rather than language. 'Tosh' and 'Text' he calls them in a letter, adding 'I teach the "tosh".') History made that kind of distinction, one felt.[17]

Scott was thus working in what were even then rather unusual, and not entirely ideal, academic circumstances. In literary subjects, research tends to be a solitary endeavour, the essential loneliness of which is usually counterweighted not only by the sociability of a department's day-to-day life but also by the department's collaborative effort in devising and running courses, and in standing up for itself against pressures from elsewhere in the university. There is also, normally, a sense that although one's colleagues work on different topics they are still intellectually close and 'talking the same language'. Scott seems to have had none of this: the shared Scottish focus seems to have been insufficient to provide a common ground. For many years in the 1950s and early '60s, even the social side of departmental life was hampered by the complete absence of accommodation. When A. A. M. Duncan arrived to occupy the Chair in 1962, there was no 'department of Scottish History and Literature' in any physical sense, merely a small side room used by lecturers before a lecture, containing a suitcase with Professor Pryde's initials on it, and a bookcase containing three novels. Lecturers had no separate offices. Nor was there much social choice within the small department.[18] (Once Scott had his own department, in 1971, there were only two of them, plus a shared lecturer in language studies. This increased to three when Roderick Lyall arrived in 1975. Thus Scott spent his academic life in what now seem absolutely tiny academic units.)

Scott's appointment, located in a department of Scottish history, might have created exciting intellectual opportunities. That this did not fully happen tells us something about Scott himself, about his historian colleagues in the 1950s and about the place that Scottish literature had come to occupy in the department's thinking. In the same way as Rait could offer competence in both aspects of his professorship, so Scott might have built upon his lifelong interest in history. But he did not seem to perceive the possibilities. Instead of responding to the interests of his historian colleagues, he preferred to participate in the multifarious literary activities opening up to him outwith the university. Had this point been put to him, of course, he would undoubtedly have replied—and with much justice—that too much 'spadework' had yet to be done before the university discussion of Scottish literature could attain the sophistication (the luxury?) of a sustained interaction with Scottish history as a discipline. Too many important Scottish authors lacked modern editions; too many leading Scottish writers had yet to be the focus of a body of modern criticism; too much Scottish writing could not easily be put into the hands of students or the general public. When Scott took up the subject, it demanded of him and his generation a willingness to work at the most basic academic fundamentals. If his intellectual isolation from his historian colleagues was due in part to temperamental reasons, it was also true that his subject was not yet at the point where it could begin to interact with Scottish history in a truly collaborative way.

Equally, one might have expected the new lecturer in Scottish literature to find academic companionship within the English department but that does not seem to have happened, either. In part, this may have been because the English department felt threatened, or at least put out, by the very creation of the post. John MacQueen was an undergraduate in English at Glasgow at this time, and can recall sensing a distinct feeling of upset, in his department, when the new lecturer was appointed. As MacQueen says, Professor Peter Alexander was 'quite amazed' by the new appointment.[19] Perhaps the English department felt that it had not been sufficiently consulted: this was certainly the reproach used by conservative elements in the faculty who complained formally to the university, six months before Scott arrived, about the creation of five new lectureships in social sciences.[20]

In any case, the post-war Glasgow English department, and indeed the Arts faculty as a whole, had an ethos that was some way from anything Scott was likely to find congenial. Several interviewees have commented on the prevailing desire within the department to replicate, so far as possible, the atmosphere and values of an Oxford college—values both academic and social. Socially, they assumed a certain high tone, and a willingness to be clubbable. Academically, Oxford sympathies implied contentment with established judgements as to what is more valuable, and what is less so, in English and related literatures. Jack Rillie, whose time on the staff at Glasgow coincided exactly with Scott's, recalls (in a note to me) the social atmosphere of the post-war English department:

> It was—to someone who had just spent six and a half years in the army—all a bit twee in the late '40s, early '50s. Club breaks were a bit like afternoon tea in, say, *Mansfield Park*. The one lady member of department was treated with great deference. We 'watched our language' and subjects of conversation (oh, indeed, even in her absence). There was a spurious kind of 'Oxford College' atmosphere whose manners I had to learn. [Alexander Scott] would not notice—or, if he did, not learn. So 'not one of us'. Not 'class' in the least—but what Paul called his Christians 'a peculiar people'....[Scott] was also...LOUD—and the physical sense would have been enough. The Professor...pulled rank instinctively, expected deference. [Scott] might not notice.

Rillie hints at another possible difficulty—although he is aware that the suggestion might be contentious! '[Scott] was like other Aberdonians I knew (hope I don't offend!)—blunt, didn't adjust to possible areas of sensitivity or show particular interest in others' concerns. Independent, but certainly not rude. Nor shy.' Furthermore, it seems unlikely that Scott, so committed to contemporary writing, could ever have been comfortable with an English department for whom (as Rillie claims) the 'story' of English literature stopped with Matthew Arnold.

On the other hand, as John MacQueen points out, the post-war English department at Glasgow was not completely closed-minded, despite its general elderliness: it was possible, for example, for Edwin Morgan, who arrived almost simultaneously with Scott, to introduce more Scottish material into the undergraduate curriculum. If the department's conservatism is suggested by the fact that Morgan believes he was the first to do so, its flexibility is suggested by the fact that the innovation was possible. And as MacQueen later discovered, the southern sympathies and occasionally precious style of the Glasgow English lecturers did not prevent them from adapting to the needs of their huge (and potentially rowdy) local classes: their clear, straightforward, strong lectures were far superior to what he encountered at Cambridge a year or two later. Nevertheless, of living poets, Hugh MacDiarmid for one was extremely unpopular with the English staff, an outlook scarcely calculated to endear them to the enthusiastic new recruit to MacDiarmid's Renaissance movement—or him to them, for that matter.

Nor was it merely the department of English which Scott might have found uncongenial. As the official history of Glasgow University makes abundantly clear, the departments of humanities and languages at this time were deeply and aggressively conservative in outlook. There was sustained opposition from within the faculty to the development of African studies and Slavonic and East European studies. The arguments used against the latter will be familiar to anyone advocating Scottish literature during the later decades of the twentieth century: 'There was opposition within the Faculty to the idea that Polish and Czech languages *were of sufficient merit to justify a place in the graduating curriculum*'[21] [my italics]. While Scott's post does not seem to have aroused quite the same level of opposition, he had entered an environment that tended to confirm his undergraduate perception of university cliquishness.

Whatever his reaction to the ethos of the faculty of Arts, there can be little doubt that his strange position within his department helped engender a sense of isolation. As Archie Duncan quickly recognised when he arrived as professor in 1962, Scott's very active and wide range of literary interests were not adequately represented by the teaching arrangements for Scottish literature. He had outgrown, as it were, courses originally shaped by the perceptions of historians. Scott, after just a few years in post, had perhaps pressed for a stronger literary presence in the Honours course: the Honours topic for 1952–3, the 'Government of medieval Scotland', prompted the following new sentence in the calendar: 'Use will be made of the literary authorities—Henryson, Dunbar, Boece, Sir David Lindsay, John Knox and Robert Lindsay of Pitscottie.' Prescriptions from later in the 1950s, however, once more give far less prominence to literary texts. Indeed, once George Pryde took over as professor in 1957, the historical side of the department's teaching seems to have become ever more professional and modernised, a process that Archie Duncan would continue in the 1960s. With the teaching of Scottish history becoming ever more highly evolved—more intensely itself, as it were—it is understandable that the solitary advocate of Scottish literature should become less and less comfortable.

A different personality, however, might have reacted to the situation more constructively. Tempting as it is to see the root of Scott's later difficulties arising from the unique circumstances of his early career in Glasgow University, it is also possible that one should look a little earlier still. There is at least room for doubt as to the intensity of Scott's commitment to the idea of an academic career. Many who knew him agree that, despite his later prominence as an academic and his sustained and conscientious hard work in his job, it was possible to feel that his heart was elsewhere. Certainly, in his account of his early years as an undergraduate, there is no hint of longing for an academic post: if anything, the opposite is true. When he was completing his degree, conspicuous academic success coincided with the urgent demands of his young family. He seems to have sought out university positions as the most obvious step to take in the circumstances in which he found himself. Cath Scott cannot recall any clear moment of decision, or of commitment to an academic career. I asked Derick Thomson, who was close to him in the Aberdeen English class, if he recalled Scott ever expressing such a commitment, or having clear aspirations in that direction.

> I don't think I can give you precise information about Alex's ambitions in his early years. I suspect that he had an open mind about jobs in his final years at Aberdeen University, and just took the first offer that came up. Like you, I suspect that he was more attracted to writing than to teaching, and I think his enthusiasm for his academic career at Glasgow was a bit lukewarm. He didn't mix easily with academic colleagues in general, and had more enthusiasm for poetry and drama.[22]

Some light on his thinking as he first entered academic employment is cast by two letters he wrote to Maurice Lindsay in the weeks immediately following graduation. The first is dated 2 July 1947:

> At present I am in a state of uncertainty about my future. I got through the Finals in English with First-Class Honours; but the question is, 'What now?' There may be an opportunity to take a research degree on Scottish literature, but that depends on whether the Scottish Education Department is prepared to finance me in a more-or-less adequate fashion.[23]

This partial confirmation of Thomson's suspicions is strengthened by a further letter (19 August 1947) after the question 'what now?' had been unexpectedly answered: 'The Edinburgh appointment was a great stroke of luck, especially as I shall be able to do research for a Ph.D. on nineteenth-century Scottish poetry at the same time.'[24] He had found a congenial job, rather than entering the career of his dreams. Equally, these comments on research fail to convey much hint of passionate desire or engagement. That said, the interest in nineteenth-century poetry was genuine and would remain with him, but (as can easily happen) his research was soon to be deflected into a quite different direction.

It seems likely that his central perception of himself as a writer above all things was not displaced or altered by the career on which he had embarked, and the inner priority he had always given to creative activities over academic demands persisted, even in his new circumstances. His contemporaries were often conscious of this. As Tom Scott wrote to him on 2 November 1967:

'You are a writer first and an academic after.'[25] Many of those to whom I have spoken also saw him in this way. Part of the justification for this view lies in the limited extent of his purely academic research over his entire career, a matter that will be examined in more detail later. Also relevant, however, is the perception by Glasgow colleagues for much of his academic career, but particularly in the 1950s and '60s, that he usually just showed up in the university to do his teaching, and disappeared off campus once again as soon as classes were over. This even seems to have been the case once the department obtained better accommodation and its lecturers had their own offices. He was one of those lecturers who are 'never around'—hard to get hold of both by students and by colleagues. And he showed no inclination to get involved in university politics and decision-making. Even after he was heading his own department, he was still perceived as someone who appeared on committees only when he had to (not entirely justly, I suggest, for faculty minutes record his presence at meetings in the 1970s far more often than they indicate his absence). To those many in Glasgow University who had no interest in, or knowledge of, his varied activities outside the university, he seemed to be just coasting along, not pulling his weight. As Rillie puts it:

> No, the university—this one anyhow—was not 'his place'. And his absence was noticed more than his presence. I really don't think anyone regarded him as a man with a 'calling' ... Most people didn't know him. Many thought him idle and apathetic.'[26]

It was a perception that eventually counted against him.

For many years, too, he seems to have lived (imaginatively) in two places at once—Glasgow and Aberdeen. An uncollected poem, 'Train til Aberdeen', recorded as written during a journey on 15 October 1948 'between Glasgow & Aberdeen', suggests his reservations about the location of his new job, and the feelings he continued to have for his home town.

> Fowr hours awa frae the grime and glaur o Glesca,
> Fowr hours o kintra droukt in October sun,
> Ower birlan burns and by a drove o mountains
> And shauven parks wi aa the hairst got in,
> Till sudden, the sea!—he's chuckit a handfu o siller
> Straucht in my een.
>
> The lichthoose sclents frae the shore, a lintwhite lassie
> Luran the wealth o trawler chiels tae lan',
> The waas get up, and spires o gesserant granite
> Dirk at the cloods whas colour mates their ain,
> Till sudden, the city!—quine wi the glamour o smeddum,
> Ye've grippit me roun.[27]

Admittedly, when this was written, Scott had been living in Glasgow without his young family at the start of his first session there. Indeed, the next few poems in the notebook, written around a month later back in Glasgow, constitute an emotional diary suggesting his tenderness and longing. On 17 November he records both 'Continent o Venus', perhaps the most forceful and powerful of his love poems, and also (on the same subject but in an entirely different mood) 'Sex Sang'.[28] The following day he records 'Bairnsang (For Crombie and Ewan)'.

But when all the family circumstances of these weeks are taken into account and discounted, there remains a charge of emotion in these lines on Aberdeen which both look back to his youthful happiness and security there, and forward to 'Heart of Stone', his major effort at writing a poem that would do justice to the city.

The 1950s were spent, for the family as a whole, 'between Glasgow & Aberdeen': Crombie Scott recalls those days vividly and confirms how important Aberdeen then was to his father.[29] He remembers his grandparents' house in Hilton Terrace as filled with emotional warmth, and confirms his mother's recollection that family holidays were usually taken in Aberdeen—and, sometimes, not just for a week or a fortnight but for most of the school holidays. He says that the family did not take so much as a tour of the Highlands until he was sixteen, and then only at the initiative of family friends. His recollection is that, once in Aberdeen, the two small boys would be given over to their grandparents, while Alex and Cath spent time with their Aberdonian circle. Crombie goes so far as to say that he still feels part-Aberdonian, even though he was essentially brought up in Glasgow. But thanks to the attachment to the northern city which his parents exuded—and thanks, also, to the loving warmth of the oft-visited grandparents— he still feels, in his fifties, as if he is partly an immigrant in Glasgow. Crombie Scott's attraction to the northern city was clearly created by his father's strength of feeling during those early Glasgow years. Many of Scott's colleagues and friends also confirm the continuing importance of Aberdeen in his life, not only those such as Edwin Morgan and Maurice Lindsay who knew him in the 1950s but also others such as John MacQueen, Thomas Crawford, Trevor Royle and Roderick Lyall whose personal knowledge of him did not begin until the 1960s or '70s. At least two of these expressed doubts as to whether or not he ever fully settled in Glasgow: indeed, Morgan (who knew him throughout his working life at Glasgow University) thinks that he'd have gone back eagerly to live and work in Aberdeen, had he ever had the chance. And in a two-page typescript, in his remaining papers, in which he outlined his life from the perspective of the mid-1980s, he wrote (surely with some exaggeration?) that, having left Aberdeen in 1947, he had 'holidayed there at least half-a-dozen times a year during every year since'.

Nevertheless, when he first took up the Glasgow post it offered him a new kind of creativity, which he grasped with some vigour. The late 1940s and much of the 1950s was, for Scott, one of his most active and productive periods of academic research. Four substantial publications appeared in the 1950s: *Selected Poems of William Jeffrey* (1951), a selection of the poems of his namesake Alexander Scott for the Saltire Society (1952), and two works on the poet William Soutar, which perhaps constitute his most important achievements in purely academic terms, namely the selection from Soutar's diaries (*Diaries of a Dying Man*, 1954) and the biography *Still Life* (1958). Apart from the Saltire selection (the initiative for which possibly came from the Society rather than from Scott himself), his research (unlike his teaching) was focused on the Scottish Renaissance and so reflected his creative involvement with the movement rather than being (in the stock phrase) purely academic. The books on Soutar lack nothing of academic merit. They do suggest, however, that from the beginning his vision of being a university lecturer was that it was one of several roles he was playing in furthering the Renaissance goal of a reinvigorated Scottish literary life. It is in some such sense that he was a writer first and an academic second. His notion of his responsibilities as an academic were very different from those held by other, more specifically focused university colleagues. His difference of approach helps explain why he was not always perceived as having produced work of the highest academic quality. It also helps explain why he felt, latterly, a sense of injustice when he was not promoted to a chair: by his own lights, he had achieved more than enough to justify the honour; from the point of view of a more orthodox academic outlook, he had not.

What was Scott like as a teacher? For much of his career at Glasgow teaching involved simply lecturing, and setting and marking essays and examinations—tutorials were seldom employed until they became more common in the 1970s. And Scott's lecture delivery was a shout, as is recalled not just by former students but also by former colleagues who could hear him if they were anywhere in the vicinity of the lecture room, which was actually quite small. As Jack Rillie writes: 'effect like shouting messages to a sinking ship (on Scottish Chaucerians); gobbets of information (mainly) repeated; he was not orating—more like dictating methodically down a very bad phone line.' Robert MacDonald, taking Scott's class in the very early 1960s, recalls the effect as sermon-like, rather.[30] The result, says Douglas Gifford, was 'impressive but slightly boring'; Gifford thinks that Scott's written criticism was better than his lectures.[31] It was, by the 1960s, a rather old-fashioned style of lecturing: he was not attempting to discuss anything with his students, but rather was informing them of what they had to know. Roderick Lyall recalls that the sub-Honours students, at least, did not have to actually read the texts: they were simply expected to pay close attention to the lectures.[32] So that they could get it all down, Scott read slowly from lecture notes which would seem to have changed little as the years went by. Scott's view of his lectures as requiring no change, which had disconcerted Joyce Lindsay while the new lecturer was her guest in 1948, is confirmed by his students, and by Professor Jack to whom Scott said, during Jack's period as external examiner in Scott's department, that a lecture, once written, was fixed.

When Robert MacDonald returned to the university in 1976 as Clerk to the Faculty of Arts, he found that he was hearing the lectures for a second time as he walked past.

In fact, a number of Scott's lecture notes survive, in long, narrow, hardbound ledgers.[33] Their finality is proclaimed not just by the solid bindings but also by the way they are written out. They are in tiny longhand, with no space between the lines or the long paragraphs. They could not have been used as a mere *aide-mémoire*: the solid blocks of minuscule handwriting can be followed by the eye and mind only with care. The occasional glance down at them would simply not suffice. The slow delivery recollected by colleagues must have been due at least partly to the nature of these scripts, which demanded to be followed with the minimum of spontaneity. Scott wrote lectures as formal continuous prose, but with vocal delivery in mind: had he used real notes, his lectures would have sounded quite different. These are very detailed, with many facts and dates. They are essays, in fact, and seem intended to contain most of what he knew and thought about their subject-matter. But equally, they are for his eyes only. Here is an extract transcribed from his lecture on Smollett:

> In talking of S's novels, 1 is continually under necess of using such phrases as 'localities thro which action of novel moves', for travel is essential ingredient of novel as S wrote it. Med poets often regarded life as pilgrimage—most famous example of this in Eng, of course, is Chaucer's Cant Tales; S appears to have treated life, at least for lit purposes, as journey. Nor is this surprising, for gt deal of his own life spent in travelling—1st from Scot to Lond in search of fame as dramatist; then to Cartagena & Jamaica as naval surgeon; then on Grand Tour on Cont before wrote Per Pickle; he was abroad again travelling Fr & Italy from 1763 to 1765, & in 1768 set out on last journey to Leghorn, where was to die ...

As regards the content of his lectures, Scott's approach was resolutely factual and historical, usually 'introductory' in nature, hardly ever straying into thinking about the subject in less obvious ways. Douglas Gifford was surprised that he did not draw upon the immense range of reading, knowledge and wit which he knew his teacher possessed. Scott saw the history of Scottish literature as a tale to be recounted, which he did over two years in the first instance. In the 1960s, the Ordinary (first-year) class covered Scottish literature 'from its beginnings' to 1707; Higher Ordinary took up the story at 1707 and continued to the early twentieth century. Surprisingly, in view of Scott's own passionate commitment to MacDiarmid's Renaissance, neither Ronald Jack nor Robert MacDonald recall Scott dealing with that or with later twentieth-century material in class—but then coverage of anything approaching contemporary literature was not, it would seem, Glasgow's way at that time. And when Honours classes came in with the new department in 1971, Scott's programme for them simply told the same story again in the Honours third and fourth years, but in somewhat greater detail. Only with Rod Lyall's suggestion of a 'double-author' paper in the late 1970s did this pattern begin to break up.

There was never a hint of anything which would now be called 'theoretical'. Professor Kenneth Newton recalls[34] Scott's lectures to the Honours English class, on early twentieth-century Scottish fiction: at their core was a simple recounting of the plots with nothing to challenge senior students, who were clearly not expected to have read the book in advance. Edwin Morgan's impression, too, was that Scott's lectures were completely 'black and white' and did not always stimulate the very best students. It was an approach, however, that Ronald Jack and Robert MacDonald felt could be justified: an introductory level of lecturing was appropriate for the vast majority of the sub-Honours students Scott was teaching in the 1950s and '60s. Surviving lecture notes confirm this: historical information and description of the text is the prevailing mode, and when value judgements are made (which is quite often) they nevertheless seem to be offered as fixed and unchallengeable, to be learned along with the rest of the information. Rillie recalls being puzzled, with Edwin Morgan, as to how someone as clever as Scott (unavoidably overheard through the wall) could be content to repeat the same simple material for so long. Perhaps Scott did find lecturing something of a chore: revealingly, Tom Leonard writes to me: 'Regarding Alex's lectures, the bits I do remember liking is when he would recite from poems—I liked that because he obviously enjoyed doing it, became himself a bit more maybe.'[35] He further comments that reading the poetry 'seemed what he was for—not just doing his job'.

The distinction between Scott the poet and Scott the university lecturer was detectable even in the lecture room, though Scott the actor obviously helped out the latter. And it is the 'drama', the theatrical opportunities, of Scott's lecturing which Jack and MacDonald recall, too, though it was never the drama of spontaneous thought. The thespian Scott did not deviate from his lines, but acting experience would regularly show through, and MacDonald recalls enjoying his lectures greatly and being enthused by them. Rod Lyall recalls that his lectures 'were a performance' which could and did stimulate students.

If further proof of this be needed, it is perhaps to be found in the mock scroll in praise of their teacher and his poetry which the class of 1966–7 presented to him at a dinner in his honour. It begins:

> BE IT KNOWN TO ALL MEN AND WOMEN by this DECLARATION, that Whereas APOLLO, the Sovereign Lord of Poetry, hath by particular predilection Singled Out from the prosaic herd of men MR. ALEXANDER SCOTT to be the special vessel of his illumination, and in consequence of that choice hath in his High Benignity shed a Generative Ray upon the naturally barren soil of his pericranium, thereby rendering it exceedingly rich of Odes and Lyrics and other Rhymical Effusions ...

And so on for a whole page, signed on Friday 5 May 1967 by twenty-two students (including Douglas Gifford). According to Crombie Scott, this document, and the whole occasion, gave great pleasure.

As a postgraduate supervisor, he was good: where necessary he stimulated, surprised and nagged, but did not try to mould a student's thinking into an extension of his own.

SCOTT HAD SETTLED, WITH WHATEVER degree of satisfaction, in the city in which he would raise his family, pursue his career and die. To some extent, the interest which his life may now hold for us is bound up with his participation in the broader Scottish literary trends of the time—the developments in drama in the 1950s, the stimulus given to writing and publishing in the 1960s and '70s, and the emergence of Scottish literature as an academic subject growing in esteem and popularity and encouraging a new readership for the work of Scottish authors. These less purely personal matters are dealt with in succeeding chapters. On the other hand, the private and domestic aspects of those forty years in Glasgow are bound up, to some extent, with his poetry, of which a brief account is also given below. Finally, it will be appropriate to round out whatever sense of the man emerges from the main body of this book by sketching, in a concluding chapter, what can be gleaned of his personality and personal impact, on family, friends, students and colleagues. Nevertheless, it may help readers make sense of the 'public' narrative which precedes that final chapter if a brief summary of his remaining life is given here. After all, there is no surprise denouement to spoil.

His marriage was a happy one, though with its share of strains and difficulties, like most marriages. At the time of writing, his widow has survived him by seventeen years. His two sons, born so soon after the war, remained his total family. His father died in 1976, his mother as late as 1988, only eighteen months or so before Scott himself. He and Cath spent their married life in the West End of Glasgow, first in Lothian Gardens, then (from autumn 1959) at 5 Doune Gardens, a spacious terraced house. Finally, in October 1980, the couple moved to a flat at 14 Kirklee Terrace.

In his immediate family circle, the demands of Scott's literary and academic callings were accorded supreme priority: the life of the precocious schoolboy writer continued, the physical and emotional space which Scott's sense of vocation demanded being granted by his wife (so far as possible) without serious dispute. As time went by, the importance of Aberdeen as an alternative to Glasgow diminished, at least to some extent, and was supplanted by a growing devotion to the holiday destinations of the eastern Mediterranean—in particular Greece and Yugoslavia. We all look forward to our holidays, but Alexander Scott seems to have lived for these escapes to sunshine and antiquity—and perhaps, too, to a degree of sexual rejuvenation—with some of the myth-making intensity which had earlier elevated the memory of Aberdeen to a visionary status.

Family life could not be entirely separated from literary and professional circumstances, however, and by the end of the 1950s there were difficulties in all three. As we shall see, Scott's hopes to develop a name for himself as a dramatist—a hope that resulted, in the decade after the war, in a stream of now almost completely forgotten plays in a variety of media—came to nothing. Towards the end of the 1950s, also, he suffered the first really major setback in his academic career, when his attempt to gain a doctorate from his old university of Aberdeen, on the strength of his new biography of William Soutar, was turned down in 1958, at around the time of the book's publication. Perhaps in consequence of these disappointments, he found that he was losing all capacity to write poems. There is a hiatus in the ninth poetry notebook when, after a brief and never-published poem, 'The Sceptics' (dated 31 May 1957), the next poem to be recorded is 'Prehistoric Playmate' (also, arrestingly, dated 31 May 1965).[36] Do we glimpse something of his state of mind in the five lines of 'The Sceptics'?

> It is the world—the world with all of us in it —
> Cries from its cross, a huge agonising groan,
> 'My God, my God! Why have we forsaken Thee?'
> And shudders against the dark eclipsing noon
> As if that night were only the dim of death.

When one turns the page, it is to be confronted by the grimly perky satire of 'Just aucht-and-a-tanner for Ayesha's immortal breist ...' ('Prehistoric Playmate'). The unhappiness resulting from this loss of an ability that he had long regarded as fundamental to his very being is eloquently vouched for by both Catherine and Crombie Scott. Crombie, in particular, looks back at that period with some bitterness. It coincided with the brothers' teenage years: their father withdrew into himself to such an extent that they felt, quite simply, that he was not there for them. Crombie refers often to his father's 'muse' and to his loss of her, a timeworn but (to Crombie) still-living formula which helps him express his sense of a jealous and cruel rival to which, for a long and crucial period, he 'lost' his father. Once it was over, in the mid-1960s and Crombie was a young adult, 'I got my happy Dad back'. Scott himself writes of those dreadful years of poetic dearth, in 'Eighteen':

> I think of a six-year silence,
> six winter trees
> with never a single bird

According to the family, the poetic log-jam was broken by Finlay J. MacDonald, a friend and programme producer for the BBC in Scotland, who commissioned Scott to write a long poem on Aberdeen, as part of a television series in which poems, focused on places in Scotland, would be married to photographs. This series was an imaginative piece of experimental television which produced several fine poems from leading Scottish poets of the 1960s. It enabled Scott to write the poem about Aberdeen which he had been trying to write since the 1940s. Gratitude resulted in Scott dedicating his first volume of poems for fourteen years, *Cantrips* (1968), to MacDonald, 'commissioner extraordinary'. Following this, from the mid-1960s to the early 1980s, Scott was able to keep up a fairly steady flow of poems so that he was once more at the forefront of the Scottish poetry-reading public's awareness. Not that 'Heart of Stone' was Scott's only encounter with the BBC at this time. On the contrary, the readings and discussion programmes which had first introduced him to the microphone in post-war Aberdeen had initiated a regular involvement which had made him, by the time of 'Heart of Stone', a frequent broadcaster on literary and cultural matters. Some of his plays, too, had been for radio.

The 1960s also brought welcome change to his position, and the position of his subject, in Glasgow University. As described in a later chapter, Archie Duncan's arrival as head of department enabled Scott to move towards the independent department of Scottish Literature which he had probably wanted from the start. Separate classes in Scottish literature were gradually brought in, until a new department (in effect) was set up in 1971. Furthermore, in 1964 he gained his first academic promotion, to senior lecturer. His hopes, however, that the emergence of a new department with himself at its head would bring him a professorial chair were not to be fulfilled, a disappointment that soured his final years at university. He eventually stepped down as head of the department of Scottish Literature in the autumn of 1983, following this with a three-year period of part-time re-engagement, for teaching purposes.

Before this, however, a further dimension was added to the new lease of life he was granted in the mid-1960s. Not only was he writing again, and realising that the prospect of his own department was slowly coming about, but also the literary life of Scotland as a whole entered a hopeful and extremely lively phase with the new Scottish Art Council's enlarged commitment to writing and publishing, a phase in which Scott played a full and active part.

However, in 1977, emphysema was diagnosed, a disease of the lung which everyone believed was related to his continued heavy smoking. The disease progressed only slowly and at first made little impact on his outward behaviour. Crombie Scott, however, remembers his father's gradually deteriorating health being brought home to him one day in Aberdeen (he cannot be sure of the date) when, on Union Street, he was suddenly asked to slow down, a thing he had never heard before from his much taller father. I myself can recall at least one occasion (probably in the early- or mid-1980s) when David Hewitt of the University of Aberdeen and I had to leave Scott leaning against a metal safety barrier some yards from the then Scottish Arts Council premises in Charlotte Square, Edinburgh, as we all returned after lunch for a meeting. Scott, gasping for breath, urgently waved us on—he did not want his painful recovery to be witnessed. From having been a near-invariable presence at every possible literary meeting from the early 1970s onwards, Scott became a most infrequent attendee in the late 1980s. According to Cath Scott, her husband's doctors had been long checking him for signs of lung cancer, a regular complication for emphysema sufferers. This was finally confirmed, probably during a visit to the doctor in June 1989. He died three months later.

Chapter 4

A Department of Scottish Literature

Scott's position at Glasgow, at the end of the 1950s, was somewhat contradictory and uncomfortable. Although committed to the teaching of Scottish literature at university level, he was far from confining himself to academic concerns. He appeared to many university colleagues to be time-serving, but was actually engaged in a range of activities contributing to the increasing health of Scotland's literary life. Despite having, in both the English department and the department of Scottish History and Literature, colleagues who, like him, were interested in literature and/or the Scottish past, he nevertheless seems to have been essentially lonely within Glasgow University. From this imperfect situation, however, something of unique and lasting value eventually emerged: the separate department of Scottish Literature. Yet few in the University of Glasgow, at the beginning of the 1960s, were predicting that this would soon happen.

To this day, the department remains the only one of its kind, despite the immense growth of academic activity in the field from the 1960s onwards. In the other Scottish universities, teaching and research in Scottish language and literature still takes place mainly within departments of English. These are home to many academics currently helping push the subject forward but who seem to have felt no need to separate themselves from traditional English departments, and one has to conclude that it is not utterly essential for a Glasgow-style separation to take place. Yet, if asked, academics in the field welcome the fact that there is at least one distinct department of the subject in an ancient Scottish university. It is an appropriate landmark in the academic landscape and, in the last twenty years or so in particular, has become a healthy and successful department by any standards, an ornament to Glasgow University. As Professor David Hewitt of the University of Aberdeen says, its existence is one from which all those interested in the subject derive benefit: it bestows a final academic credibility on the subject and helps maintain its presence in the courses of other departments.[1] Furthermore, the department has built links with scholars all over the world and has established itself as a major academic player. It is now a key centre for the subject, one of a very few across the globe. And Alexander Scott's presence on the spot, with his particular personality, were among the principal factors in bringing about this unique development at Glasgow.

The creation of the separate Glasgow department did not merely give the subject an outward, institutional credibility. The development there of a full undergraduate programme in Scottish literature, both sub-Honours and Honours, has meant that the total narrative of the subject has been finally articulated as a taught subject. Teaching elsewhere, focusing on portions of the story, or on individual authors and texts, had hinted at the totality of the subject only by implication. What Scott, however, and the various colleagues who later joined him had to do was to set forth the total picture. It was the first time this had been done in a modern, post-MacDiarmid context: the few printed surveys of Scottish literature then available dated, at best, from only the early years of the century. Scott and his department moved Scottish literature, as a university subject, from piecemeal snapshots to a unified perspective. Whatever the brilliance, in the 1950s and '60s, of the work being done elsewhere on aspects of the subject, it was at Scott's Glasgow that a total modern picture began to be given to undergraduates.

When the still fledgling Glasgow department of Scottish Literature was at a particularly low ebb, and when Scott himself was completing his last few months teaching there, he wrote to the *Glasgow Herald* (4 April 1986) commenting on the current controversy concerning the scandal of the Gayre Chair (see p. 83). The letter is notable both for the way in which he combines an understated pride in his major academic achievement, namely the establishment of the department itself, with an understanding of its importance when commitment to the subject elsewhere is otherwise a matter of chance and goodwill. Even now, when Scottish Literature would appear to have a secure place throughout the Scottish university system (as well as in many corners beyond it), his essential point still holds good.

> Only in the Scottish Literature department at Glasgow is it possible for undergraduates to study the subject in depth, over a full four-years joint Honours[2] course. Again, only here is Scottish literature established in its own right, without having to rely on the personal interest of lecturers in English and their ability to persuade their colleagues to allocate some time to an optional course in Scottish letters.

Even now it is still possible for the study of Scottish literature in other universities, popular as it currently is, to fall victim to fashion, or to the preferences of new members of staff in departments of English. It is less likely to disappear again at Glasgow, and its embodiment there helps its status elsewhere, as Hewitt maintains.

As we have seen, Scott, from an early age, married a love of solitariness with the need to create round himself an environment of friendship and sharing which reflected and supported his literary interests and goals. At Glasgow, he was out of luck: his strange and isolated situation in the faculty of Arts failed to provide him with the support he instinctively sought. This was possibly the fault of no one, including Scott himself, though it is conceivable that a different personality might have created closer and more intellectually productive ties, in the 1950s, with both the English department and the Scottish historians. Scott stood apart, however, as he had done when the other children played street games in Cattofield Place; he had his own agenda. In the past, he had made a home in whichever educational institution he found himself by joining a drama group and by projecting himself in the role of 'writer': at school and as an undergraduate these tactics had earned him plaudits alongside his academic successes. As a professional academic in the 1950s, however, only success in the core activities of teaching and research counted: his efforts as a creative writer, as a dramatist and as a literary journalist no longer helped him crack open his new academic institution. Consequently (it is tempting to speculate) his inability to find a ready-made supportive society within the university may well have encouraged him to desire a separate department of Scottish Literature which, with luck, would give him what existing university departments could not. Such a department, which he could infuse with the vision and priorities of MacDiarmid's Renaissance, might make Glasgow University the academic and institutional home it had not been hitherto. Be that as it may, it must have been more and more obvious to any observer, surveying the growth, modernisation and specialisation of the post-war University of Glasgow, that the curious academic compromise of the chair of Scottish History and Literature was increasingly anachronistic. Change was clearly needed. How might it be brought about?

In 1962, a new professor and head of department arrived at the department of Scottish History and Literature. Archibald (Archie) A. M. Duncan, a medieval historian, was half a dozen years younger than Scott, who by this time had been fourteen years in the department. Some saw the personalities of the two men as rather similar and their day-to-day working relationship was cordial enough, but differences of background and approach maintained a distance between them which, while perhaps regrettable in personal terms, was nevertheless fruitful. Duncan was conscious that he had been promoted ahead of the older man; his university background, too, was Edinburgh and Oxford. Even more significant than the difference in ages, however, was the difference in approach to academic life itself: Duncan (as Rod Lyall[3] and others point out) embodied a younger, more dynamic and more overtly professional attitude to teaching and research than did Scott, academically shaped in the 1940s. Duncan was, temperamentally, a moderniser; Scott's approach to teaching, research and university life in general were beginning to look old-fashioned. So far as involvement with faculty and university affairs were concerned, the pair could not have been more different: beside Duncan's committed participation, Scott's (at that time) near-complete disengagement showed up ever more clearly. Duncan is still impatient at the memory of Scott's swift daily departures once the teaching was done.[4] He also fails to sympathise with Scott's lack of interest in university decision-making and with his resulting naivety as regards the *realpolitik* behind many of those decisions.

Yet although the interaction between the two was less than perfect, it did include a mutual willingness to find a better place for Scottish Literature in the university's arrangements. On this matter at least, Scott was as keen to innovate as was his new head of department and the two seem to have worked well together. Duncan's energetic support for the development of teaching in the subject, long desired by Scott, appears to have been one of the decisive factors in the eventual emergence of the department of Scottish Literature in 1971. As Jack Rillie says: '[Duncan] had the influence and the energy to get it through. Alex would never have managed it on his own.'[5] Rillie recalls that though Scott had often talked about the need for a separate department: 'I was never aware of him "campaigning" for it.' Even so, by the time David Hewitt (for example) was an undergraduate in Edinburgh in the early 1960s, there was an awareness in Scottish literary and academic circles of an intention in Glasgow (in effect, on the part of Alexander Scott) to establish a separate department of Scottish Literature and to teach the whole historical range of the subject.[6]

The emergence of the subject, in the form of a distinct department at Glasgow, was not, however, solely the result of Alexander Scott's stubborn and solitary championing suddenly teaming up with Archie Duncan's administrative energy. There was a growing feeling, throughout Scottish academia, that the subject's time had come. Interest in it had not been lacking in the other Scottish universities, although what was visible during the period of Scott's academic career was a shift from the teaching of individual Scottish authors and texts to the teaching of 'Scottish literature', with all the implications of context and continuity which the phrase implies. But at Edinburgh in 1948, for example, W. L. Renwick had intended that specifically Scottish literary topics should be taught by Scott and when the latter decamped to Glasgow Renwick, far from dropping the idea, appointed an alternative Scottish specialist, James Smart, in his place. He, in turn, would be succeeded by John MacQueen in 1959, who was appointed as a lecturer in 'medieval English and Scottish literature'. MacQueen also testifies to the fact that Renwick's successor, John Butt, was interested in Scottish material and encouraged its teaching.[7]

At Aberdeen, Alexander Scott himself had been briefly taught medieval Scottish literature, in his two immediate post-war years, by Matthew P. MacDiarmid. MacDiarmid had been an assistant lecturer there when war broke out, becoming a full lecturer in 1946 but moving to Belfast in 1952.[8] By then, however, he had been joined by two young Aberdeen graduates, Walter A. S. Keir and James Michie, both of whom had strong interests in Scottish literature. Indeed, from 1951 onwards, the syllabuses of both the first- and second-year classes at Aberdeen always contained a number of Scottish texts, the list changing and expanding slowly as the 1950s unfolded. In 1953, Aberdeen students began to be able to offer a complete Honours paper in Scottish literature. By session 1959–60, the texts being taught included the poems of Burns, Dunbar and Henryson along with others drawn from an anthology of medieval and Renaissance Scottish poetry, *Rob Roy*, *The Master of Ballantrae*, *The House with the Green Shutters*, plays by Bridie, and the *Satire of the Three Estates*. To this core were added other occasional texts and authors—Carlyle, ballads, Boswell, *A Scots Quair*, etc.

Examination papers from Aberdeen reflect an even greater awareness of the subject: in 1955, students could answer not only on such canonical authors and texts as those just mentioned, but also on a range of women writers from Jane Welsh Carlyle to Catherine Carswell and Agnes Muir Mackenzie. Questions were also being set on Livingstone's journals, George MacDonald's sermons (!) and the diaries of William Soutar (newly available in the 1954 edition by Keir's close friend Alexander Scott). How many students chose to answer on any of this is another matter, but the lively interest of the academic staff of Aberdeen in the broad sweep of Scottish literature is clear. By the time M. P. MacDiarmid returned from Belfast as a senior lecturer in 1964, Scottish material had become (thanks to Keir and Michie) a firmly established and prominent feature of the Aberdeen course.

The team of Scottish specialists was further greatly strengthened with the arrival, in January 1967, of Thomas Crawford. This was due to the energy of Professor G. I. Duthie, whose Shakespearean sympathies did not prevent him from being willing to allow the Scottish angle to develop and who had entered into keen competition with his Edinburgh counterpart John MacQueen (by then promoted to a chair) to secure Crawford, who had signalled his desire to return to Scotland from New Zealand. Duthie took great pleasure in snapping him up, thereby gaining for his department the author of a recent (1960) ground-breaking study of Burns. This book, in itself, played an important part in creating the realisation that Scottish literature was becoming academically mature. By the time of Crawford's arrival, the Aberdeen staff also contained two assistant lecturers, David Hewitt and Isobel Murray, who would contribute substantially to the department's reputation in Scottish literature in the decades to come.

At St Andrews, similarly, Scottish literature was securely represented in the post-war syllabuses of the English department, though less extensively and more narrowly than at Aberdeen. The Honours focus, so far as Scottish material was concerned, was on medieval literature in the form of texts such as *The Kingis Quair* and *The Testament of Cresseid* and such authors as Dunbar. At sub-Honours, there was almost always a Waverley novel set—in some years, more than one. Other individual texts made their sporadic appearances: the ballads, Scott's *Border Minstrelsy*, Burns's poems, *Humphrey Clinker*, *Annals of the Parish*, *Heroes and Hero Worship*, *Past and Present*. From 1955, however, an Honours paper in Scottish literature was introduced, which, a year later, was made compulsory for students specialising in literature as opposed to English language. Its focus at first seems to have been confined, unlike at Aberdeen, to literature before Sir Walter Scott. Scott himself was added in 1959. As the 1960s progressed, these papers tended to become a little shorter and a little thinner: it may be (as Professor Douglas Gifford suspects) that these papers were 'on the books' but not necessarily always taken or taught.[9] A change is visible, however, in the paper for May 1967: questions on nineteenth- and twentieth-century novelists appear for the first time, as do questions on Barrie, Bridie and on twentieth-century Scottish poets (though MacDiarmid was yet to be mentioned by name—this only two years before Aberdeen students were to be given an opportunity to write on 'concrete poetry in Scotland').

One is aware that examination papers do not necessarily reflect what was actually taught, and that in those days examinations sometimes seem to have been designed partially with a view to spurring future students on to more abstruse explorations. The present author, who must have encountered (but cannot recollect) the 1969 paper from Aberdeen which included the question on concrete poetry, can vouch for the fact that in the course that the paper examined no extended attention was given to concrete poetry, nor to the Christ's Kirk Tradition as such, nor to James Thomson ('B.V'), nor to John Davidson, despite their presence in the exam paper. (He does have, however, a faint recollection of Desmond Stewart's *The Mamelukes* being touched upon in a lecture!) Even so, some sense of the attitudes towards Scottish literature prevailing in the various Scottish departments can be gleaned from examination papers and what they reveal is a strong groundswell of interest and activity in the teaching of the subject.

Nor would this brief sketch of the state of the subject in the post-war decades be complete without an acknowledgement of the significant contribution made by important academics working furth of Scotland. These included David Daiches whose writings arguably initiated the post-war discussion of Burns, Scott and Stevenson, James Kinsley who was particularly important for his editorial work on major Scottish poets up to and including Burns, and G. Ross Roy whose initiatives at Columbia, SC established a major research resource and created the first academic journal devoted to Scottish literature.

But just as Glasgow, in the early 1960s, was contemplating developing the subject and the other Scottish universities were also showing increased interest in it, so the conservative attitude which would cause hesitations in Glasgow was being replicated elsewhere in Scottish academic life. And even when the subject did not provoke outright hostility, there was (and is) still a division of opinion as to whether Scottish literature is best taught as a separate subject in a separate department, or whether it should be taught within departments of English as part of a degree in English literature.

There are, as ever, things to be said on both sides. One understands, for example, the point of view of Scottish patriots who look at other nations, large and small, studying and teaching their native languages and literatures with pride. Why should not Scotland do the same, especially as the Scottish literary heritage is long and valuable? Why should Scottish literature not be taught, free-standing, outwith the umbrella of English literary history? Rod Lyall points out, furthermore, that he and his colleagues in the new department in the 1970s discovered with pleasure that they were no longer discussing Scottish writing defensively.[10] The perpetual underlying comparison with England and the stressing of Scottishness fell away: the subject no longer had to be defined with respect to its differences from English but could be offered simply on its own terms. On the other hand, it is nevertheless possible to feel either that the corpus of Scottish literature is too small to provide an adequate literary education or that in its very nature it demands a breadth of knowledge of writing from outside Scotland which is best acquired in the course of an undergraduate degree in English. As Professor Tom Craik succinctly puts it: 'Its dangers as subject of a whole degree: parochialism and politicisation.'[11] Lyall puts the same problem in different terms: the danger for the 'new' subject was that it might be ghettoised.

In the early 1960s, however, the separate department was still some way in the future. At the time of Duncan's arrival, Scott seemed to many in the university to be merely coasting in his job, but in fact he was as concerned about the place of Scottish literature at Glasgow as ever. Even before Duncan arrived in the university to take up his new post, Scott made a point of travelling through to Edinburgh to discuss with him the place of Scottish literature in the department's curriculum. They rapidly discovered that neither was knowledgeable about, nor terribly interested in, the other's sphere of expertise. Both recognised, however, that the current position of Scottish literature, in reality a very subsidiary add-on to the history teaching of the department, was inappropriate. Scott was keen to develop it and Duncan was supportive. Wasting no time, Duncan put in train the discussions that would lead to the start of an Ordinary Class (i.e. a first-year class) in Scottish literature in the autumn of 1963, separating the two subjects for the first time, as the minutes of meetings of the Arts faculty reveal.[12] At his request, a committee of the faculty of Arts was asked 'to consider the teaching of Scottish literature'. Although the faculty's arch-conservative, Professor Christian Fordyce, was a member of this committee, at the faculty meeting of 5 February 1963 it reported back that it 'was of the opinion that a new Ordinary course in Scottish literature should be instituted'. Nevertheless, familiar doubts and opposition immediately began to emerge: 'In the discussion which followed, objection was raised to the proliferation of Ordinary courses and doubt was expressed about the suitability of Scottish literature as a subject of study of an Ordinary course'. A decision was postponed until 5 March: 'After a full discussion it was decided by a majority vote that, for an experimental period of two years, there should be an Ordinary course in Scottish literature. The whole matter would be reviewed again in the session 1964–5.' Which it was, on 4 May 1965, when 'the faculty agreed to continue for session 1965–6 the present arrangement whereby Scottish history and Scottish literature are separated, thus extending the two-year trial period for a further year.' Despite the tentativeness of this start (or perhaps because of it), another committee was instituted 'to consider the teaching of Scottish literature', and it is clear from its report that by this time there was a considerable groundswell of opinion in favour of developing the subject properly. This committee included, among others, professors Archie Duncan, Peter Butter (English) and Derick Thomson (Celtic), and it reported back on 7 December 1965. Its report was accepted by faculty, who agreed to make a number of recommendations to the university authorities. The first of these historic recommendations was not only a major landmark in the academic development of the subject but is also highly significant as regards Alexander Scott's remaining career at Glasgow. The recommendation was:

> (1) That there should be a chair of Scottish Language and Literature. The professor should be responsible for the development of the subject in consultation with the professors of English and the professors of other closely related subjects. The existing chair in Scottish History and Literature should be renamed the chair of Scottish History and its incumbent should cease to be responsible for the subject of Scottish literature.

At the end of the minute, however, what might seem a potentially ominous note was struck: 'The faculty agreed to consider later the priority to be given to the proposed new chair.' This, however, was merely a sensible acknowledgement that in a decade of expansion and innovation many new subjects merited the creation of chairs and that not everything could be done at once. Even so, it is startling to remember that, in fact, it was not until 1995 that an established chair of Scottish Literature eventually came into existence, a delay that caused considerable tension between Scott and the university. For the second half of his working life, the prospect of a chair was dangling tantalisingly before him and he must have believed that, with these decisions of 1965, he had moved very close to obtaining it. The fact that, in the event, he was never given a chair certainly pained him during his final years as a teacher, as many who knew him testify. In December 1965, however, it must have seemed to him that a whole new academic future was opening up and that things were suddenly moving quickly.

A further recommendation was no less cheering: 'An additional lecturer in Scottish Literature [should] be appointed and ... an appointment be made of a lecturer in Language to be shared with English Language.' Indeed, this same meeting approved a further tangible equipping of the emerging department: faculty agreed to Professor Duncan's request for £50 to buy a bound copy of the *Scottish National Dictionary*. (This followed a much earlier request from Duncan, on 4 February 1964, for a grant 'to enable him to build up the Scottish literature resources of his class library', a request that had produced £30 each year over the two sessions 1963–5.)[13]

Although differing perceptions of Scott's personal worthiness as an academic probably played a part in delaying the filling of the proposed Scottish chair in the 1970s and '80s, it seems clear that in the 1960s the proposal just had to take its chances amidst a host of competing claims from other disciplines. But as the years passed, it slipped further and further down the list. Discussions of the faculty's priorities as regards chairs were a regular item in the 1970s, but by then it would seem that the Scottish Literature chair was no longer even being thought about. It simply disappeared from view, although a few years later it would re-emerge in a blaze of publicity. In the mid-1960s, however, these disappointments were far in the future.

Scott was made a senior lecturer in 1964 and seems to have felt that he was beginning to make some professional progress once more. A letter from C. M. Grieve to Scott reveals the extent to which the pair were actively discussing the way things were going at Glasgow, somewhat confirming one's suspicion that Scott regarded his university work as a facet of the Scottish Renaissance project.[14] They were also discussing Kenneth Buthlay, whose permanent return to Scotland seemed desirable to both Scott and Grieve, and who would soon be appointed by Scott to the new post of lecturer in 1966.

Buthlay was a quiet, sensitive scholar then performing much of the best early academic research on MacDiarmid. Scott had encountered him in Sao Paulo, at a British Council conference. They had even known each other, at least slightly, at Aberdeen University immediately after the war, where Buthlay had rather looked up to the older, prominent and energetic ex-officer. By the mid-60s, however, Buthlay had published a ground-breaking short study of MacDiarmid (1964), which managed to be both an excellent general introduction to, and a subtle and penetrating analysis of, that challenging subject. As letters in the National Library make clear, Scott was extremely keen that Buthlay apply for the post[15] and Duncan recalls that the decision to appoint him was essentially Scott's. (A very young Ian M. Campbell, now Professor of Scottish and Victorian Literature at Edinburgh, was also interviewed for the post. After Campbell's unsuccessful interview, Duncan went out of his way to commiserate with him and to indicate that the decision to appoint Buthlay had essentially been taken by others on the appointing committee.)[16] The warm relations between Scott and Buthlay cooled, however, as they worked together in an extremely small department with its day-to-day pressures. Edwin Morgan conjectures that Scott, in addition, may have been conscious that Buthlay, unlike himself, was producing ground-breaking research on a really major Scottish author.[17] On the other hand, Buthlay was no more of a committee man or university politician than Scott, who does not seem to have found him a huge help as regards the new and increasing administrative burden with which Scott was grappling.

The next logical development in the subject's growth at Glasgow was the introduction of Honours papers. Duncan (still, in the late 1960s, Scott's head of department) was also supportive of this step but felt that it would necessitate a final break between the component parts of his department: as much as anything else, his own lack of knowledge of Scottish literature would put him in a completely false position of titular responsibility for it.[18] So he backed the move to create a new and separate department of Scottish Literature, which was agreed in principle before the onset of the major university cuts of the early 1970s. The world's first department of Scottish Literature started its independent existence in the academic year 1971–2. As the University moved to this decision, however, it was not assumed that the new department required the filling of the proposed chair (now half a dozen years after it was first agreed in principle) nor that Scott as its head required to be further promoted at that point. Furthermore, in that period of suddenly increasing financial difficulty for UK universities, there would be no additional full-time teaching staff. As Scott put it in a letter to Alastair Mackie:

> Afraid there is no university cash around—due to the 'squeeze'—for a Scott. Lit. chair or more staff. Ken Buthlay and I will just have to double our lecturing load. But the great thing is to have established a precedent, which the other Scottish universities can't afford to ignore.[19]

The combination of pleasure and resignation expressed here was appropriate for the time, not just because money was short but also because responses within the university to the development were still diverse. As Duncan recalls, there was a strong strand of feeling that the new department was just a lot of nationalistic nonsense. There was apparently, for example, one notorious occasion after senate had approved the Honours degree in the subject when two professors of the physical sciences were heard denouncing the innovation in the college club bar, claiming that there was 'no such subject' as Scottish literature. This view was taken even by some in the English department, though not by Peter Butter nor by Edwin Morgan, both of whom generously agreed to help out with some of the teaching. Jack Rillie, too, was supportive. He recalls, however, that:

> there was indeed a general feeling in English that there really was not enough in Scottish literature to provide the breadth for a four-years Honours course. And although one or two may have doubted whether there was enough to justify a separate appointment there was no real opposition to AS on these grounds...But AS was enough. Then there were two more staff and Sc Lit was a dept claiming a place in Combined Honours. That was a bit harder to accept....But no organised opposition to the introduction of the Sc. Lit. dept.[20]

Furthermore, the English department's view of Scott as a colleague was far from rapturous. For example, in 1985, Archie Duncan argued for consideration to be given to the bringing together of Scottish and English literature under one umbrella. (He was writing during a period when Glasgow University was under particular pressure to combine cognate departments across the board, and also at a time when the English department under Peter Butter was a much more co-operative body generally than it had been in the 1960s.) Making the case, though, he commented bluntly to the principal, Sir Alwyn Williams, on how Scott's perceived personality had been a factor in the decisions taken fifteen years earlier:

> I do not think we should follow this [i.e. the establishment of a Gayre Chair in Scottish Literature—see below] through without first deciding whether Scottish Literature should continue to be a separate department. It would seem to me that if it formed a department within English Literature both subjects would be greatly strengthened. I think it is no secret that this would have been seriously considered when the department was set up were it not that Mr Scott was such an abrasive personality that the English department were reluctant to have him in their midst. Now I think we should ask ourselves: if we were setting up Scottish Literature in the university where would we put it? The answer seems surely to be in the English Literature department.[21]

If Duncan's energy, capability and goodwill were essential to the establishing of the separate department, so (by Duncan's own account) was Scott with his blunt, uncompromising personality and his refusal to accommodate himself to the conventions and expectations of university life, at least at Glasgow. In so far as Duncan was motivated to remove from his department a subject that he himself did not profess, it is obvious that, all other things being equal, his readiest solution would have been to transfer the subject and its teacher to the department of English. But all other things were not equal: the teacher was Alexander Scott. As David Hewitt says, Scott was the necessary thorn, whose prickliness resulted in departmental independence for the subject.[22] Scott's 'thrawnness' enabled him (in Rod Lyall's phrase) to 'hold the fort' for Scottish literature's academic status in the university world at large.[23] But while that 'thrawnness' was, in one way, merely a personal characteristic and part of his style, it was also a reflection of his undeviating commitment to, and prioritising of, his subject. If Scott regarded his university teaching as an aspect of his greater mission on behalf of the Scottish Renaissance and its priorities, that also meant that his strength of feeling for the wider movement stiffened and sustained his commitment to his educational task.

Scott soon discovered, though, that his attainment of his long-held desire to head his own department of Scottish Literature did not suddenly render his university life free of trouble or disappointment. Despite the help of sympathetic colleagues in English Literature, the teaching load was substantially increasing. Furthermore, he was discovering that, even though they had known each other for so long, he and Buthlay did not really get on well as colleagues. This situation had already became apparent to others such as Robert MacDonald who, having been a student of Scott's in 1961–3, arrived as Clerk to the Faculty of Arts in 1975. MacDonald's sense of the new department was that, despite its youth, it was not really very dynamic and 'didn't seem to be going anywhere very far, or very fast'.[24] It is a view held by some that Scott's choice of Buthlay, whatever the solidity of his work on MacDiarmid and despite his great personal humanity (a virtue that my own contacts with him, over a number of years, fully confirm), was an opportunity missed when someone of a younger generation could have been brought in. As it was, the new department was originally staffed, on the literature side at least, by two men both around fifty whose outlooks on their subject and how it should be taught had been formed a generation earlier. The dream Scott was realising was already twenty years old.

The appointment of Rod Lyall in 1975, however, brought a much younger and highly dynamic personality into the department. As the first Honours students completed their degrees, it had become apparent that a medieval and Renaissance specialist was required. Scott's wide-ranging coverage of all periods of Scottish literature had been sufficient, for more than a quarter of a century, for sub-Honours work but effective Honours teaching requires more precise research expertise on the part of the teacher. Lyall's arrival was of huge significance: not only would he eventually prove an innovative head of department after Scott's retirement in 1983, but unlike his older colleagues he also proved to be a natural university politician, eager to get involved in the decision-making processes which increasingly impacted on their work. So prominent and effective did he become in the faculty's committees that, while still an un-promoted lecturer, he was elected dean of the faculty. It was at Lyall's instigation that the first major breakaway from the purely historical approach to the department's teaching of the subject was introduced: he pushed for the introduction of author-centred Honours papers alongside the old-style 'period' papers used hitherto.

In the still tiny department, there was always the uncomfortable suspicion that the English department in particular still tended to look down on Scottish literature, both as a subject and as a rival department. In the 1960s, even the undergraduates could pick up that Scottish literature was being looked down upon, to some extent, by academics in other departments. Rod Lyall voices the belief that, as a whole, the English department viewed the new department of Scottish Literature with 'genial contempt' and says that Scott was fully aware of the feeling. Lyall believes that Scott confidently regarded that attitude to his subject as quite unjustified but was unable to fight back against it.[25] He lacked the political skills to make headway in such a situation, and although he was now attending meetings of faculty often he spoke infrequently and made little impression. His energy was still focused on teaching—and on the activities outside Glasgow University in which he was as heavily involved as ever.

The simmering mistrust between the two literature departments came to a head in the dispute as to the degree to be awarded to the poet Tom Leonard in

1976. In the normal course of events, the only occasion in the academic year when two departments (in any university) actually sit down together in the same room is at the examination board meeting which decides the degrees to be awarded to joint-Honours candidates. The meeting to decide Leonard's degree proved to be so bitter that even now, thirty years on, it is still a painful and sensitive recollection to anyone who was there. Leonard himself (though not, of course, present at the meeting) still gets understandably angry about what took place, and even now members of the two departments approach the subject in conversation with extreme tentativeness, keen not to mention Leonard's name. Leonard, however, is prepared to have the matter raised in public, provided that the following is made clear:

> I don't mind you mentioning my name as you ask, so long as you make it absolutely clear that in my own estimation the attempt to give me a third was personally spiteful, and in my opinion was certainly outrageous. I was shocked at the time, though also at the time I thought: 'How typical – they would, wouldn't they.'[26]

The difficulty arose because the two departments had come to the meeting with diametrically opposed preconceptions about what degree class should be awarded to their shared student. For English, Leonard was deserving of nothing less than a First—he had been awarded the Bradley Medal as Best Student of the Year in English, and his papers in the subject confirmed that view. Of his Scottish literature papers, however, not all had been completed and he admits that his answers on one or two writers he found unsympathetic—he mentions Sir Walter Scott—were below his best. Yet he insists that elsewhere in his Scottish answers he was writing at or near his best.[27] All on the Scottish side, however, including the external examiner, saw him as meriting no more than a Third. After much bitter arguing, the English team, strongly supported by *their* external examiner, succeeded in gaining for Leonard a Lower Second (2.2).

Thankfully, the justice or otherwise of this decision need concern us not a whit. What is relevant, however, are the undercurrents between the two departments which became visible during this dispute. The members of the Scottish Literature department felt that the meeting (and its outcome) showed the attitude of superiority towards them held by their English colleagues: to them, the larger department seemed to be taking the view that English literature (as a subject) is far more important than Scottish literature, *therefore* the English point of view should prevail. It is a version of events that Jack Rillie, however, from the English Literature side of the argument, does not fully endorse. He thinks that the difficulties at moments such as this arose, rather, out of problems of personality: Scott could seem over-stubborn in examiners' meetings and (he suspects) there were occasional worries, in the faculty as a whole, about the marking standards being applied in the new department. The Scots often seemed to be marking too high—except when they 'badly undermarked' (in Rillie's view)

Leonard. For whatever reason, marks being given by the new department often seemed inaccurate to faculty colleagues, and a doubt about Scott himself, as an academic, seemed to play its part. Rillie wonders if Scott's lack of experience in working as part of a large literature department left him unsure about marking standards.[28] Against this, however, it has to be said that neither of the Scottish academics from other universities who acted as external examiners for the department of Scottish Literature during Scott's headship, and to whom I have spoken, expressed any worries about his competence in these matters.

Ideally, the dispute should have ended with the decision to award the Lower Second but not only were those present left with bruises, which lasted for many years, but also Leonard's desire to proceed to postgraduate work on the nineteenth-century poet James Thomson added to the ill-feeling. While still ignorant of the Scottish Literature department's view of his Finals performance, Leonard attempted to phone Scott to ask to be taken on as a research student. Scott was unavailable, so Leonard called Edwin Morgan, in the English department, instead. Morgan instantly agreed to supervise him and the arrangements were made without further reference to Scott's department, a matter about which Scott complained bitterly at meetings of faculty and of the university's Higher Degrees Committee where Peter Butter, as head of English, eventually apologised for the apparent discourtesy. The whole episode both revealed and exacerbated the strains between the two departments and added to Scott's embitterment. (Leonard's research resulted not in a further degree but in an award-winning study of Thomson, the research materials for which Glasgow University subsequently purchased. Leonard relishes the irony.)

The development of the subject in the 1960s and the setting up of the separate department in 1971 kept the issue of possible promotion for Scott very much alive. Letters to fellow poets during the lead-up to 1971 show clearly that he had been hoping that the chair first envisaged by the university in 1965 would be created along with the new department—with the implication that he should occupy it. He took over as head, however, still with the rank of senior lecturer. He was first considered for a readership in 1972, when referees' perceptions of him were divided along lines that remained fixed throughout his remaining time at Glasgow and, indeed, that remain to this day. His old teacher, M. P. MacDiarmid, took the view that the range of Scott's contribution to the literary life of Scotland justified promotion. As Principal Williams noted in 1976:

> MacDiarmid's opinion on Scott when sought in 1972 was summed up 'it seems to me that the sum of Mr Scott's literary activities, if considered along with his departmental responsibilities, justifies the conferment of a readership.' The other two referees at that time...were not enthusiastic.[29]

One of the two unenthusiastic referees confirmed to me that he recognised the range of Scott's general cultural activities but that, in his view, a substantial academic promotion such as the one proposed requires a substantial published academic achievement and that (again, in his view) Scott always lacked that. In recent decades, we have become familiar with the demand for solid research publications (which has come to mean publications which carry weight in the periodic Research Assessment Exercise) as practically the only justification for academic promotion, but in 1972 such outside pressures were not yet in view: nevertheless, Scott's academic weight was in doubt—and the doubt was relevant—even in those pre-lapsarian days. Yet it was part of Scott's awkwardness that he could not be simply dismissed as a straightforward non-performer. When his name again came forward for a readership in 1976 (probably at his own instigation, stung as he was by Edwin Morgan's promotion to a titular professorship in 1975),[30] even the hard-headed Archie Duncan was giving serious and sympathetic consideration to the case for taking Scott's 'creative side' into account and was looking around for helpful and sound referees, amongst whom he suggested the poet George Bruce, knowing he would speak up strongly for Scott.[31] In other words, Scott's activity as a poet and writer was being seriously considered as part of his academic case, and he became a reader in October 1976.

Scott was then proposed for a titular professorship by his old friend Derick Thomson. This failed, as did Thomson's further attempt the following year.[32] As Thomson's letter on this second occasion makes clear, the university authorities were beginning to contemplate the distinction between Scott and the department he headed. It gives, as one of the justifications for Scott's promotion, the opinion that: 'I am strongly of the view that his subject should be further supported ...', at which point someone, possibly Principal Williams, has underlined 'his subject' but added the comment 'But not the man?'

A year later still, Scott apparently thought that he had found the answer to the blockage of his further promotion. The death of C. M. Grieve in 1978 had prompted the setting up of a Hugh MacDiarmid Memorial Fund: Scott and other literati found themselves discussing possible uses for the hoped-for money at a meeting at Scottish Arts Council headquarters. Douglas Gifford recalls suggesting that perhaps a chair of Scottish Literature might be the best use for the money, and noticing a look of new interest passing across Scott's face—a gleam in his eye—as the idea was floated.[33] The result was a letter from Scott to Principal Williams, informing him of the fund's existence and of the proposal, and pointing out that Glasgow was best placed of all the Scottish universities to take advantage of the opportunity, thanks to its already having a department in place. Williams replied to this, arguing that Scott's sums did not quite meet the requirements: Scott had thought that if another university were to set about establishing a chair from scratch, £150,000 would be needed—far more, Scott was prepared to admit, than the fund was ever likely to raise. He tried to persuade Williams, however, that Glasgow (uniquely) would need far less than this: 'All that would be required here would be a much smaller sum in order to "top up" the present departmental arrangements.' Williams' cautious reply indicated that a chair now demanded a fund of £230,000, and succeeded in flushing out from Scott the admission that what he was really asking for was the elevation of 'the present head of the department of Scottish Literature here to the proposed chair. I'm sorry if this point was obscure in my original letter, where I was attempting to make it in as impersonal a way as possible.'[34]

In the end, the fund was put to quite a different use, but Scott's intervention at this point brought the issue of his possible elevation under discussion once more. In an exchange of notes between Principal Williams and Archie Duncan, the latter made no secret of his own doubts about Scott's worthiness of a chair, and in discussion with me has admitted that it was also his political sense that such a promotion would not have had strong support in the relevant committee.[35] The old complaint about Scott's non-presence on campus was now being overtaken by a belief that he lacked organisation and efficiency as a departmental head, and by a perception within the university (and not merely on Duncan's part) that his department was among the least dynamic in the university. Furthermore, it was a period of particular financial stringency across the whole university sector and the number of students taking the subject was very low, so that (within the department, at least) there seemed the serious possibility that it might be one of those closed in any 'rationalisation'.

Nevertheless, a further attempt was made at this time to put Scott forward for a chair by Kenneth Varty, the dean of the faculty of Arts.[36] Varty had reviewed the previous failed attempts and recognised that Scott's earlier applications had been extremely poorly prepared. And indeed the 1977 application contains a curriculum vitae of less than one page, entirely lacking in detail and very poorly laid out. It is jolly hard to read, in fact. Varty, trying hard to be helpful, says of this:

> Mr Scott's way of listing, laconically, pel-mel [*sic*], his many publications and editorial activities, gave an unclear impression of the quite extraordinary wealth of research and involvement which one expects of a professor.

He now gave Scott detailed advice on how a CV might be better structured 'so that the members of the committee may see more clearly his very real achievements'. He, too, is anxious that the department be bolstered by such a promotion, and implicitly acknowledges the importance of Scott's creative writing:

> a strong case for it with a view to the long-term promotion and development of the teaching (and practice) of Scottish Literature in this university ... it seems to be generally agreed that he has done much to stimulate and advance significantly the study of his subject.

The pencilled comments on this letter include: 'Acceptable as scholar/poet' and in the documentation the detail 'MC—1945' is picked out and asterisked. On the other hand, the Principal (?) has also scribbled, against the passage about the laconic, pell-mell listing, the query: 'Does this reflect the way he deals with dept?' This letter is accompanied by a new list of publications which is, indeed, much longer and fuller than before, and undeniably impressive. Its very first item, however, is: '"The red planet calling red circle". Science-fiction short story. The Hotspur, 1934'—a detail that Rod Lyall recalls as disastrous, revealing as it does Scott's surprising lack of a sense of what is relevant to include in an academic CV.[37] Scott the creative writer continued to be extremely conscious, and proud, of his schoolboy achievements, especially this earliest publication, but once more his perception of himself as, first and foremost, a writer came in conflict with the demands of his academic career.

There occurred one final opportunity for a chair to come Scott's way. In June 1980, Lt.-Col. Robert Gayre of Gayre and Nigg, a rich Scottish ethnologist who had previously given gifts to the universities of Edinburgh and Oxford, contributed £10,000 to the university's Whistler Appeal (to prevent the sale of the university's collection of Whistler's paintings earmarked to help fund the new Hunterian Art Gallery). Gayre followed this in October with an offer of a further £30,000 to support 'the Scottish Arts' in the university. Archie Duncan, considering how the money might be applied to the university's needs, proposed to the Principal that they suggest the financing of a chair of Scottish literature.[38] He did this despite his criticisms of Scott and his current department, seeing the offer, in a completely pragmatic way, as a chance not to be missed. Pragmatism prevailed, too, in the university's ignoring of Gayre's known racialist views. And pragmatism pointed the way to the arrangement agreed between the university and Gayre for the provision of the money: Gayre would donate an annual sum of £10,000 for five years, from 1981 to 1985 inclusive. Invested, this sum would produce an amount sufficient to enable the founding of a chair in 1986. Staggering the money not only helped the university persuade Gayre to increase the total amount, but also sidestepped the issue of the problem embodied in Scott. Alert to the possibility of controversy within the university, Duncan believed that the perception of Scott was such that the chances of successfully establishing a chair in Scottish Literature would be higher if Rod Lyall were to be the beneficiary. Alexander Scott was due to retire in 1985.

The first that Scott and his department knew of developments that so intimately concerned them was in a letter to Scott from the Principal.[39] Carefully worded to imply that Scott would doubtless rejoice in the approaching creation of the long-desired chair, the letter makes no acknowledgement of the personal message to Scott which it silently conveyed. Other material in the Principal's papers makes it clear that Williams was conscious, nevertheless, of the hurtfulness of the arrangement. Rod Lyall recalls the meeting at which Scott produced the letter.[40] That things had been arranged so as to bring the chair into being as soon as Scott had departed was obvious to all. It was, says Lyall, a perfect insult: 'an appalling slap in the face'. Student numbers had dropped to an alarming extent and Scott growled bitterly: 'It would be ironic, wouldn't it, if they appointed a professor and there were no students for him to teach?' It was the conclusive proof to Scott that he was never going to be granted a chair, and the immediate trigger for his early retirement. Lyall is full of sympathy for Scott, although, like many of the other academics involved, he sees why the university acted as it did. He cannot shake off the feeling, however, that Scott was handled insensitively. To the best of his knowledge, the letter produced at the department meeting was the first Scott himself knew about Gayre's money and how it had been decided to use it. Archie Duncan acknowledges that he and Scott never discussed the matter, and Lyall is reasonably sure that the Principal did not call Scott in to give him an explanation or to sweeten the pill. As Duncan says: 'He just had to lump it.'[41]

Scott's reply to the Principal's letter was laconic but far from pell-mell:

> Dear Principal,
> Very many thanks for your most welcome letter on the Gayre benefaction, and for your own good offices in the matter. We must hope that when the gift is made public it will stimulate other benefactors to join in the project.
> Yours sincerely,
> Alexander Scott[42]

I am assured that, despite appearances, Scott's treatment was in no way the product of vindictiveness on the part of anyone in the university. As Jack Rillie says, he was regarded by some in the university as 'an awkward bugger' but he genuinely seems to have had no particular enemies.[43] Duncan insists that there was *no* feeling that people wanted rid of Scott—'none of that, at all'.[44] Having discussed the matter with several Glasgow academics in a position to know, I have been convinced that Scott's failure to be given a chair was in no way due to the desire of anyone to do him down. Rather, it was a reflection of the reality of academic life and the circumstances in which all universities found themselves from the 1970s onwards. From then on, it was more urgent than ever before that a professor should have a proven track record of esteemed academic publication, that the university could be assured that a new professor would continue to publish well, and that he or she would offer a department strong academic leadership both through publishing and through close involvement with staff, students and the university community as a whole. In the modern world, as a result of the premium now placed on academic research productivity, no chair can be offered to anyone who cannot fulfil those requirements. It would be a grave, indeed irresponsible, disservice to the academic institution to do so. This was becoming an inescapable feature of academic life in the later years of Scott's time at Glasgow.

Of course, chair appointments had always implied high academic standards, and it is clear that at no stage in his career had Scott been widely perceived within the university as a likely candidate for a professorship. His record of strictly academic publication, though stretching back to the beginning of his career, was patchy and, while respectable enough, it was always perceived as lacking the distinction justifying a chair. Furthermore, his reputation in the university as someone who came in just to do the lecturing did not make him an obvious professorial role model. Nor had he turned out to be a dynamic head of department after 1971.

Scott himself, however, maintained his hopes of a personal chair throughout the first decade of the new department's existence. That he did so reflected not just his slowness to appreciate the newly urgent realities of university life, but also the fact that he viewed himself with a double perspective: partly he saw himself in the context of academia, and partly as prominent in Scotland's literary life in general. And he never disentangled these perspectives. Conversely, both communities had perceptions of him. If, by and large, most inside the university saw him as little deserving of a chair, very many outside the university, especially those who knew him personally and worked with him on any number of cultural projects, could not understand why he was not promoted. To fellow poets and collaborators Maurice Lindsay and Duncan Glen, for example, it was inconceivable that a lifetime of promoting Scottish literature both outside and inside the University of Glasgow should fail to bring its due reward. From the time that the department of Scottish Literature began in 1971, it was widely expected in the Scottish literary community that Scott would be promoted, and it was not understood why he was not. The view persists to this day. Paul Scott's comment in his recent autobiography puts it clearly: 'It is a reproach to Glasgow University that he was never made Professor of Scottish Literature, a post for which he was so well equipped and for which the time had come.'[45]

In the same vein, Maurice Lindsay has recently written as follows:

> Alexander Scott ... founded the Department of Scottish Literature at Glasgow University, though—much to that august body's disgrace, in the opinion of many—he remained reader in Scottish Literature, the distinction of occupying the first Chair in the subject eventually going to one of his students.[46]

Tessa Ransford, whose dealings with Scott have left her with mixed feelings about him, nevertheless recalls how she and all her literary friends were shocked when it sank in that he would not be given the chair so long expected to be his.[47]

Although it is not hard to understand why this view should have been so prevalent, anyone with experience of the difficulties facing decision-makers in modern universities will also understand that the matter was actually far less clear-cut. That said, however, the issue does not simply arise from a division between knowledgeable university insiders and well-meaning outsiders. It is not hard to find academic contemporaries of Scott who, while admittedly not party to all the minutiae of the case, feel that, on balance, he was hard done by. Occasionally, some felt that, even as late as the 1980s, to specialise in Scottish literature was to be regarded as an academic lightweight. Rod Lyall recalls how, during his time at Glasgow, an Edinburgh academic once went into print describing Scottish literature as a 'second-class subject for second-class minds'.[48] David Hewitt recalls how, when he was acting as the department's external examiner soon after Scott's departure, he felt that he and his Scottish literature colleagues were being treated to something like discourtesy by some of their English department opposite numbers, a discourtesy that, once more, seemed to reflect a judgement upon the subject itself.[49] The point is sometimes made, also, that other scholars and critics of great distinction in the field of Scottish literature, including M. P. MacDiarmid and Thomas Crawford, failed to gain chairs in the 1960s and '70s, to the surprise of many who knew their work: suspicion of prejudice can still be found. It should be acknowledged, however, that practical local considerations in the University of Aberdeen appear to have been decisive in the failure to promote MacDiarmid and Crawford.

It is probably necessary, in these matters, to guard against a swift adoption of dark suspicions: when monolithic institutions appear to do down deserving individuals, it is only too easy to cast the institution as a villain. In Scott's case, however, the balance of justice and injustice still seems exceptionally finely poised, and even those of my informants with knowledge of the complexities of promotion in their own institutions are sometimes able to feel that Glasgow University failed to appreciate the strengths of Scott's lifetime achievement.

And as has been pointed out to me by more than one person, Scott was perhaps merely unlucky in his timing. In his day, it was seldom that publishing poetry or fiction contributed to academic advancement, an attitude that was carried over into the early years of research assessment in the period immediately following Scott's retirement. In the first Research Assessment Exercises, only strictly academic publications by university staff 'counted': creative writing of the kind Scott had long been producing was not even considered by the early assessment panels whose judgements played such a major part in determining a department's reputation and funding. That position no longer holds good; published poems and novels are now accepted as a possible part of an academic's 'research' output. As Ronald Jack says, nowadays someone with Scott's mix of publications would be worth his weight in gold to any literature department.[50]

Disgusted by his treatment and increasingly troubled by his health, Scott consulted with Rod Lyall and decided to avail himself of the early retirement scheme then on offer. He ceased to be head of department when he retired at the end of September 1983, but (like so many other senior academics encouraged to leave early in the interests of university finances) he took part-time re-engagement for a further three years, for teaching purposes.

The Gayre bequest, furthermore, ended happily for no one. The university pushed ahead with its plans to establish the chair, advertising the post and getting to the point of inviting candidates for interview. But it had made the mistake of publicly naming the chair after Gayre, thus drawing attention to the source of the money. Early in 1986, a major controversy blew up about his racist views. The furore reached an astonishing pitch and at an extremely late stage the university decided, after all, that it could not accept his money. Archie Duncan had to travel to Gayre's home and personally hand over a cheque for the sum Gayre had contributed. This debacle coincided with Scott's last months as a university teacher, and left the tiny department in an extraordinarily exposed position with one senior member leaving, another due to retire in a very few years, and Rod Lyall left with no assurance that new colleagues would be appointed to join him. Indeed, he was urged to agree to join the English department, letting the department of Scottish Literature disappear.[51] This did not happen, of course and Lyall was awarded a titular chair. An established chair in Scottish Literature was not created, however, until 1995, when T. Douglas Gifford, the student of Scott's referred to by Maurice Lindsay, was appointed to it.

Scott's achievement at Glasgow, however, cannot be simply reduced to the question of his promotion or lack of it. In personal terms, he was a considerable success. If he minimised his accessibility to students by being often out of his office, he was nevertheless capable of providing them with strong support when the need arose: Tom Leonard found Scott sympathetic and understanding when personal difficulties were made known to him. Immediate academic colleagues usually found Scott straightforward to work with. Indeed, Rod Lyall stresses that Scott was 'a good boss', clearly glad that his new appointee was so energetic in all areas of academic activity. Scott welcomed Lyall's youthful and fresh approach, encouraging him to 'rethink a lot of what we were doing as a department'. Scott, says Lyall, was very open to change and put up no barrier to any new initiatives—'though if he *was* against something, you knew!'[52] Indeed, it seems likely that this youthful energy was part of what Scott was looking for, by the mid-1970s. The two had first met at an Edinburgh conference in 1974 during which, at a party, Lyall had accidentally spilled beer over Scott. When the chance to appoint a medievalist arose soon after, Scott contacted Lyall and told him to apply; Lyall believes that Scott must have known that he would bring change to the department.

Not that Scott was always lacking in initiatives of his own: it seems to have been through his efforts that George Bruce, who had retired from his senior position in BBC Scotland in 1970, was appointed as the university's first creative writing fellow attached to the department of Scottish Literature in 1971. At first, however, the appointment was surprisingly controversial: younger writers complained of cronyism.[53] What they did not know was that Scott's first impulse was to have Iain Crichton Smith, who twice turned down the opportunity.[54] But then Bruce proved an outstanding success. This was one of the earliest appointments of its kind and was one which, says Trevor Royle (literature director of the Scottish Arts Council during much of the 1970s), set new standards for holders of similar positions.[55]

The fellowship was one of the more obvious successes in Scott's time as head of the department. On the whole, under Scott's leadership in the first dozen years of its existence, the department was regarded as a modest rather than a resounding success. Scott had achieved one of his most important professional goals, but the doggedness which had finally brought it about was not necessarily the ideal quality to enable the department to take off spectacularly in what was an increasingly difficult environment for everyone in academic life at that time. The substantial drop in student numbers in the later 1970s, though far from afflicting Scottish Literature alone, was an especially worrying problem. Only under his successors as head of department, Rod Lyall and Douglas Gifford, did the department begin to thrive and expand once more. Fortune was on their side, as they would be the first to admit: not only did student numbers generally begin to pick up, but also across Scotland (and, indeed, elsewhere) Scottish literature as an academic subject really began to take off both in terms of academic prestige and student popularity. It became easier, too, to publish in the subject. Equally important, however, was the fact that both Lyall and Gifford were completely comfortable in the cut and thrust of university life. Both were able to make an impression on the Glasgow University community, in personal and social as well as administrative terms, to an extent that Scott had failed to do.

Yet both are full of praise for their former head of department, and teacher. Gifford stresses how Scott's unwavering commitment to the subject, over many years when it was far from fashionable, was crucial to the establishment and development of the department.[56] Lyall sees him as important more as a cultural activist than as an academic; but in the academic sphere 'he created a space, an opportunity'.[57] They and others in the field know that it was a later generation which was able to take advantage of Scott's doggedness in his university role, but 'he held the fort'. Scott may not have been the occupant of the first established chair of Scottish Literature, but no one can deny him the honour of being the first head of the world's only department of the subject.

Although Scott's uncomfortable academic career tells us little, in general, about the relationship between practising poets and universities in modern Scotland, it does tell us much about the man himself. Post-war Glasgow University was not inherently inhospitable to serious poets, as the careers of Derick Thomson and Edwin Morgan demonstrate. But Thomson and Morgan, in their different ways, saw themselves as academics as precisely as they saw themselves as poets. Scott, it seems, did not. One comes to the conclusion that, firmly as he believed in the importance of his subject, his teaching was part of a wider enterprise on behalf of literature in Scotland, an enterprise that drew its strength from a world of creativity and nationalism with different rules from those of academia.

The tension between the two spheres of commitment is also visible in Scott's patchy career as a publishing academic. This was an area where many, both inside and outside Scotland's universities, looked for more from him than they received. There is no academic 'big book' with his name on it, putting his mark on the history of the subject. In this respect, his two major publications on Soutar, from the first phase of his university career, constitute his most substantial achievements. (Nor, indeed, at the time of writing, have they yet been supplanted.) By the 1970s, many would have agreed that Alexander Scott, by then equally senior as a poet identified with the Renaissance and as a prominent Scottish academic, should have been producing the definitive account of MacDiarmid and his poetic and cultural revolution, for his own generation at least. No such account appeared, though there is much evidence that Scott had just such a plan in mind. One can only speculate why no such book appeared. Even Rod Lyall, by then a colleague close to him and professionally concerned to know what academic work Scott was engaged in, does not know what happened to the much talked-about project.

Part of the problem was one that, to an extent, still afflicts academics (in these days of the Research Assessment Exercise, even more than in Scott's): what does, and what does not, constitute academic publishing? Even apart from the question of what weight ('research weight', that is), if any, should be given to the published poetry of an academic poet, there is the question of where literary and cultural 'journalism' ends and 'proper' academic publishing begins. It was an issue that Edwin Muir had stumbled upon when, moving to St Andrews in 1935, he expected to build a career on the merits of the copious and highly respected cultural 'journalism' he had published by then. 'Surely by this time I've done some work that should count', he thought, but found that, without the proper academic accoutrements, it didn't.[58] Similarly, in the 1970s, Isobel Murray found that the substantial book reviewing she was then doing in *The Scotsman* was far from helping her academic career—if anything, the opposite.[59] Alexander Scott instinctively regarded the context, or medium, of his comments and criticism as utterly irrelevant but took the perhaps simple-minded view that the value of the comment or argument, wherever published, was all that mattered. The result was that much of his 'critical' commentary appeared in various cultural journals with no particular academic weight or aura—or on that still more ephemeral medium, radio.

Nor is the matter sufficiently described by saying that Scott simply published too much of his academic material in non-academic places. His whole temperament was such that, wherever he published, his writing was often going to strike other academics as journalistic. It can be hard to define the difference between 'the academic' and 'the journalistic', yet the difference was crucial to the way he was perceived by university colleagues, and therefore also vital to the health or otherwise of his career. 'Journalistic' suggests superficiality and a merely temporary interest; it implies speed and sketchiness instead of sustained research (in libraries, or in the slow development of ideas and insight). In himself, Scott was not like that—above all, he had an expert knowledge of Scottish literature, from start to finish, acquired and intensified over several decades. Furthermore, he was particularly steeped in his areas of especial expertise. Yet his quickness and decisiveness of mind, his long-standing habit of writing hurriedly and against deadlines, and his preference for writing conversationally and in a lively, witty fashion, resulted in writing that has both the virtue and the drawback of momentary, spontaneous utterance. Even that does not fully explain the difference, however, at least in his case. Whereas most academic writers appear to write as if contributing to a scholarly debate (even if a particular debate is not directly invoked), Scott's manner often failed to imply debate but offered, instead, *ex cathedra* pronouncements. It was as if Scott's imagined reader was the general literary enthusiast for Scottish writing; most academics, on the other hand, write as if for a narrower, more specialised community. So, for example, the pieces from the *Scots Independent* published in 1996 under the title *Sing frae the hert* preserve much that is welcome and uniquely characteristic of him, but also illustrate the difference between literary comment and 'literary criticism' in the accepted academic sense.[60] They are the products of the chance literary encounters and impulses of a Scottish man of letters; they are not the produce of a programme of sustained, investigative scholarship or intellectual commitment. The primary reason for this characteristic manner lay, no doubt, in Scott's personality, but it might be usefully remembered, also, that as one of the modern pioneers of the academic treatment of Scottish literature, he would sometimes have had no written academic debate to which to contribute. Sometimes, he would be making a case (for a work or a writer) for the first time. Often enough, in the 1940s and '50s especially, he would be thinking and writing in a near-vacuum of criticism from others.

Another way of illustrating the issue is to compare Scott's edition of the poetry of his namesake Alexander Scott (*c*1515–83) with the anthology *Ballattis of Luve* edited by John MacQueen, a collection containing a substantial number of the earlier Scott's poems.[61] It is not simply a matter of the different decisions, by the two editors, on whether to offer a modernised or an original language text, fundamental as that choice may be. Scott's decision to modernise was part and parcel of his desire that these poems be accessible to as wide a readership as possible, with the minimum of impediment. MacQueen's edition was also 'popular' in format and pricing, but there was no compromise in scholarly ideals and the text is unmodernised. If anything, however, it is in the respective introductions that the opposition is starkest. Where MacQueen's is wide ranging and packed to overflowing with scholarship and close interpretation, Scott's emphasis is on reading the poems as a direct expression of the poet—a poet, moreover, whose apparent emotional contrariness enlists him (in Scott's eyes) as a product of the second Scottish Renaissance as much as he undoubtedly was of the first. Many will feel that, on the bookstall, there is a place for both approaches, but a comparison such as this brings out how easy it was for other professional academics to feel that there was an amateurishness in Scott's approach to his business. Not that this critical response to the volume was universal: it is Duncan Glen's view that the decision to modernise the text was 'brave' rather than amateurish, and the late Professor Philip Hobsbaum recalled buying the book as a student, tickled by the conjunction of the name across the centuries, thereby making the acquaintance of both poets for the first time—and valuing the book, and them, ever after.[62]

His *Poems of Alexander Scott* for the Saltire Society was a product, of course, of his first years as a lecturer and no one, looking back, would claim that Scott's strengths lay in sixteenth-century textual scholarship. His particular fields of Scottish expertise were in the twentieth-century Renaissance, of which he himself was now part, and in nineteenth-century poetry, especially Romantic poetry. His periods of active research on these areas arose not simply from the inner compulsion of his personal curiosity about them—the purest academic motivation. Rather, his energy was stimulated to the point of publishing effort at particular turning points in his academic career or, to be more precise, by temporary periods of especial enthusiasm for the academic element in his portfolio of interests. Thus, his first decade at Glasgow was an especially fruitful one as regards academic writing, and so was the early 1970s. The former, clearly, was when he was striving to make his mark as a young academic, while the latter surely reflects his gush of enthusiasm at being, at long last, in charge of his own department.

Disappointment seems to have drained both those bursts of energy. As mentioned in the previous chapter, his application in 1958 for a higher degree on the strength of his new book on Soutar was turned down by his old university, Aberdeen. It is not clear why this occurred: the award of a higher degree on the strength of published (or about-to-be-published) work was an acceptable procedure at that time, and there is no obvious reason in the book itself why it might be judged to be wanting. Scott had undoubtedly 'done the work' for a doctorate. At around the same time he was denied the opportunity to produce an edition of Soutar's poems as he expected and thought he deserved, after having recently produced two substantial works, *Diaries of a Dying Man* and *Still Life*, which had done much to sustain and raise the poet's reputation. In the National Library of Scotland there is a small school jotter entitled 'Wm Soutar: Verses' in which Scott appears to have been systematically putting together a picture of Soutar's writings and which looks like an embryonic selected poems.[63] Soutar's father, for reasons best known to himself, asked the scholar and librarian W. R. Aitken to undertake the task and his selection of poems appeared in 1961.[64] Scott and his wife regarded this as an act of Machiavellian opportunism by Aitken, the ill-feeling lasting until Scott's death (and beyond, as Cath Scott's still hurt account made clear to me). Impartial observers, however, discount the idea that Aitken acted improperly and accept that the initiative for the 1961 edition was the poet's father's. Nor is it a prevalent view that John Soutar's choice was a bad one. It seems likely, however, that Scott was treated insensitively and that greater consideration of his service to the dead poet might have been appropriate. In any case, the 'loss' of the poems to Aitken was a bad blow: it came, too, at a time when not only had Aberdeen University snubbed him but also his career as a dramatist appeared to have no future, and his poetic inspiration was drying up. It is not surprising that, for a while, his academic publishing largely dried up as well.

The second burst of academic research activity in the 1970s petered out also: this time, one suspects, the reason was the dawning realisation that no professorship would be forthcoming. Teaching loads for Scott and his colleagues, too, had gone up in comparison with what had been demanded in the 1950s and '60s. Additionally, as we have seen, it was a period of great difficulty in the new and struggling department. Indeed, it was a time of crisis and low morale in the profession generally.

William Soutar was the focus of much of his research in the 1950s, and as has been indicated elsewhere he had Douglas Young to thank for the opportunity of access to material held by the poet's family. Soutar and his family first encountered Young in October 1940. A decade later, Young, by now a kenspeckle figure in the Scottish cultural firmament, agreed to undertake the editing and publishing of the diaries of the deceased poet, although, from the outset, he proposed that he would require assistance and had mentioned 'Mr Scott and Edwin and Willa Muir' in a letter to John Soutar.[65] He was also considering involving Helen Cruickshank.[66] It is not clear that any firm arrangement was ever made with the Muirs, though Young discussed the diary material with them at Newbattle. Scott had agreed to be involved by early December 1950. By 1954, however, when the edition finally appeared, he had taken over the bulk of the work, keeping charge of Soutar's notebooks and manuscripts so that John Soutar, anxious as to the exact whereabouts of his son's material, asked W. R. Aitken to write to Young to find out what was happening.[67] When the volume was published, Scott was the sole editor named. Until very recently, this was the only edition of Soutar's diaries available. It is a volume that retains its usefulness, as so far nothing has supplanted it, including Heidelinde Prüger's idiosyncratic study of 2001.[68]

One assumes that Scott began on the biography promptly after the completion of work on the *Diaries*. Certainly, by April 1956, full of energy and optimism, he was writing to George Bruce: 'I'm roaring on with Soutar—have just piloted him through 1927. The book may be finished this year after all.'[69] He was underestimating how long it would take him, however: as he said in a letter to Mr and Mrs William Mackenzie, who had lent him some correspondence and who chased him up regarding its return when *Still Life* was published: 'I'm sorry to have kept the letters so long, but the book was a bigger job than I imagined it would be when I began.'[70] Nevertheless, his work was accepted for publication by October 1957 and had provided him with the excitement of discovering a considerable body of material (including two collections of poems by Soutar) hitherto unknown.[71]

The other scholarly product of these early years was his *Selected Poems of William Jeffrey* (1951). This, too, seems not to have been supplanted in the half-century since its publication though that has probably got less to do with the quality of Scott's work than with the near-complete lack of interest in Jeffrey since his death in 1946. Although Scott produced a substantial selection with a workmanlike introduction, there is an air of dutifulness about this modest project which the young academic was no doubt glad to add to his list of achievements, while at the same time making generally accessible another Renaissance author. It does not look as if it could have taken him too long to do, but it will have fitted well into his familiar routine of marrying his Renaissance enthusiasms with professional demands, combining university work with extra-university priorities. (His commitment to Soutar, to whom he must have immediately turned, was of a different order.) And one must not forget that Scott was also teaching, was producing poetry and a string of plays, was editing the *Scots Review* and then (for several years) the *Saltire Review* and was broadcasting regularly. Academic research was only one priority among many, and when it resulted in the major disappointment of Aberdeen's rejection it seems to have become less important to him for a few years.

With his promotion to senior lecturer in 1964, however, and the growth of his subject within Glasgow University during the 1960s, Scott had a fresh lease of academic life, something that can be seen in his contributions, in the 1960s, to the new academic journal in the field of Scottish literature, *Studies in Scottish Literature*, which first appeared in July 1963. This was founded and edited by Professor G. Ross Roy, then of Texas Technological College but soon to be established in the University of South Carolina at Columbia. Ross Roy soon became a friend, and as the 1960s progressed and the university study of Scottish literature produced a generation of scholars and teachers markedly willing to co-operate in the development of their subject, Scott found himself at the centre of an alternative academic community, which proved far more congenial to him than Glasgow University, on its own, had done. Then, with the new decade, came the new department.

Suddenly, he was engaged in academic publishing once more. Not only was he general editor of Calder & Boyar's new series of editions for university use, but he was also busy creating substantial contributions to it. The anthology *Contemporary Scottish Verse 1959–1969*, valuable as it was, was perhaps less 'academic' than *The Hugh MacDiarmid Anthology* (1972), and both were, in a sense, teaching texts rather than the results of pure research. Both were jointly edited, also, as was *Neil Gunn: The Man and the Writer* (1973), the extremely valuable collection of essays on Gunn, which Scott produced with Douglas Gifford. But with this volume, and with his two contributions to a major international conference on Sir Walter Scott in 1971, he was suddenly presenting himself as high-profile scholar and critic in an international arena—a role that, despite his having been at Glasgow for almost quarter of a century, must have had a certain novelty for him. (But without souring, nocht is sweet: despite being the only contributor at the Scott conference to deliver two papers, on *The Lay of the Last Minstrel* and on Hogg's verse, he was disgusted to find that neither was chosen for the subsequent volume of selected papers.)

These academic activities, however, in no way supplanted his usual contributions to the literary life of contemporary Scotland, namely the writing of his own poems, the submitting of essays and comment to journals such as Glen's *Akros*, and the editing of periodicals and anthologies. When his weekly arts column in the *Scots Independent* was suddenly brought to an end, Glen gave him the opportunity to write and edit a newsletter supplement called *Knowe*, though that ran for only a few issues. Even now, in other words, Scott was failing (or refusing) to distinguish between the kind of publishing that would (say) clinch his case for a chair, and that which would be discounted in a university system which was increasingly having to lay greater emphasis than ever before on formal research publication. He continued to produce publications slanted heavily towards his own likes and personality, such as his entertaining and erudite but scarcely long-desired anthology of Scottish erotic poetry, *Scotch Passion*. Somewhat more of a contribution to our knowledge of the Scottish literary past, and to the availability of effective modern versions, was his edition, prepared with Maurice Lindsay, of *The Comic Poems of William Tennant* (1989). This last was the product of his final years when ill-health must have forced him to leave much of the work on the volume to his old friend. Tennant was very much a poet after his own heart, and this volume represents the major outcome of that enthusiasm for nineteenth-century Scottish poetry, which he had acquired as an undergraduate. He first proposed Tennant's poems as an annual volume for the Association for Scottish Literary Studies in 1982, clearly intending to produce the edition himself: it was the deterioration of his health which induced him to ask for Lindsay's help. It eventually appeared only weeks after his death.

Once again, however, a major academic publication was the product of collaboration rather than being solely his own. No doubt part of the explanation for this pattern lies in the incorrigible multifariousness of his interests and activities. It is clear, too, that Scott liked to work in a team whenever he could—though he always had to be top dog. One wonders, though, if there was also a surprising insecurity, an unease about his own capacity to pull off academic success unaided, after the surprising rejection of his greatest single-handed effort by his home university where, at the outset of his career, academic plaudits had come to him with insouciant ease. One is tempted to amateur psychology, also, when contemplating the 'big books' he envisaged but never produced. The first of these can be glimpsed in the period immediately after he was made a senior lecturer in 1964, and when separate classes in Scottish literature were beginning. In a letter to George Bruce, he says that he is currently engaged on 'a study of Anglo-Scottish literature during the period of middle-class domination (*c*.1830–75).'[72] A year later, he was discussing the project with Douglas Young.[73] A few years later still, in a CV that was prepared during the period of his arts column to the *Scots Independent* (i.e. January 1968–February 1970), he described himself as 'at present engaged on a critical study of *Anglo-Scottish Poetry from Scott to the Present*'. In the National Library of Scotland there is an undated jotter with the heading 'Anglo-Scottish literature 1830–1875', which appears to contain the opening (Preface and Chapter 1) of a book which, says the first sentence, will eventually be volume one of a three-part study of Anglo-Scottish literature from 1830 to 1960.[74] By the 1970s, and by the time Rod Lyall joined him as a colleague, this project had become one on 'Modern Scottish literature: A critical history'.[75] It was this twentieth-century volume, essentially (one assumes) a history of the Renaissance of MacDiarmid and his followers, of which he would talk to friends and colleagues. For example, in a letter to 'Alastair' [Mackie?], he wrote:

> The first 3 titles are lined up for the Carcanet Press series, and I'm at work on my own book for it, a critical study of Modern Scott. Lit (from 1920). But as the whole book is only 250 pages, and covers fiction and drama as well as poetry, I doubt there will be room for more than a single chapter on the verse of the last ten years. However, the work of Alastair Mackie will figure prominently in that. The book should be out next winter.[76]

Seventeen months later, in another letter to Mackie, he refers to being: 'on the home stretch of my book on *Modern Scottish Literature* for Carcanet Press'.[77] And in a CV he prepared on applying for a titular chair in the university's promotion round of December 1979, he lists (rashly) among 'critical books': '*Hugh MacDiarmid and Modern Scottish Literature.* 1980 [sic]. Critical study of the poet and his influence on modern Scottish poetry, drama and fiction. 200pp.'

No such volume ever appeared, of course: I am not aware of any complete, or near-complete, typescript, nor was Rod Lyall ever aware of precisely what happened to this long-cherished project. Scott's most extensive accounts of the period are to be found in his essay 'The MacDiarmid Makars 1923–1972' (published by Akros in 1972) and the introduction to his anthology *Modern Scots Verse: 1922–1977* (1978). (In the CV of December 1979, where he is palpably straining to make his case look overpowering, 'The MacDiarmid Makars' is described as being 20,000 words long—apparently a small book. In fact, the Akros pamphlet looks and reads like a long essay, and is more of the order of 13,000–14,000 words.)

Duncan Glen sees his old friend as having been 'lazy about getting on with big jobs', and believes this to have been the reason why Scott's history of the Renaissance movement never materialised.[78] Glen is probably correct, but it is also noticeable that Scott's approach, in the many short accounts and surveys he wrote on modern Scottish poetry, was invariably cumulative and descriptive, rather than analytical or discursive. He simply reported what he saw; he did not often analyse to any great depth, nor did his underlying assumptions and ideas develop far beyond the account of these matters which he gave in 1946 in his brilliant prize-winning undergraduate essay, 'Scottish poetry between 1918 and 1939'.[79] In the main, he described the scene he saw, and told his readers what was happening out there—he acted as a journalist, one might say. Might he have found that his approach was not conducive to creating a book-length discussion?

His surviving letters hint occasionally at other projects which never came to fruition, such as the anthology of Scottish Romantic verse he envisaged contributing to the Calder & Boyars series, as he mentions to David Morrison.[80] It would have begun, it seems, with Scott's *Minstrelsy of the Scottish Border* and ended with *Sangschaw*. But then, academic lives are full of ideas for projects that do not happen. Despite his mysterious failure to complete the studies he seemed destined to write, the volume and variety of Scott's writing and publications, over several decades, certainly amounted to 'some work that should count'. If much of it was addressed, one way or another, to his contemporaries rather than to posterity, he still produced material, especially the publications of the 1950s and the later volumes on Gunn and Tennant, which remains useful to readers and students a generation later. The volume of scholarly and critical work in Scottish literary studies will have to grow much further yet before his contribution can finally be completely ignored.

Chapter 5

Renaissance Man

This chapter deals with Scott's involvement with the post-war Scottish Renaissance group and with his participation in Scotland's literary life. It considers his growing commitment to the movement, his personal relationships with other writers, and his contribution (a substantial one) as editor of a number of small magazines. It thus sketches the context for his activities as committee man, broadcaster, dramatist and poet, and attempts to conjure up a little of the world of Scotland's public literary arena during the quarter century or so after the war.

It is possible to trace Scott's growing identification with the Scottish Renaissance movement in some detail. For this, we have to thank the *North-East Review*, the Aberdeen-based periodical fired with quixotic opposition to the journalism then on offer to north-east readers from the Kemsley group of newspapers.[1] Its need for talented local writing mated intimately with Scott's need to get into print and, as in many other marriages of the time, consummation was hastened by the pressures and uncertainties of war. Indeed, just as the imminence of D-Day had clearly everything to do with Scott's sudden decision to marry Catherine Goodall, so the appearance of his first published poem in the *North-East Review*, just as he was called up, seems anything but coincidental. The amount that Scott wrote and published during his years in uniform is astonishing, and testifies to more than mere enthusiasm for writing. One begins to suspect something of cause and effect: was his sustained and tenacious immersion in writing a response to army life and to the dangers he had to face? Service life seems to have stimulated his writing as much as it impeded it. It is as if he was driven to insist on his selfhood, and to strive for the fullest possible self-fulfilment, when he found himself in circumstances pressuring him towards selflessness and, if necessary, self-sacrifice. No doubt he was prepared for the latter if necessary, but his opposite-facing instincts towards life and self-preservation took a decidedly intellectual and artistic turn, along with his commitment to his new wife. The war seems to have been utterly formative so far as he was concerned, turning a hitherto immature young poet, slowly and blindly finding his way through the alternatives dangling in front of him, into a focused adult determined to press on eagerly with life. Just as his swift wartime nuptials were the beginning of a successful and sustaining forty-five year marriage, so also his habit of getting into print wherever and whenever possible began at this point. Similarly, his rapid espousal of the Renaissance argument for Scots as a modern poetic medium set him on a literary path from which he never essentially deviated thereafter. The crucial commitments of his life took place in 1943–4.

The fact that he did not subsequently deviate from them suggests, of course, that they were the right commitments for him. Nevertheless, one wonders if there was something about him requiring the extraordinary pressures of wartime to help him take the very biggest decisions. He never again took quite the same transformative grip on his life as he did in those war years when it was most obviously threatened. Scott's impulsive and quixotic grasping at his future when the certainty of any future at all was most in doubt was in marked contrast to his general unwillingness to mould his life—to take life-transforming decisions—both before and after this moment of crisis. In his student autobiography, there is a passage of self-analysis which, while reflecting in part a certain youthful aesthetic languor and Shelleyan self-absorption, seems to embody much that was true of his whole approach to life.

> All my life I have been like a leaf, blown now here, now there, by the winds, now buffeted by the storm-blasts, now wafted gently by soft breezes. Of my own initiative I have done little; indeed, the only thing I have done off my own bat is start to write—and that was an unconscious, and not a conscious, urge. But for the most part I have been content to fall in with the plans of others. Only in my writing do I stand alone, taking orders from no man—and precious little advice, either. Otherwise, though I make an excellent lieutenant, I am no leader. Which makes life, on the whole, much simpler, though there are times when I have resented it...[2]

In later years, Cath Scott would often be his 'leader' in domestic matters (finding a house, deciding when to move to another one, providing most of the daily disciplining of their children, deciding when to throw a party, etc.). Similarly, in university matters, it was Archie Duncan who provided much of the drive which enabled Scott's aspirations for Scottish literature to develop into a real department—Scott's major contribution lay as much in what he was as in what he did. There was often a part of Alexander Scott withdrawn into the world of his own writing, letting the world of decision-taking look after itself, though even there one recalls that it was the intervention of Finlay J. Macdonald, with his BBC commission of 'Heart of Stone', which helped break up the poetic logjam of the early 1960s.

In that world of writing, the commitment to Scots was a decisive turning point. That strangely isolated poem in Scots, 'In Manus Tuas', indicates that he was aware of the possibility of writing in the language as early as 1938, just as it indicates his natural proficiency in it.[3] We may never know what prompted it then. It is easier to ascribe his next attempt, 'Frae Steel A Sang', to the nationalistic influence of the undergraduate Derick Thomson and to the substantial exploration of Burns' poems in the summer of 1940.[4] Nevertheless, his inner journey of commitment to the Renaissance movement arose primarily from his involvement with the *North-East Review*, as he himself indicated to Alan Bold.[5] That journal, at first weekly then (from June 1940) monthly, was far from being a narrowly literary periodical. Indeed, in its earliest issues it attempted to provide news coverage like the local newspapers it was avowedly challenging, but it evolved into a general cultural and current-affairs review. In the early days, poetry was often confined to a single poem per issue, usually of the 'Doric' kind—in other words, written with the local Aberdeenshire speech mannerisms and reflecting the country life of the Aberdeen hinterland either in an amused but self-congratulatory way, or in sentimental, elegiac mode. It was 'kailyard' verse, one might say, but it fitted with the *Review*'s goal of giving the inhabitants of the North-East their own voice. Here is an example by Alison Mill, from the issue of 15 March 1940.

'Bonnie Meen'

Bonnie Meen! bra' Queen o' Nicht!
Danderin' a' yer leen for oors,
Is the lift yer cas-tle *[sic]* yaird?
Are the stars yer gairden flo'ers?

Is the Milky Wey a bank,
Faur the sma fite gowans bla'?
Mars a rose o burnin' reid?
T'evenin star a bud like sna'?

Fyles ye're dwinin'. Are ye feart
O' the scufflin' Muckle Bear?
Dis Orion, wi' his sword,
Fricht ye affa, staunin' there?

Though ye're weary, Bonny Meen,
Danderin' roun' yer far-aff track,
Dinna halt! These darksome nichts,
We counts the days till ee'll be back.

This is scarcely 'The Bonnie Broukit Bairn'—though, perhaps, not entirely unrelated to it, either. So, although one or two poems by Hunter Diack showed a bit more irony and awareness of modern trends, a whole new level of literary sophistication and ambition was revealed when Scott's first poem in *North-*

East Review, 'At Summer's End', appeared in December 1941. Thereafter, he contributed a flow of writing of all kinds, beginning with a review of a volume by Vernon Watkins in the January 1942 number, in which he attacked as meaningless the New Apocalypse school but indicated approval for MacNeice. Poems and reviews were followed from mid-1943 by discursive articles and short stories. The first of these, 'Fatal Bellman' (August 1943), is a fictionalised account of the bombing raid that had claimed his parental home in April of that year. There can be no doubt that it is by Scott, but its author is given as 'Lancelot Mackie'. (Mackie, of course, was his middle name.) Scott used both this and his real name, sometimes for contributions on adjacent pages, until he added a third persona, 'Alasdair Cheyne', in January 1945. (Cheyne, of course, was his mother's middle name.) Indeed, the issue of September 1945 sported all three names, by which time he and Jessie Kesson had emerged as the two writers of special talent to have been nurtured by the journal. Scott's account of his literary response to the war, in his letter to Bold of 19 February 1979, is entirely borne out by the journal:

> While it was still going on I acted as unofficial (and anonymous) war-correspondent for the Aberdeen political/literary monthly, *North-East Review*, which published regular articles of mine hot from the cannon's mouth, as it were, until I was demobbed in December '45.

So it was that Scott was full of confidence when, in the issue of July 1943, he contributed 'Emptiness in Alban', his attack on the very idea of writing contemporary verse in Scots. It implies that his exposure to new Scots verse, up to that date, had consisted largely of the poems in *North-East Review*—in which case, his attitude contained a lot of sense.

> If Scotland is to produce any literature worthy of the name, that literature must be written in English. English is a highly-developed, highly articulate language, whereas the Scottish dialects are limited in vocabulary and in emotional and intellectual range.

He was still defending his rejection of Scots in correspondence published in September 1943. Yet only a month later, in October, he wrote appreciatively of the Penguin *Scottish Short Stories* edited by Theodora and J. F. Hendry, praising 'the vein of wry-mouthed, sometimes almost grudging, and always sardonic humour which runs through many of the stories and makes them characteristically Scottish products'. Scott then reviewed the first of Maurice Lindsay's *Poetry Scotland* volumes in the issue of March 1944, along with a selection of Burns, and also MacDiarmid's *Lucky Poet*. This review was his moment of recantation when he proclaimed himself convinced, after all, that Scottish poetry had awakened: '[*Poetry Scotland*'s] appearance, in the fifth year of war, is a portent of the days of hope and endeavour which lie ahead of us in the peace to follow.'

This, written several months before he first saw action in what was possibly going to be a long, hard, bloody campaign, suggests how much his own ambition to survive was tied up with his commitment to a literary future. In the same March 1944 issue, he contributes an account (part fictional?) by 'Lancelot Mackie' of a conversation with the battalion padre, 'Benefit of Clergy', which touches on the strengths and limitations of modern literary Scots. Here he argues that Scots cannot carry a lot of intellectual argument but is good at conveying individual and emotional emphasis.

In his letter to Alan Bold about his growing interest in Scots, he continues:

> Of course it was the encounter with the poetry of Soutar and Chris which convinced me, imaginatively, that it was still possible to write poems on contemporary themes in the Scots which was my native tongue but which my academic education had led me to regard as an inferior patois that should be ignored for serious literary purposes.

Thereafter, his enthusiasm for the best that contemporary Scottish poets were producing was plain to see. In April 1944 he reviewed *The Scottish Poems of Violet Jacob*, singling out 'The Jaud' as 'a work of genius'. This period clearly saw the emergence not only of Scott the Renaissance poet but also of Scott the reviewer, with his preference for poetry of immediate emotional impact. By May 1944, he was seeing Scots as a medium which, by its very nature, encourages terse, effective utterance: he rejects almost all the poems in the collection *Last Leave* by B. J. B. Macarthur as weakly Tennysonian, except for one. '"Eight Gaed Oot", the first, the shortest and the finest poem in the book, escapes these strictures by being written in Scots.'

Nevertheless, he had not swallowed the MacDiarmid doctrine of 'synthetic Scots' in its entirety. In a sense he never did, despite a post-war phase of using some dictionary-derived words and of following the linguistic leads of Soutar and Douglas Young. The issue of August 1944 contains an important letter from 'Lancelot Mackie' arguing that even MacDiarmid could not really synthesise a Scots language. Here, Scott argues that the way forward is to use a local dialect (such as the Buchan dialect, which he had used in a short story printed in June 1943) and to fill it out with English terms when necessary. He believes that a poetically useful 'synthesised Scots' will come about in future only as a result of slow, everyday use. As his response, a generation later, to Tom Leonard's work indicates, Scott's preference was for change to come about gradually, naturally, and not as the product of drastic, individualistic innovation.

From mid-1944, Scott's contributions to *North-East Review* reflect an ever more obvious Scottish Renaissance commitment, especially in his short stories and in the books he reviews. Authors he discusses include Nan Shepherd, Eric Linklater and Douglas Young. His December 1944 review of the latter's *Auntran Blads* sees it as a weakness that so many poems require resort to the dictionary to be understood, and voices a preference for the poems in English.

Reviewing *Scots Writing*, a short-lived journal of the 1940s, in the same article, he implies that to write truly Scottish poetry the poet must look back to an age of Scots writing *before* MacDiarmid. Here, perhaps, is the beginning of Scott's difference from MacDiarmid as a poet in Scots: where to MacDiarmid the twentieth-century Renaissance had been all about affiliating Scottish literature to the international Modernist movement, to Scott the world of international contemporary poetry was infinitely less relevant than the uniquely Scottish poetic tradition.

April 1945 brought his essay 'Some Reasons for Regionalism', referring not to Scotland's internal variety but to the diversities within Great Britain as a whole: essentially an anti-London statement, it expresses ideas which, though naïve-seeming, continued, to some extent, to guide his own choices:

> Regionalism, a federation of regions each with its own centre of government and culture, instead of a centralised state dominated by the colossal capital city, will put an end to this metropolitan monopoly of the nation's talent. When each region has its own parliament, its own newspapers and publishing houses, its own dramatic schools, repertory theatres and music festivals, its own film studios and broadcasting stations, there will be no need for local boys to head Londonwards if they want to make good. There will be seats for them in the regional parliament, the regional newspapers will print their articles and the regional publishers their books, the regional theatres will produce their plays and the regional orchestras will play their music.
>
> Intelligence and initiative will stay at home ... The present centralized state of Great Britain is fully alive only at its centre, but the federal union of the regions will tingle with life to the finger-tips.

At first glance, this is a surprisingly political statement from someone who latterly struck friends as thoroughly non-political. The benefits he envisages, however, are destined primarily for artists and performers: already his nationalist instincts are primarily those of a cultural nationalist.

Two months later, in June, his essay 'History begins at home' argues that Scotland has essentially been a province since 1707 and that the absence of the teaching of Scottish history in schools is wrong. The essay underlines his strong commitment to Scotland's future but it is a commitment, once more, founded upon the necessary knowledge of Scotland's past. And in September 1945, he publishes 'The Sleeper Awakes', a literary article trumpeting forth the reality of Scotland's new literary Renaissance. Two months on, however, in a review of *Poetry Scotland 2* and George Bruce's *Sea Talk*, he is still inveighing against the use of obscure and ancient Scots words, a practice that he seems to bracket with the obscurity of some contemporary English verse. In the December 1945 issue, the first for which he was himself editor, he introduces a new column entitled 'British bards and Scots reviewers': in the first one he praises the variety of languages being used in Scotland and stresses how Scottishness need not be associated with just one form of speech. Indeed, he is still obviously drawn, in part, to English as a poetic medium, and declares himself appreciative of what he calls 'English with a Scottish accent' as found, for example, in *A Scots Quair*.

In the CV in the National Library of Scotland, he described himself as editing *North-East Review* 'from the "Scottish Renaissance" viewpoint'.[6] What this meant, in practice, was not simply more discussions than previously on matters of poetic language, or more concentration on contemporary Scottish writing on the review pages (though this last is particularly marked). It meant adopting a more explicitly anti-London stance, in place of the cheerful Buchan regionalism of the paper's early years. It also involved persuading figures such as MacDiarmid and Douglas Young to contribute. The latter produced a particularly notable Renaissance utterance in the form of an article on Burns, for the February 1946 issue, written entirely in Scots. Not surprisingly, the editor was now unstinting in his praise of Young (a 'Scottish poet of the first rank') and of *Auntran Blads*. His tune was changing somewhat, also, with regard to Synthetic Scots and to obscurity in contemporary art. In a 'Lancelot Mackie' article on 'The Modern Idiom' in the same issue he stresses the complete independence of the artist, who is seen as someone who creates 'because he *must*, because something within himself drives him irresistibly towards creation, and not because he has to earn his living.' And he now insists that obscurity in modern art arises primarily from the public's lazy impatience with the new and unfamiliar: 'obscure' artists are not 'fakers'. This view is backed up by a letter from Hamish Lawrie, making the case for the obscurity of contemporary verse. Furthermore, in a review of R. Crombie Saunders's *Selected Poems of Hugh MacDiarmid* Scott now unhesitatingly argues the case for Synthetic Scots and ascribes to MacDiarmid 'a record of achievement perhaps unmatched in modern letters'. Scott includes, too, a poem of his own, in Scots ('Sang for Robert Burns') for which he provides a gloss at the foot of the page.

North-East Review continued until its last issue in October 1946. It had always made a loss: by the editor's own account it simply did not sell enough copies. For Scott, though, it had provided invaluable experience in the editing of small literary periodicals, a task to which he would return, despite its pressures and disappointments. Clearly, it had given him a place amongst a lively literary community, a position he always relished. The journal had not only brought him into the centre of just such a group—Diack and Mackenzie, Park, Mackintosh, Foster, Simpson and Kesson—but had strengthened his bonds with several other friends who contributed during his editorship—Lawrie, Main, Thomson, Keir. And it pointed forward as well, because that last issue also contained material by two younger Aberdeen students, Kenneth Buthlay and Iain Crichton Smith.

For the next two years, Scott's life was dominated by the business of getting a foothold in academia. However, by the time he had settled into the Glasgow

University post in the autumn of 1948, he clearly felt that he was firmly part of exciting new developments in Scottish writing. At the end of his first year there, in 1949, he published his first small volume of poems, *The Latest in Elegies*, dedicated to the memory of the two greatest writers of the Scottish Literary Renaissance to have died up to that time, 'Lewis Grassic Gibbon' and William Soutar. Such a dedication in a first book looks like a declaration of intention to pick up where they had left off. Furthermore, he was able to feel part of Edinburgh's literary circles, thanks to the year he had spent networking there. He was still at home, too, in Aberdeen, where Walter Keir was living (and adding intellectual and alcoholic stimulus to every visit home Scott made), where Jessie Kesson was regularly to be encountered and where James Burns Singer would soon dwell briefly. The excitement was all for a new literature built from a contemporary commitment to an old language. As he later recalled, in a letter to Lindsay, it was 'a time when I was mad keen on everything Scots'.[7]

Nevertheless, the old tension between his two areas of endeavour, the academic and the literary, emerged instantly, as his letter to Douglas Young indicates.[8]

> Thank you for your letter. I should be glad to do anything I can for the Makars, but this year, unfortunately, I'm too busy ploughing through the whole of Scot. Lit. and trying to cut it up into lectures to be able to undertake the executive work you suggest.

The writing of the lectures, by the sound of it, was a chore which he was keen to get out of the way, though its oppressiveness clearly arose from sheer quantity and urgency rather than from any lack of engagement with the subject. In the late 1940s, nevertheless, his creative ambitions were strong and powerful, and it is perhaps no wonder if the routine of teaching preparation and delivery seemed to conflict with the goals to which so much of his energy was naturally tending. Now, the long slow prelude was over: the youthful poetic immaturity and uncertainty, the educational hurdles, war service, the emotional storms and turmoils of the pre-marital state, the quest for security in steady employment and domesticity—all were now behind him. The time had clearly finally arrived for him to *be* the writer he had long aspired to be. This meant constant writing, and an active involvement in the social and fraternal life of Scotland's writing community. On the other hand, however, he could no longer treat the claims of the academy with the same confident insouciance as sometimes in the past. That said, it is astonishing how much work and literary socialising, not related to his Glasgow post, he undertook in his first dozen or so years in it.

Not the least time-consuming was his editing of *The New Alliance & Scots Review* (better known simply as the *Scots Review*) in its last year, 1950–1. Like the *North-East Review*, it was not aligned with any particular political viewpoint and claimed as its policy that 'there is much to be said for Scotland and that it ought to be said as gracefully as possible' (Vol. 7.7; October

1946). Scott's first contribution to it, apart from individual poems, seems to have been a letter (December 1946) during the Plastic Scots controversy, but this was followed in April 1947 by an article on 'Byron as Scotsman' which contains some insights into his conception of Scottishness, including 'a stubborn Scottish thrawnness, a refusal to bow to any and every authority, a hatred of all orthodoxies irrespective of their merits, a thirst for rebellion'. As so often, too, he praises 'passion', which seems to him, in Byron's work at least, a transforming power:

> In the intensity of the passion one accepts as a triumphant revelation what might otherwise seem pessimistic nihilism. The voice is the voice of Isaiah, of Knox, of the Covenanters—the voice of Byron, the voice of the 'damned Presbyterian conscience' endowed with song.

The issue for January 1948 contained his article 'Return to reality' in which he again defended Plastic Scots, insisting that obscure medieval words formed only a small proportion of the vocabulary of recent Lallans poems, which were soundly based, he insisted, on living Scots speech. He also claimed that the Scots tongue was currently a better medium than English in which to raise a new and vital tradition on the rubble of Modernism's fragmentation. He saw the English scene as consisting of isolated individuals giving voice to their privateness, whereas in Scotland there was the possibility of a shared culture. Scotland, he insisted, still retained a literary tradition which, though rusty, was not worn out: 'Damaged by neglect that tradition may be, but the poets are now setting about its repair.' That impulse towards a community of artist friends—to be a significant part of a shared culture—dwelt deep within him.

By the looks of it (the names of editors were not listed), Scott took over the editorial reins of *Scots Review* with the issue of May 1950. From then on, not only were his own contributions more frequent, but suddenly so were those of his friends from the days of *North-East Review*. Reviews and articles by Walter Keir, George Main, Vincent Park and Derick Thomson become noticeable. So, once more, do the abundant contributions of 'Alasdair Cheyne', with his stablemate 'Scott Mackie' (no doubt, Lancelot Mackie's little brother). Furthermore, Moira Burgess has suggested to me that a third pseudonym, 'Robert Gordon' was also used: if so, he was impudently appropriating the name of the school with which various of his colleagues were associated. Hamish Lawrie contributed a short story, as did I. C. Smith. Two interesting features, however, reflect Scott's new Glasgow environment. One is a series of articles by Alexander Trocchi chronicling his observations of France on his first foray there: they were lively and observant, and give little hint of the *enfant terrible* to come. The other is his increasing use of talks originally given on the radio. This not only reflects his own new intimacy with the world of Scottish broadcasting but also underlines the closeness of the domains of radio talk and serious print journalism. Scott was not the only intellectual to see the two as having parity of weight and substance, and he published, during his year in this particular editorial chair, material originally broadcast by Robert Kemp, Edwin Muir, Sydney Goodsir Smith, Cedric Thorpe Davie and himself.

The *Scots Review* folded with the issue of September 1951, but only a few years later Scott was editing a new, but somewhat similar, journal, the *Saltire Review of Arts, Letters and Life*—i.e. the *Saltire Review*. His first editorial made explicit that he saw the new venture taking over from where the *Scots Review*—and *Poetry Scotland* and *Scottish Arts and Letters*—had left off. Once more, Scott was responding to what he saw as a cultural need, though there is also little doubt that he loved being in charge of such publications, and that he saw them as occasional publishing opportunities for his own material. The *Saltire Review* came out three times per year and was able to call on Scotland's leading authorities. As was to be expected, the emphasis was literary, but there were also worthwhile essays on such topics as architecture and broadcasting as well as on the other fine arts. Scott's own circle of friends was less in evidence than they had been in the *Scots Review*, though many familiar names appeared at one time or another: Walter Keir was a fairly frequent contributor and reviewer. Scott's own contributions were less numerous than in his earlier journals; nor does he seem to have resorted to pseudonyms. A few of his poems were published there, as was a shortened version of *The Last Time I Saw Paris* (in No. 12, autumn 1957). More unexpectedly, he published two short stories in Scots, derived from plays. One was 'MacGregor despite them' (No. 8, autumn 1956), essentially the short play of that name presented as a story. The other, 'King Dod's dilemma' is more curious: it takes two of the characters from *Right Royal*, King Dod himself and the archdruid Ake, and places them in a completely new short tale. The mood and humour of the stage play are revisited here, and the story is an unexpected spin-off from that earlier success. Scott was joined in the editorial role by J. M. Reid from the issue of autumn 1956 onwards and seems to have given up editorial responsibility with the issue of winter 1957.

Such responsibilities continued to be woven through the remainder of his life: motivation for his repeated willingness to take on what many would regard as a thankless chore seems to have come, ultimately, from his desire that his vision of appropriate standards and cultural correctness prevailed. He itched to be in charge, and to have the job (any job) done properly by his lights. This is visible in the plentiful correspondence which survives relating to the annual (or as near-annual as possible) *Scottish Poetry* anthologies, which Edinburgh University Press began to publish in 1966.[9] Scott would eventually become one of the trio of editors for the last three issues (Nos 7–9) but when Maurice Lindsay started the series in the mid-1960s Scott had been silent, poetically, for a number of years and possibly less of a familiar name to readers at that time. The original editors, his friends Maurice Lindsay, George Bruce and Edwin Morgan, seem to have used the early issues as an encouragement to him to start writing poetry once more. The first volumes in the series coincided with his enthusiastic return to the writing of verse, and he took the keenest interest in the volumes as they appeared. In letters to Lindsay and Bruce in particular, he analysed their editorial labours, partly to keep them up to the mark, but partly because he was anxious (as ever) that a significant enterprise such as this should both reflect what was best in current writing, and also nurture the Scottish poetic future that he wanted to see. Thus he was disappointed in the average standard of contribution in the first volume, and was constantly on the lookout for signs that poetry in Scots was being discriminated against. Indeed, it was one of his worries that none of the three editors used Lallans in their own current verse. His unasked-for criticisms, perceptive as they could be, were sufficient to irritate occasionally even his old colleagues, as Lindsay revealed in a letter to Bruce:

> Pope Alexandrius Scotus, self-ordained Primate of All Scottish Letters, has been taking me to task about the 'amount of rubbish' in *SP1*. I explained that with a tri-partite voting system, width of choice was inevitable. All the same, he's not so far wrong. I hope Eddie won't push his rubbish demands [?] too far this time! ... But I'm sure we must concentrate on quality rather than quantity this time, though if we get both, good and well.[10]

In the flow of letters between the three editors as they made their choices for each succeeding volume, however, they were equally blunt about some of Scott's submissions. He was a looming presence in the background of the early volumes of the series, though his primary claim to involvement was purely over the choice of his own poems. The satirical 'pop' poems on the icons of popular entertainment, which featured prominently in his new phase of poetry in the mid-1960s, caused the editors some difficulty, most especially in the case of 'Prehistoric Playmate', which was accepted with some hesitation by the editors but then pulled from the volume by the Secretary of Edinburgh University Press (EUP), Archie Turnbull, for fear of litigation. Scott was outraged. The other great issue for him, as regards the early volumes, was how much of 'Heart of Stone' could be included: a substantial selection was offered in *Scottish Poetry 2*.

Lindsay was correct, though: Scott did see himself, to some extent, as 'primate of all Scottish letters' and when the arrangement with EUP began to run into difficulties he did not hesitate to offer to include future volumes in his 'Scottish Series' of Scottish editions, which by then had moved from Calder & Boyars to Routledge.[11] It was not until the original editorial trio began to split up, however, that he got his chance to participate directly: Morgan offended his two colleagues by entirely omitting them from an account of twentieth-century Scottish poetry, and Bruce, less chained to a desk since he retired from the BBC, was not going to be available to help plan No. 7. By the early 1970s, too, the Scottish Arts Council, which had strongly supported the series by guaranteeing it against loss, was pressing for a policy of editorial rotation. Roderick Watson was brought in as a fourth editor as a result, and with No. 7 the team consisted of Lindsay, Watson and Scott. The series ended with *Scottish Poetry 9*, in 1976.

By 1976, however, Lindsay and Scott were involved in a new venture, namely the quarterly periodical *The Scottish Review: Arts and Environment*, which first appeared late in 1975. Published jointly by the Scottish Civic Trust and the Saltire Society, it had the air of belonging to an earlier age. It is true that, by then, *Scottish International* (see p. 125) had been and gone, but it *had* been. And by the time *The Scottish Review* folded in turn in 1984, *Cencrastus*, with its new youthfulness of style and format, was well established. *The Scottish Review* was a quality production, but its neat style, its stance of conservative opposition to much that was contemporary (as its opening editorial made clear), and perhaps even the seasoned expertise of its contributors, combined to align it with an older generation. At the outset, Lindsay and Scott were listed merely as members of the editorial board, and it seems to have been, in concept, a group effort. But by 1978 Lindsay had become editor, with Scott as deputy editor; later still, with the twenty-fourth issue (August 1981), the two became joint editors.

Scott also undertook yet another onerous editorial task as joint editor of *New Writing Scotland*, the creative writing annual first published in 1983 by the Association for Scottish Literary Studies (ASLS). As the present writer recalls, this was a bold innovation by ASLS, and was intended to supply a felt need in Scottish publishing and to round out the association's portfolio of publications with a view to confirming the case for continued Scottish Arts Council support. It was important that the publication be a success. Choice of editor(s) for the early numbers was particularly crucial, and the ASLS felt that Scott, senior as he was, would be the best person to establish the newcomer—as was said at the time regarding Scott's judgement about new writing: 'Say what you like about Alex, he can spot winners.' And so he could. He was teamed with James Aitchison, with a view to his handing over to another co-editor after a couple of years, once his decades of editorial experience had made their contribution. In the event, it was Aitchison who first had to hand over to another after three issues: Scott co-edited a fourth. When he relinquished *New Writing Scotland* in 1986, there came to a close four decades of idealistic labour amongst Scotland's little magazines, enterprises in which he heartily believed. As he and Carl MacDougall wrote in the introduction to Scott's final issue: 'The more small magazines there are, the better the opportunities for new developments.' This simple concept, and priority, guided Scott through many hours of effort.

EVIDENCE OF SCOTT'S PERSONAL INVOLVEMENT with writers of the Scottish Renaissance in the late 1940s and '50s is less copious (at least so far as surviving correspondence is concerned) than it is for the 1960s onwards. Yet what exists suggests the same business-like intimacy with which he always seems to

Alexander Scott with his parents.

A senior group at Aberdeen Central School. Scott is on the extreme left.

Marriage, a month before D-Day.

A platoon of 5/7th Gordons during the Battle of the Reichswald. It is believed that the figure immediately to the right of the central post is Alexander Scott.

Photograph courtesy of the Imperial War Museum, London. B14411.

Scott's graduation photograph.

Alex and Cath Scott at a wedding in the immediate post-war years.

The joys of family holidays:
Cath, Alex and Ewan at John o' Groats.

Scott with his parents (late 1950s?).

All that remains of the large drawing by Gregoire Michonze which once adorned the French Institute in Edinburgh. The group of poets (centre foreground) are (left to right) Norman MacCaig, Douglas Young, Sorley Maclean, Alexander Scott, Christopher Grieve ('Hugh MacDiarmid'). The lady on the extreme left, whom they are toasting, may be Isobel Nicolson, and the figure to the right of MacDiarmid may be Sydney Goodsir Smith.

Image courtesy of Ian Begg

Gregoire Michonze: *Alexander Scott, b. 1920* (Scottish National Portrait Gallery) PG 2824

Portrait of Alexander Scott by Gregoire Michonze. Edinburgh, summer 1948.

Scott, photographed by Crombie Scott in Doune Gardens, Glasgow.

The Department of Scottish Literature in the 1970s: Kenneth Buthlay, Caroline Macafee, Roderick Lyall, Alexander Scott.

Image courtesy of *The Herald & Evening Times* picture archive.

A Mediterranean holiday (1960s?).

Scott with the committee of the Scots Language Society, in the 1980s.

One of the last photographs of Alexander Scott.

have conducted his literary life. In many of his relationships, friendship and the Renaissance cause seem to have been indissolubly linked. For example, his sense of being part of an Edinburgh-based self-aware group of writers is suggested by the continuation of the letter to Young quoted earlier:

> I shall contact MacDiarmid about alternate meetings of the Makars in Glasgow and Edinburgh, though for various reasons I'm not very optimistic about results. Even in Edinburgh, when people had only to take a tram to the Abbotsford, attendance at meetings was bad, and I can't see it improving if a train-journey is involved. Moreover, if Kincaid, Blytheman and the others are brought in, the Makars are bound to split, politically, into Marxists and non-Marxists, a consummation devoutly not to be wished. Without any such split, there's a wide enough crack in our façade already, with Albert Mackie publicly tearing to shreds everything Maurice Lindsay puts in print.[12]

Here, one notices that MacDiarmid is not yet 'Chris', as he would later become in Scott's correspondence, also that Scott is already gravitating towards the secretarial-organisational role he would play so often in later years, and that the mixture of literature and politics is something he already abhors. One also detects a faint air of banishment, as if fate had removed Scott from the literary nerve-centre and relocated him on the fringes. The letter ends with a hint of a sigh: 'Thanks for the offer to put me up some night in Edinburgh—I hope to be able to accept it one of these days.'

Young was among Scott's principal points of contact with the Renaissance movement in the late 1940s and early 1950s. The arrangement whereby Scott would assist him in the preparation of an edition of Soutar's diaries was not agreed until December 1950, but that mark of Young's respect was preceded in the same year by his request in March for copies of Scott's recent verse for inclusion in his anthology *Scottish Verse 1851–1951*, and by his invitation to Scott to join the PEN Club and to 'take part in a public symposium for broadcasting on 19 May in Edinburgh, on problems & tendencies in Scottish poetry'.[13]

In the post-war period, Young appears to have been performing the role that had been MacDiarmid's before the war—that of the central and dominating figure impelling the Renaissance forward as much by personal contact as by writing and poetic example. Under his influence, 'The Makars' briefly strived for a near-formal organisational structure (or at least for the public appearance of one), as is suggested by their contributions to the 'Plastic Scots' debates in the *Glasgow Herald* and the *Scotsman* in 1947 and 1948. Thus, in a letter of 30 April 1948, the group (here, A. D. Mackie, Hamish Henderson, Maurice Lindsay, J. Ritchie, Alexander Scott, Sydney Goodsir Smith and Douglas Young) responded to a speech by James Bridie with a letter purportedly sent from 'The Makars' Club, Edinburgh'. A second letter (7 May) from Henderson, Lindsay, Scott, Smith and Young claimed to emanate from 'The Makars' Club, at Edinburgh'.[14] Lindsay underlined this usage in an angry letter prompted by an article by Lewis Spence attacking 'this farrago of pidgin Doric' in the Rothermere-owned *Scottish Daily Mail*. Threatening Rothermere with legal action, Lindsay insisted that the group of poets complained about called itself 'The Makars Club'.[15] By 16 November 1948, Young was pushing for a completely formal organisation to the extent that he was writing to Lindsay, 'The meeting of 19th will be only exploratory, but a draft constitution and rules might well be considered. Please tell Alec [sic] Scott the time is 6–30.'[16]

Lindsay was the other great activist and organiser for the group at this time, having given the post-war Lallans movement a major impetus with his *Poetry Scotland* anthologies from 1943 onwards. His eagerness and willingness to take a lead is clear from the following, as is the instinct (a feature of the period) to institutionalise the group in more formal structures. Writing to Goodsir Smith on 8 January 1947, he proposes to deal with the economic problems of publishing new Scottish poetry by setting up a:

> Scottish Renaissance Society to undertake publication on a cheap, small-scale basis. Perhaps four 5/- books of verse a year ... The idea is worth thrashing out, and perhaps we might meet to discuss it? I thought on including Douglas, A. Scott, G. C. Hay, S. MacLean, Chris, and ourselves in the scheme ...'[17]

This suggests also, as do so many other scraps of evidence of this sort, the perceived centrality of Alexander Scott in the group, confirming the impression conveyed by the Michonze drawings. At the time Lindsay wrote to Goodsir Smith, however, Scott was still only half-way through his final year at Aberdeen University.

Scott himself conveyed a sense of a group strongly aware of itself in a letter to the radio producer Robin Richardson: discussing possible reviewers for his *The Latest in Elegies*, Scott suggested—in place of John Speirs—Kerr Paxton 'who is, like Speirs, himself outside *the movement*' [my italics].[18] That both self-perceptions and public perceptions of these poets *as a group* were strong is suggested by a sensitive letter to Lindsay from Norman MacCaig. In it, MacCaig diagnoses the dangers of being part of a group such as the Lallans Makars: it can lead, he thinks, to inauthenticity and 'learnt' feeling:

> I can't help suspecting the bad influence of such facts as being a member of a 'group', with its insidious tendency to regulate one's own reactions to things and events, a situation doubly dangerous to you since you are a member both of a literary and a political group. The fact of being the target for unsympathetic abuse which results from being a member of a minority group is bound to increase the self-consciousness of one's work, the exaggerations and obstinacies and similar falsifications of one's intentions.[19]

But if MacCaig found his own poetic salvation in standing well away from the group's agenda, Scott—for a time at least—found his in eager participation, so far as his new Glasgow location permitted it. That the group existed, in his mind, as a clear-cut 'club' is confirmed by his reference to 'The Makars' Club' and its members' creation of the Scots Style Sheet in the foreword to *The Hugh MacDiarmid Anthology*.[20] The Style Sheet was primarily Young's project, as McClure's discussion and Lindsay's conversation with me make clear.[21] Scott's poems from the late 1940s show the influence of the Style Sheet, as a comparison with (say) the poems in Scots in the *Selected Poems* (1950) with McClure's account of Young's spelling practices at this time quickly shows.[22] Admittedly, the *Selected Poems* appeared in a Saltire series edited by Young and Lindsay, but the presence of the same spelling features in the notebook versions of the collection's poems suggests that the orthographical decisions were authorial, not editorial.

So, by the early 1950s, Scott's perception of himself as a Scottish Renaissance poet was justified by the personal friendships he had established with other leading Scottish poets, and also by the distinctive contribution he was making in his academic teaching and research, and by his journal editing, his broadcasting, his drama and his poetry. All contributed, in his eyes, to the cause. The story of his role as a Renaissance poet and man of letters becomes simply that of his varied activities and personal relationships. These last permeated everything he did outside his university work: the bond between literary commitment and personal or group allegiances, first visible during his school years, remained. Not that this particularly marked him out from his fellow writers: coteries were the order of the day. Scott's had Grieve at its centre. As we have seen, he was in direct communication with Grieve at least as early as his post-war editorship of *North-East Review*, and he was one of those who lowered Grieve into his grave in 1978 (see his poem, 'Cords'). He never wavered from his view that Grieve was the most important Scottish poet of the century, thanks to his Scots poetry of the 1920s and '30s, yet even in his *North-East Review* days Scott had his reservations about the later verse. As he wrote in the issue for September 1946, he saw the Scottish Renaissance as MacDiarmid's single-handed achievement, but regretted his 'more recent polyglot prolixities'. Thirty-six years later, while trying to persuade Maurice Lindsay to allow Alan Bold, then preparing his edition of MacDiarmid's letters, to print a couple in which MacDiarmid had viciously attacked Lindsay, Scott says:

> They are all part of the history of the period and of Chris's peculiar (in every sense) contribution to it. He was *a great poet for a decade* [my italics] and (I fear) a wild man always.[23]

(Those in the University of Glasgow and elsewhere who saw Scott as simply—in Jack Rillie's words—'an awkward bugger' would have been astonished to see the tact, sensitivity, thoughtfulness and generosity which Scott brought to this delicate negotiation between Bold and Lindsay.) And if this quotation reveals some detachment in Scott's attitude to the great man, it seems confirmed by statements such as this from George Bruce, in a letter to Scott in 1968, telling him that: 'You never fell over yourself to be a Disciple of the Great Hugh.'[24] Bruce, here, is referring specifically to Scott's practice as a poet in Scots, but he seems aware of his friend's total response to MacDiarmid.

Both Duncan Glen and Maurice Lindsay have made the same point to me, Glen differentiating Scott's judicious if consistent hero-worship of MacDiarmid from Goodsir Smith's unbounded veneration. Lindsay does not believe that Scott ever had a really close personal relationship with MacDiarmid.[25] Yet their friendship and mutual respect were strong, as testified by countless letters, Scott's writings on MacDiarmid, and family recollections of numerous get-togethers (particularly in The Pewter Pot) when MacDiarmid was in Glasgow. The two men worked well together over a great span of years, and MacDiarmid was always uppermost in Scott's mind when some literary initiative was being organised. Thus, when Scott was trying (in his turn) to initiate a poetry book club in 1967, MacDiarmid was his inevitable choice as chairman. MacDiarmid responded thus:

> I would of course be willing to serve as Chairman of such a Scottish Poetry Book Society as you propose. The composition of the Committee you indicate—viz. Norman, Sydney, yourself (as Managing Editor) and Stewart Conn seems to me OK.[26]

(There is a strong whiff of the coterie in this latter sentence.) Two years later, there was talk of the two collaborating on a play that MacDiarmid had been proposing:

> I hear from Alec McCrindle that the Scottish Actors Coy. would like to include in their next year's plans the play I asked you to collaborate with me in writing—viz. a sort of conflation of Brecht's Threepenny Opera, Gay's Beggars Opera, Burns's Jolly Beggars, Graham's Skellat Bellman, and Chambers on the Lord of Misrule. So we'll having [sic] to begin planning it in some detail.

Six weeks later, the idea was fizzling out despite MacDiarmid's optimism: 'I quite understand about the avalanche of literary chores ... Your suggestion re the play is O.K. and I'll hope to get something drafted this month and then in February we may be able to complete the job.'[27] This burst of optimism is the last one hears of it.

Scott's view of MacDiarmid, and of their respective perches on the emerging vista of modern Scotland's Mount Parnassus, is perhaps summed up in the following, once more in a letter to Alan Bold, in which Scott surveys the considerable (by 1979) bulk of his own work:

> In the light of all this work, together with eight collections of verse (and another pending), you must forgive me if I demur from your estimate of the Scots scene as a mountain (Chris) surrounded by molehills (the rest of us). The difference in scale appears to me, if still striking, rather less dramatic than you suggest.[28]

This ability to combine deep, affectionate respect with critical honesty and judgement permeated and sustained those lifelong friendships which were so important to him—with perhaps Sydney Goodsir Smith, Norman MacCaig, George Bruce and Maurice Lindsay in particular, as well as with MacDiarmid. His relationships with other Renaissance luminaries could be less stable, however. Douglas Dunn's 'coteries' implies not only bonding within each little group but also (to some extent) conflict between them.[29] In this fissiparous milieu, Scott had a reputation as something of an aggressive and cantankerous bruiser. Once more, it is worth pointing out that he was far from unique in his willingness to lash out in letters or print—and to resort to law, if things went too far. Even that benign and supportive midwife to so much Scottish writing from the late 1960s onwards—Duncan Glen—could be exasperated occasionally by the perpetual crossfire. On 15 July 1980, for example, Glen wrote to another of Scott's friends, the poet Alastair Mackie: 'I don't think I can explain Alex Scott's actions. I gave up trying to know what to expect from that literary generation—Tom Scott, Alex Scott, Maurice Lindsay—long ago.'[30]

A FULL ACCOUNT OF THE LITERARY conflicts of the time would be tedious in the extreme, even were it possible. Here, brief accounts of three of Alexander Scott's jousts will have to suffice.

Long before 1980, Glen had written to Mackie in, if anything, even more heartfelt terms:

> I was a good friend of Douglas Young when I printed Alex Scott's poem attacking Douglas and it cost me my friendship with Douglas to a large extent. So also have I printed Tom Scott attacking people whom I admire and in terms I dislike; and Alex Scott attacking people I like and all this makes enemies for me![31]

Glen's reference here is to 'Supermakar Story', Scott's satirical treatment of the argument which raged for some weeks in the correspondence columns of the *Scotsman* newspaper in the late summer of 1966, following the production at the Edinburgh Festival of *The Burdies*, Young's Scots version of the comedy by Aristophanes. Young's text was strongly attacked by the *Scotsman*'s drama critic, Allen Wright, and the production instantly became the great controversial talking-point of the festival's first week. Wright's initial review of 23 August was followed up by several days of epistolary dispute, as well as by public defences by Young and others, but it was not until Wednesday 31 August that Young wrote to *The Scotsman* in the following terms:

> I have heard of only one criticism of myself as author, or co-author, whatever a translator and adaptor should be termed. That was vented after my press and television appearances, and came from Mr A. Scott on the BBC *Arts Review*. He objected to the use of Scots from various periods and social strata. But Aristophanes used Greek from various periods and social strata, with parodies of epic, tragedy, dithyrambic lyric, and 'officialese', and with slang...Mr Scott might have known that by reading page 50 of the second edition of *The Puddocks*, seeing that he is supposed to be a specialist in Scottish literature. If he lacks enough Greek...

Young's letter also refers to Norman MacCaig, who apparently thought well of Young's use of Scots, as 'the finest critic among Scottish poets'. This judgement seems little likely to have endeared itself to Scott, despite his closeness to MacCaig. Consequently, Scott's first letter on the subject appeared in *The Scotsman* of Saturday 3 September. In it, he insisted that his essential objection was not to the notion of using differing varieties of Scots but arose because in this particular case the technique, in his opinion, had failed to produce an effective work. But it was to the more personal thrusts that he eventually turned, the jibe that he is 'supposed to be a specialist in Scottish literature' producing a touchy, rather pompous summary of his status and achievements in the literary and academic spheres. This was followed by two further letters from Scott and three from Young, in which Scott insisted on his own more native grasp of Scots while Young continued to hint, patronisingly, at Scott's lack of competence in the classical languages. It was in his third and last letter (Tuesday 13 September) that Scott insisted: 'he mustn't expect the rest of us to regard him as Supermakar, free of the subjective fallibilities of lesser mortals.' As a note on the published poem explains, the coinage 'Supermakar' transforms the nickname of the then prime minister Harold MacMillan, 'Supermac', into an embodiment of Scottish poetic invincibility *par excellence*, in the unlikely style of the comic-strip hero Superman. It is a typical flash of Scott's creative punning wit. Looking at the newspaper exchange in isolation, one can feel a certain amount of heat arising between the two old friends and colleagues, but nothing to suggest that the two, having trod on each others' corns, would be henceforth at daggers drawn.

Nor were they, although both, for the moment, believed passionately in their side of the argument (laying aside purely personal pique). Duncan Glen in 1971 thought that Young had been permanently offended by the publishing of the poem, but when interviewed in 2002 he felt that of the two men it was Scott who felt the more deeply during the exchange. Glen senses that something really upset Scott in the 'Supermakar' squabble but does not know what it might have been. Perhaps the following, from a letter to George Bruce, who had clearly been made uneasy by the confrontational nature of Scott's new poem on the affair, which Scott had just sent him, may reveal part of the answer:

> If 'Supermakar Story' amused you, I'm pleased. But why refer to the poem as 'Douglas Young stanzas'? Let us all hope, for the sake of Scottish poetry, that Supermakar is an entirely fictitious character.
>
> I entirely agree when you say, 'We Scots are too good at dissension.' But I'm professionally concerned with the craft of criticism, a difficult craft to practise in a country as small as ours, where 'aabody kens aabody else', and where there is only too much temptation to indulge in mutual book-scratching. I've tried to avoid this; but if a writer whose work is criticised on purely stylistic grounds is to be allowed to get away with writing letters to the press in which he tries to escape from criticism by denigrating the professional standing of the critic ('supposed to be a specialist in Scottish literature'), then we might as well cease the attempt to apply critical standards to work produced north of the Border. It may be, of course, that Young regards himself as a kind of licensed buffoon, entitled to behave as he likes; but if so, it's time he was disabused of this illusion—there has to be some kind of minimal courtesy between writers and critics, and when Young oversteps the mark he must be prepared to take as good as he gives ... Anyhow, 'S.S.' has helped me to get D.Y. out of my system ...[32]

The mixture of purely personal offence and (at the same time) genuine care for the health of the Scottish literary world was typical of Scott and perhaps goes some way to explain his frequent public combativeness. Several of my interviewees, however, are also inclined to believe that he actually enjoyed public disputation, perhaps to the detriment of an inner calm of mind, which enables poetry to be written. One also suspects that Scott had resented the patronising flavour of Young's letters, perhaps feeling that they contained too strong an echo of the Batman-and-Robin nature (to conjure up an alternative superhero) of their relationship in the first years of Scott's academic career. In any case, there is probably a danger of exaggerating the anger against Young in 'Supermakar Story', which is not so much an assault as a send-up. The poem itself contributes only half of the total effect; the other half is derived from the notes which, while providing some explanation in case the reader had not been following the row in the papers, are primarily a parody of Young's characteristically academic manner as he glosses his own poems. An example is the scarcely less copious notes to his 'Ice-flumes Owregie Their Lades' in *A Braird o Thristles* but such annotation was a feature of several of Young's poems in the *Poetry Scotland* collections of the 1940s.

Nevertheless, it can come as a surprise to readers of Scott's verse that this memorably antagonistic (if lightweight) poem should have been followed, in January 1974, by 'Lament for a Makar', written in Young's memory. I have known those who, mindful of the Supermakar spat, declared themselves shocked by what seems the crocodile tears shed in the later poem. But 'Lament for a Makar' can be felt as carrying a genuine burden of grief because the squabble of 1966, public as it was, was only one moment in a lifelong professional friendship. By the early 1960s the two appear to have been less close than in the 1940s but still on good terms: a letter from 1962 survives in which Young comments: 'I hope your Muse is kind'.[33] (Written when Scott's muse was being as unkind as she was ever to be to him, might this indicate that Young was privy to Scott's poetic dearth and trying to be gently supportive?) And in the years after 1966, the two men seem to have quickly resumed a good working relationship on both the professional and personal levels. Scott was becoming heavily involved with the ever more proactive Scottish Arts Council in 1967, around the time when Young took over the chairmanship of the Literature Committee. Letters survive from this period which discuss, amicably and at length, issues arising from its work, but in which Young also refers, in the most complimentary terms, to Scott's own current writing, including: 'a piece about Aberdeen, which sounded utterly authentic, and had a lot of pull-out about it. I hope you will be printing it somewhere, say in your new collection with Duncan Glen.'

A few months later, Young wrote:

> I trust you will be able to come to the Arts Council gathering on Friday 26th to talk about getting Scots works printed & bought. And, if so, I hope you will take the lead in listing priorities ...[34]

It sounds as if they had both got the Supermakar episode out of their systems. Thus, the context in which 'Lament for a Makar' must be read is far bigger and more friendly than readers, knowing only the earlier poem, might assume. And it is worth mentioning another possibility, put to me by Duncan Glen who says that he has always felt that 'Lament for a Makar' was really about Scott himself. Like Scott, Young had always been denied a university chair in Scotland, despite his striking and multifarious talents: he finally became a professor with his move to Canada's McMaster University, from where he went to his final post as a professor of Greek in North Carolina in 1970. Scott's poem is about the fate of talent in 'our ain owre thankless country', a fate 'sair, sair to thole'. No crocodile tears here, it would seem, only bitter fellow-feeling.

At the height of the *Scotsman* 'debate' about *The Burdies*, one of the letters of support Scott received was from fellow Lallans poet Tom Scott. For anyone who can personally recall that generation of poets, the feuding between the two Scotts probably seems the quintessence of its astonishing and apparently endemic capacity for civil war. Or is that quintessence to be found, rather, in

Scott v. Bold, or Scott v. Young, or Scott (T.) v. Lindsay, or Grieve v. Lindsay, or any one of a dozen others—all of them echoes (in style if not in substance) of Grieve v. Muir? As we have seen, Duncan Glen, for one, could be reduced to despair by it all.

Of these Homeric combats, the one between Alex Scott and Tom Scott was one of the best known. Its *casus belli* was Tom's reprinting, in *Catalyst for the Scottish Viewpoint* (a journal started in 1967 by the 1320 Club, a radical wing of the Scottish nationalist movement), of an earlier (1963) article. In this, he had deplored the lack of teaching of Scottish literature in Scottish universities and also the non-existence of any separate university department of Scottish literature. When Alex picked up on this, for his regular feature 'Around the Arts' in the *Scots Independent* of 9 March 1968, he denounced the article's mistakes, pointing out that Tom's account, not entirely accurate in 1963, was now even more wide of the mark, especially in view of the recent developments in the teaching of Scottish literature at Glasgow. In one sense, of course, Tom was correct in that an independent department of Scottish Literature would still not come into being for another three and a half years, but Alex was clearly right to challenge the imputation that next to no university teaching of the subject was being done anywhere. Indeed, he was stimulated to write a radio talk on the matter, which was printed in the *Scots Independent* on 6 and 13 July 1968. With recent important appointments in Scottish literature around Scotland's universities, the Scottish Arts Council's promising initiatives in the field of literature, and the establishment of the Universities Committee on Scottish Literature, there had indeed been important progress which the original article could not possibly reflect. The article of 9 March was still referring (however conventionally) to 'my friend Tom Scott'. That friendship apparently came to an end soon after, however, as Alex Scott himself later explained in a letter to John Broom:

> I set the law on Tom Scott and the editors of *Catalyst* because, after I had written adversely in *S.I.* [*Scots Independent*] about a reprint of a T.S. [Tom Scott] article on the Universities, they accused me of being part of a political conspiracy hatched by the S.N.P. against the 1320 Club! This was a gross libel on my critical independence and professional sincerity which I was amply justified in demanding to be withdrawn. My comments on T.S., on the other hand, have always been concerned with his competence as a writer, not with his political commitments.[35]

The pair had been friendly, nevertheless, for most of the 1960s, as is clear from correspondence relating, in particular, to the emergence of *The Oxford Book of Scottish Verse* in 1966, and to the great debate about *Scottish International*. Despite the growing number of anthologies of twentieth-century Scottish verse then emerging, and despite the spirit of nationalistic independence which animated so many poets of Scott's generation, the prestige of an Oxford anthology was still all-powerful. *The Oxford Book of Scottish Verse*—the definitive statement, as it seemed, of who was a Scottish poet of substance and who was not—was the collection that they all wanted to be in. The result was a certain amount of lobbying of the editors, John MacQueen and Tom Scott, as MacQueen recalls—his recollection being slightly at odds with Tom Scott's statement below. (Alex Scott, MacQueen says, was 'conspicuous' by *not* writing to the editors—rather, he seems to have been 'rightly confident' about inclusion.)[36] By and large, Tom Scott dealt with these importunings, but confided in Alex Scott, of whose friendly sympathy he was clearly sure:

> Apart from the only-to-be-expected disgraceful behaviour of the self-exposed non-poetic mob of Finlay fans, only one person touted for a place in the anthology—no, there was another. You will have no difficulty guessing who. But, on the whole, the Scots poets have been true to type. And I have erred on the side of charity where my contemporaries are concerned. I might even have included Finlay—an early piece of whimsy, but not entirely despicable—if his claque hadn't cooked his goose for him.[37]

Previous to this, the two Scotts had been amicably discussing the choice of poets, poems and editions of poems which should appear in the modern section of the volume, and Tom had also consulted with Alex about the glossing of early Scots. And during the same period, Tom was sounding out Alex on the possibility of his entering the teaching profession, though admitting that he did not really fancy it. Alex Scott, however, attempted to persuade him to think about it seriously, in terms that suggest that he himself was far from disillusioned about his own teaching.[38] And in his efforts to find funding for his mammoth unpublished volume on the history of Scottish literature, Tom turned to Alex for academic support, and received it. Furthermore, in Douglas Young's long letter of 9 August 1967, it is clear that he and Alex had been sympathetically discussing Tom Scott's funding problems for some time. Indeed, a few weeks later, Tom was thanking Alex profusely for proffered aid on the matter:

> I very much appreciate your offer of help over the history. The sheer isolation of my position at times daunts me, the insecurity, the wall of indifference and hostility; and I will be glad of any co-operation I can get, from the right people.[39]

By the time Trevor Royle became involved with the cross-currents of Scottish poetic politics early in 1971, however, Alex was no longer one of 'the right people' and the two Scotts were bitterly opposed.[40]

The precariousness of the relationship between the two Scotts was partly due to their utterly different *poetic* personalities, suggests John MacQueen.[41] Where Alex's poems in Scots tend towards surface liveliness, swiftness, wit, sudden piercing jests or equally sudden pangs of emotion, Tom's are slow, rolling, with a sonorousness which perpetually courts ponderousness. So Alex Scott could write to Maurice Lindsay:

> Like yourself, I find Tom Scott's work in Scots a quagmire of clotted nonsense. However, there's just one poem of his which seems to me to pass muster, and that is 'Orpheus' ... Would that the rest were silence![42]

Five years later, in a letter to Charles King, then preparing a new anthology of twentieth-century Scottish poetry, his views had not changed: 'Tom Scott. "Ithika" is awful—turgid, clumsy, bathetic. Please, please, please substitute "Orpheus" and "The Bride", the only fully-achieved poems in *The Ship*.'[43] Also contributing to the break between the two men was Tom Scott's personality: he was passionate, inclined to see things in black-and-white terms, and capable, recalls MacQueen, of sudden and complete reversions of attitude. Whatever the underlying tensions, however, the quarrel over the *Catalyst* suggestion of Alexander Scott's political bias not only showed up in the *Scots Independent* column but also spilled over into Duncan Glen's briefly surviving newsletter *Knowe*, and got as far as the letters pages of the *Times Literary Supplement*. And this was all before the row about the Goodsir Smith volume in the mid-1970s (see p. 163).

According to Trevor Royle, Alex Scott's other great enemy was Alan Bold (1943–98), which was difficult for Royle because he was close to both men.[44] He felt, however, that they could scarcely bear to be in the same room together; they were, he says, a 'nightmare'. Royle is unsure why Scott disliked Bold: it may have had something to do, he thinks, with Bold's closeness to MacDiarmid, of whom he wrote the standard biography. Perhaps, too, Scott resented the younger man's early success in publishing his poetry with Chatto & Windus. Bold was also published in a 1969 Penguin Modern Poets volume with Edwin Morgan. Not only was Bold's experience with publishers, from the start, immensely more favourable than Scott's (though Duncan Glen and others feel that Scott possibly made no attempt to find a London publisher for his verse, believing instead that Scottish publishing should be supported), but Bold also had an ability to write and publish books at a rate that any other author might envy, especially one such as Scott afflicted with periodic bouts of lost creativity. Deeper than all, though, is likely to have been Scott's dislike of Bold's verse, especially his verse in Scots. On at least one occasion, Scott bluntly said so in a letter to Bold which usefully touches on several topics including Bold's complaint that he had been omitted from Scott's anthology *Modern Scots Verse, 1922–1977*, which was published in 1978.

> You do yourself no good by going on and on about my *Modern Scots Verse* anthology. Everybody knows that none of your own attempts at Scots were included, and everybody (except yourself, apparently) knows

> the reason, your lack of command of the idiom and the movement of Scots. You also make yourself a laughing-stock by the claim that 'The Ship' is a masterpiece, followed by a quotation of a piece of pedestrian doggerel additionally marred by the ludicrously inappropriate image of Europe as a squeezed lemon. Your excellent study of Mackay Brown's work shows that you have admirable taste, and a fine ear, when considering verse and prose in English; but when you consider work in Scots, both your ear and your judgement become lamentably uncertain.[45]

Yet although Scott shared with many of his fellow-poets the refusal to take prisoners in a dispute, he also demonstrated here, and elsewhere in the same letter, the capacity to be fair and even generous. This suggests a detachment and a critical self-awareness lying alongside the personal outrage and passion which generated many of these verbal blows. At one moment he can respond to Bold: 'Your reference to "spiteful vituperation" is not only abusive but libellous. You might remember, too, the old adage about people who live in glass houses.' Yet in the letter as a whole Scott took considerable trouble to explain to Bold the various mistakes he sees him as having made, amplifying his points at some length with something akin to patience and helpfulness. As we can see, he could even suddenly offer a generous compliment where he thought it justified, and there is more than a hint of friendly amusement and ironic self-awareness in his *envoi*: 'Yours in irascible pedagoguery, Alex'. Although he was capable of bruised feelings and sustained enmities, it is seldom that one cannot also detect in Scott's conduct in these affrays a trace of principle, and of passionate commitment to standards and values in the literary matters about which he argued.

Nevertheless, it is clear that while Scott was often capable of co-operative and even friendly encouragement to Bold the relationship between the two was always precarious, a notably low point being the publication of the latter's *Modern Scottish Literature*.[46] The present writer can recall Scott's outrage at Bold's comments and judgements on the work of his close friend and colleague Maurice Lindsay. There is a particularly angry letter from Scott at this time:

> My opinion of the inadmissibility of the attack on Maurice in your *MSL* is shared by everyone who has discussed the book with me. (Incidentally, both Maurice and I began our various unpaid labours in the Scottish literary vineyard when we were in our early twenties and earning chicken-feed. What comparable contribution have you ever made, that entitles you to suggest that either of us is a moneygrubber?)
>
> If there's a grudge between us, it must be on your side, as everything you have written about me and my work in recent years is a mine of misinformation, much of it apparently malicious. The sentence in your headnote for the MacDiarmid letters, describing *Cantrips*, is a characteristic example of half-truth mixed with total error. 'Acerbic humour' is

> only one of the qualities (according to MacCaig) of the *Cantrips* poems, where he also finds passion, sympathy and tenderness, and none of those poems shows any 'enthusiasm for Aberdeenshire Scots'. Some are in English, and the others in the aggrandised Scots which I've been writing since 1945. I have never written in Aberdeenshire Scots, although a few of my short stories (and one poem) written in 1943/4 are in the artisan Scots (as Garioch called it) spoken in Aberdeen city. Your sheer gall, in setting yourself up to judge my work in Scots when you are totally unaware of the nature of the medium in which I write, goes far beyond the forgivable.[47]

This, however, is not the resounding end to the letter, as one might have expected. It actually closes with an apology (admittedly a little perfunctory) for being unable to supply Bold with any contact details for the widow of William Jeffrey. Nor was even this angry outburst the end of Scott's relations with Bold: still later correspondence exists showing the two co-operating while Bold was preparing his biography of MacDiarmid.

Why were there so many quarrels amongst Scott's generation of poets? Part of the answer has to be the obvious one: chance brought together a group of sensitive, emotional individuals, some of them with very short fuses. Scott was certainly among the latter: his capacity for anger is one of the characteristics that Thomas Crawford, for example, particularly recalls.[48] Ellie MacDonald, looking back upon the early 1970s, agrees that it was a time when poets were especially prone to doing each other down.[49] Scott was in the thick of it all. Nevertheless, says MacDonald, he was characteristically more direct than many: he usually went for an open, frontal attack rather than adopting the snideness of some others. Scott himself seems eventually to have regarded the poetic temperament as occasionally over-sensitive: attempting to persuade Maurice Lindsay to allow publication of one of MacDiarmid's more abusive letters, he commented: 'But then all of us who are poets suffer from having at least one skin too few—Chris included.'[50]

I suspect, however, that a more historically based explanation may also exist. The Scottish poets of Scott's generation felt themselves to be at something of a turning point and believed that what they did, and stood for, mattered. Something was actually at stake. Living and writing in the shadow of MacDiarmid's decisive intervention in the development of Scottish poetry, poets were particularly aware that they were contributing to an unfolding history. The question of where MacDiarmid's revolution would go next—or if it was going anywhere at all—was an urgent one. The liveliness of the 1960s, in all areas of culture, encouraged a hope that Scotland was turning into a land slightly less inimical to the artist. There was a feeling that Scottish poetry actually had a future. However, from the early 1960s onwards, it was becoming gradually less certain that that future would be the one projected by MacDiarmid's original revolution.

Scott belonged to the generation that consciously took up MacDiarmid's torch. By the 1960s, however, a still younger generation desired no future dictated by any older poet, however great. Tensions in the period, furthermore, were also the result of the Arts Council's kraken-like stirring in the mid-60s—a development that, by the early 1970s, was beginning to produce some real money for distribution to writers, publishers and publications. The result, in practice, was a new competitiveness amongst poets and publishers—for grants and subsidies. In the heyday of MacDiarmid and Muir, competition was purely for the soul and future of Scottish writing; in the 1960s and 1970s that competition took on a specifically financial dimension.

Even without the spur of financial competition, however, the world of Scottish poetry was infused with the spirit of the age. The 1960s was famously a time of rebellious, cocky youth, and of discomfort and affront amongst older generations. In this period of cultural revolution, some amongst the older generations adapted better than others. Edwin Morgan, for one, had apparently little difficulty in changing. His Glasgow colleague, Alexander Scott, had more. We shall examine his purely poetic response to the times later. Here, our concern is with his response to the broader literary challenges of the period. The 1960s brought a pervasive, optimistic but unsettling awareness of unfolding but unexpected futures. Consequently Scott was becoming less certain about the survival of the Scottish Renaissance to which he was devoted.

If it was a time when Scottish poets were worried about where poetry in general was going, it followed that they were particularly anxious about how their own work was being judged, and would be viewed by posterity. And in that phase of heightened self-awareness, groups, alliances and (to borrow from Dunn yet again) coteries naturally emerged. Their sense of group identity derived partly from their personal friendships, from respect for MacDiarmid as the key figure in their generation's landscape, and from their heightened awareness of the long narrative of Scottish poetic history. One might even speculate, too, that, as the generation that confronted Hitler, they were also aware of having been part of a yet larger, and even more crucial, turning point. They were particularly alive to history. Each had played some part in great, world-shaping events while at around the same time they had made their various commitments to the kind of poetry they wanted, choices that demanded of them that they take a larger view. Furthermore, part of the perspective bequeathed to them by MacDiarmid and his achievement was the revived possibility (the poverty of Victorian and Kailyard writing having been banished) of once more writing Scottish poetry of value, of stature, of greatness. But what should such poetry be like? In the wrangling of the 1960s and 1970s, much seemed at stake, both for the future health of Scottish verse, and for individual reputations.

War-forged commitment; a historically grounded hope for the future; an uncertainty as to what contemporary Scottish poetry ought to be like; an insecurity about the stature, the 'greatness' or otherwise, of one's own verse—

whether or not these were widely spread conditions for the poets of Scott's generation, they were certainly aspects of Scott's own awareness. Great events had forced him to major choices and to choose sides; in the controversies of these later decades he conducted himself with some of the same sense of rectitude, the same willingness to fight *à outrance*, the same consciousness of important principles at stake. He was fully aware of how the war had 'shuke me intil a shennachie'; if his war experiences did not leave much overt mark on his later poetry, they may well have contributed considerably to how he conducted himself as a poet as well as having helped him, in that era of whole-hearted commitment, to choose what sort of poet he would be.

It is worth exploring a little more how the language question, which had been central to the controversies arising from MacDiarmid's innovations in the 1920s, retained the power to divide later generations of poets. Where disputes such as that between Grieve and Muir in the 1930s, however, had been essentially a matter of theoretical interpretation and spiritual leadership, the tensions of the post-war decades increasingly involved those potent practicalities, money and power.

Duncan Glen touched upon this as long ago as 1964, in his *Hugh MacDiarmid and the Scottish Renaissance*. There, he pointed out how in the 1950s the Lallans (or 'Rose Street') poets seemed to dominate the positions of literary power, as editors and anthologists, so that there was a perceived bias towards poetry in Lallans:

> In January 1962 Tom Wright ... attacked the 'attitudes and dogmas of the older poets' and in particular their nationalism and insistence on the importance of Lallans and suggested that since the 'Lallans boys' held most of the editorial and critical posts the inevitable result was that the younger poets 'found a massive road block in their way'.[51]

As the 1960s progressed, however, Scott and his friends among the 'Lallans boys' became increasingly defensive, deploring the slow loss of prestige and popularity which verse in Scots appeared to be suffering. A notable straw in the wind was Maurice Lindsay's preface to his collection *Snow Warning* in which, Muir-like, he turned his back on Scots:

> It is utterly unthinkable that this poor wasted and abandoned speech, however rich in theory its poetic potential, can possibly express what there is to be expressed of the Scottish *ethos* in the age of the beatnik and the hydrogen bomb.[52]

Lindsay comments in his autobiography:

> This preface brought down fury on my head from several quarters. My good friend Alexander Scott (who had, indeed, a few notable unfired Scots arrows still in his quiver) thundered roundly against the error of my ways. So did Sydney Goodsir Smith ... who likened my changed

> views to 'les trahisons des clercs'. But time, I believe, has since shown that I was right ... Very little written on Scots since 1962 has disproved my claim. Twenty years on there is not a single Scots-writing poet under fifty producing work of real distinction in the old tongue.[53]

The issue of what younger poets were or were not doing was one with which Scott was increasingly concerned. Nor was he alone. In 1965, MacDiarmid responded to Scott's new clutch of poems (ending his years of dearth) as follows:

> Many thanks for your letter and typescript of poems. I have been delighted to read these—and at your continued fealty to Scots. I think a real effort must be made soon to register a new phase of the effort to prove Scots a valuable literary medium, and I myself find I must recur to it and try to refill a barrel whose bottom I have been scraping rather forlornly for too long now.[54]

In writing his new poems in Scots (many of which would appear in *Cantrips* in 1968), Scott was conscious of his increasing isolation as a practitioner in the language. For example, Goodsir Smith and Garioch seemed less prolific than they had been, while Duncan Glen's poetry had yet to appear in any bulk. Furthermore, Alistair Mackie had not yet re-emerged and Donald Campbell had yet to produce his first volume of poems. Scott's sense of the current health of poetry in Scots is made clear in comments in two letters to Lindsay:

> If I am 'likely to be the last of the Scots-writers with an individual voice,' it's a melancholy distinction. What a way to go down to posterity! It makes me feel like the Last of the Mohicans—but this particular redskin doesn't mean to bite the dust just yet.
>
> ...
>
> You are probably right about Mitchell. It may very well be that I incline towards his work for no better reason than that it shows there was at least one other writer in Scots who hove on the scene later than I did. It's depressing to have to consider oneself as 'the end'. Still, I suppose it would be even worse if one had to consider oneself a dead end; and anyhow, the only thing to do is to keep on keeping on.[55]

The 'Mitchell' here is probably David Mitchell, born in 1932; some of his poems were published by Glen in 1975. Once Glen established *Akros* in 1965, he and Scott commented to each other periodically on what they felt to be the increasing bias against Scots in, for example, the new annual *Scottish Poetry* volumes. A letter from Glen mentions how Scott had been contributing to a radio *Arts Review* programme with some 'vigorous remarks' on his, by now, pet subject of how poems in Scots were being too frequently rejected by the *Scottish Poetry* collections and by *Lines Review*.[56] But around this time, Glen himself had sensed (rightly or otherwise) that the Scottish Arts Council (SAC) itself was becoming less sympathetic to poetry in Scots.[57]

Most worryingly of all, Scott himself increasingly recognised that the Scottish Renaissance case for a literary Scots as a modern poetic medium was being rejected by younger Scottish writers. As Edwin Morgan says: 'he was always looking for younger writers to carry things forward.'[58] Scott's poem 'Mak It New', dedicated 'til Alastair Mackie—and the younger Scots makars', eloquently expresses his hopes and desires in this matter. Mackie (1925–95) was almost Scott's age but had returned to Lallans verse only in the 1960s, so Scott appears to have thought of him as belonging to a future generation and as a potential torchbearer. Mackie, however, feared for the future of literary Scots as much as Scott did. Congratulating him on the news about the new Glasgow department and his imminent headship, he thanks Scott for a favourable review in *Akros* which, he says:

> comes at a time when I was feeling rather bitter and despondent—I thought of giving up—after reading a notice in the recent [*Scottish International*] of your anthology and the current *SP5* ... I am now totally convinced that no good can come out of that quarter to Scots letters; that the young and modish are in control and that—what is a constant for those writing in Scots—the battle simply continues. You are hardened to all this; but sometimes it takes a while to accommodate the obvious.[59]

The reference here was to a new initiative which seemed particularly ominous to the Lallans poets. At the meeting of the SAC Literature Committee of 28 June 1967, there was discussion of a proposal:

> to establish a new quarterly magazine in Scotland under the editorship of Mr. Robert Tait (presently editing *Feedback*), Mr. Edwin Morgan and Mr. Robert Garioch. The Professors of English (at the Universities of Glasgow and Edinburgh) were also involved (although not editorially) in this move to start a new literary magazine.[60]

This would be *Scottish International* about which its first managing editor, Bob Tait, insists: 'the Scottish Arts Council did, as a matter of deliberate policy and intervention, bring *Scottish International* into being.' As the literature group within the newly energised SAC realised, there had been a gap in the array of Scotland's literary and cultural journals ever since the demise of *New Saltire* in 1964: 'they wanted to provide for a regular (originally, a quarterly) journal of cultural comment and opinion and creative work.'[61] Not being permitted to publish such a journal themselves, the SAC turned to *Feedback* (a fledgling publication that Tait—still only twenty-four years old—and his colleague Jack Regan had initiated, with the encouragement of Father Anthony Ross of the University of Edinburgh) and to Tait as its editor, proposing that it be converted and expanded. Tait was always seen as part of the editorial team, although he insists that, at the outset, he saw himself as the 'gofer' for more distinguished colleagues. Who those colleagues were to be was not a foregone conclusion. In a recent interview, Philip Hobsbaum said that he was invited by Peter Butter to become involved but declined, feeling that it was a task for a Scot: Edwin Morgan was then invited.[62] Tait admits both that Alexander Scott probably wanted to be an editor, and (furthermore) that he undoubtedly had a claim. In the end, an editorial triumvirate of Morgan, Garioch and Tait was installed, and Tait was surprised to find that his was soon the guiding, rather than the subordinate, hand. He had complete editorial freedom as managing editor, with neither the SAC nor the board of directors (initially, professors Butter and MacQueen, Father Anthony Ross and the actor Iain Cuthbertson) interfering at all with editorial decisions. Opposition to the new venture, however, from the Scottish Renaissance wing of literary Scotland began even before the first issue appeared. Attacks also came from those who, while less committed to cultural nationalism, were nevertheless wedded to a notion of 'culture' as being what Tait calls: '*higher-order* expressions of ideas and *mores*, expressions that should be dominated by certain genres of literature and discourses'.[63]

Scottish International turned out to be a publication of some historical importance, for it polarised Scotland's literary community and brought to the surface the deep divisions amongst those concerned with contemporary writing. As Edwin Morgan says, it was 'a crucial moment in Scottish culture', and Alexander Scott was one of those involved in the battles which raged around the *Scottish International* flag.[64]

Alastair Mackie's sense that *Scottish International* (apparently so powerful and so well funded by the SAC) was fundamentally opposed to the furthering of the Scottish Renaissance poetic agenda was a view shared by many prominent and vociferous voices on the nationalist wing of Scotland's literary world at the time. Tom Scott, for example, wrote thus to Alex Scott:

> I will write to Ronald Mavor [director of SAC] telling him I have no confidence in the magazine whatsoever under its present editor and editorial set-up, when I know my facts better. The presence of Morgan and Tait is almost enough, but not quite. It looks as if it will be a cross between Anglo-Yanko voguism and Christian morguery. In any case, dead as mutton to the real Scottish tradition. They'll get nothing from me. Duncan Glen is the man who should have been supported.[65]

At this point, the plans for the new journal had merely been announced: its first issue was that of January 1968. Tom Scott was one of the most prominent opponents of the new venture, along with (as Bob Tait recalls) William Neill, Ronald MacDonald Douglas and Tom MacDonald ('Fionn MacColla'). And over-riding all (and giving the lead to many) was the opposition of Grieve: as John Herdman has written: 'Hugh MacDiarmid was convinced that the whole project had been set up to counter the literary national movement.'[66] (The editors particularly relished Grieve's description of Morgan and Tait as 'beatnik cosmopolitans'.) Tom Scott's opinions, quoted above, contain the essence of the complaints of the nationalist opposition. *Scottish International* was seen as an attempt to supplant Scottish tradition, as the determinant of future Scottish writing and culture, with the influences and tastes of the literary scenes of England and America. The 'internationalism' flaunted in the title was seen as a cover for a London-centred orientation of taste, and sometimes as a yearning after an americanisation of culture. Particularly loathed was the 1960s vogue for 'concrete' poetry, of which the leading British practitioner was Ian Hamilton Finlay, an old friend but now inveterate enemy of MacDiarmid's, while Edwin Morgan was also known as a sympathiser with, and occasional dabbler in, the 'concrete' movement. Furthermore, there was a sporadic whiff of religious prejudice stimulated by Ross' involvement—though John MacQueen also recalls the trouble caused by the joke of the first cover illustration, which displayed another kind of 'international', the footballer Ronnie Simpson playing in his Celtic jersey at Celtic Park. As MacQueen says, 'a whole culture' was embodied in the chosen photograph, and it was a culture that some partisan readers found objectionable.[67] John Herdman, too, is conscious of deeper issues at stake than mere literary preference: he sees the 'establishment' support for the 'internationalism' of the venture as prompted by the unfolding political situation following the Hamilton by-election of 1967 when Winnie Ewing gained a historic success for the Scottish National Party.[68]

Both for those cheered by a looming nationalist political upsurge and those appalled by the prospect, the late 1960s and early '70s was a period of particular sensitivity. An 'establishment'-maintained cultural organ, not conspicuously supportive of MacDiarmid's 'Renaissance' project, therefore, could easily seem a voice of the opposing camp. On the other hand, there are those such as Bob Tait himself who see the possible root of the opposition as lying in Christopher Grieve's personal feud with Iain Hamilton Finlay, whose poems and art works seemed to sum up the radical innovativeness of the 1960s—and (in the eyes of many) the emptiness of 60s culture. Tait and his journal certainly championed Finlay—Tait still insists that Finlay is one of the very few artists of true international stature produced by modern Scotland. A further cause for complaint, however, especially among the editors of other, less well-endowed literary periodicals, was the extent of the SAC's financial support for *Scottish International*. Where other journals simply received an annual grant, *Scottish International* was given a guarantee against loss and its editors were able to aspire to production values of which others, such as Duncan Glen, could only dream.

When all was said and done, however, it remained a root complaint that the new magazine was not sufficiently committed to the nationalist cause, a fact that, to many, made its support by the *Scottish* Arts Council seem a paradox—or a dereliction of duty. Tait admits that while he and his colleagues had no trace of an anti-Renaissance agenda (MacDiarmid was the first person invited to join the board, though his refusal was not unexpected), they desired to create a new voice, expressing a wider vision for the future, rather than a narrow reinforcement and justification of the past. The impulse to break new ground, while retaining cordial relations with existing periodicals, is clear in the first editorial. After acknowledging the continuing importance of a diverse range of other journals—*Akros*, *Gairm*, *Lines Review* and *Poor.Old.Tired.Horse* are listed—it continues:

> There is surely a clear need for at least one critical review such as *Scottish International* to supplement what these other magazines and the daily press can do...Nor should one forget that the Scottish arts don't exist in a Scottish world of their own. A colourless or promiscuous internationalism is to nobody's advantage. But a self-conscious cultural nationalism can lead to bad habits of stereotyped thinking and unwillingness to look at the situation as it really is. Our policy will be to look for what is really there, and to call people's attention to it. Everyone is aware, to a greater or lesser extent, of how cultures other than Scottish impinge upon us, through publishing and the mass media. It is important that this awareness should be sharpened and extended critically, so that more opportunity can be given to compare Scottish work with work done elsewhere. To define ourselves, we believe it is necessary to define many other things, for that is the nature of the world we live in.

So, in the first issue we find articles on Stravinsky and on Voznesensky's poetry, but there is also Garioch on 'The use of Scots' and A. D. Mackie on 'The spelling of Scots'—an article which reproduced that gonfalon of the 'second generation' of Lallans makars, the Scots Style Sheet, stitched together all those years previously in the pubs of Rose Street. It also contained verse by a widely eclectic group of poets—including Alexander Scott.

A glance through the pages of *Scottish International* now prompts one to wonder what all the fuss was about. Many later periodicals share its mixture of breadth of subject and attitude, its desire to interpret 'culture' widely, its occasional journalistic boldness, its commitment to the new, the youthful and the avant-garde. A crucial moment in Scottish culture? Perhaps—certainly a sign of a cultural shift. It signified a democratisation of taste and cultural value judgements, and reflected the new cultural world community which 1960s youth embraced. The new journal embodied the future in its relaxed openness to—indeed, eager interest in—cultural and political developments across the globe. This inevitably placed it at odds with the emphases of the Lallans poets, who had tended to concentrate on firmly rooting Scottish cultural life in older Scottish traditions. The split reflects, perhaps, the paradox at the heart of MacDiarmid's Renaissance, which had aimed to draw new life from both a healthy Scottish past and a healthy internationalism. Not everyone, it seems, could live (like MacDiarmid) where extremes meet. Tait's view is that his journal came a decade too soon—too soon to be able to take advantage of the flowering of Scottish writing talent (especially among women writers) as the 1970s progressed. Too soon, also, to be properly funded for what he wanted to achieve—despite the brouhaha about its comparatively well-funded state in comparison to its rivals, Tait insists that money was always extremely tight and that it was only his penny-pinching approach to the journal's finances which kept it going through his editorship. It was left-wing in flavour, also, and it was another of the complaints against it, and against the SAC for supporting it, that politics (other than cultural nationalist politics) infected it.

Alexander Scott complained about *Scottish International*, as did so many of his friends and associates, especially in its first couple of years. He attacked it in letters, and in print. Its appearance coincided with his period as a weekly columnist in the *Scots Independent*, a newspaper/journal issued by the Scottish National Party, and his column would return to it whenever a new issue appeared. Furthermore, correspondence between him and Duncan Glen reveals that, once a couple of numbers of *Scottish International* had appeared, he was beginning to float the idea of himself instigating a rival publication, along the lines of the 1950s' *Scots Review*.[69]

Yet his attitude was more complex than this. He seems to have initially agreed to act as an adviser to *Scottish International*, but broke with the venture even before the first issue appeared. Hence Tom Scott's growl:

> No mention of you in *Scotsman*'s announcement of the new review, which sounds sheer hell—'The Scottish International Review'. Normally 'international' means English only this time it's likely to mean 'concrete' also. The board mentioned includes Peter Butter, John MacQueen and (in the name of all that's mysterious, why?) Antony Ross, S.J. Did they manage to elbow you out?[70]

Three weeks later Tom Scott wrote again saying: 'Sorry to hear about your resignation. What were the "developments"?'[71] This is filled out a little by a letter from Bob Tait which reveals that Alexander Scott had formally resigned as an adviser to the journal on the day after Tom's letter of the 7th:

> Thank you for your letter of October 8th, and for the enclosed poem. We are sorry that you feel you must break all connection with us as an adviser and that my letter of the 6th, written to confirm this matter, arrived just after you had decided to do so.
>
> We still hope that you will be willing to review for us on occasion as well as contributing in other ways too, and I would like to repeat now, in the same terms as before, our invitation to you to contribute to the first issue.[72]

It is not clear exactly which 'developments' prompted Scott to withdraw. Nevertheless, 'Justice', the poem Tait mentions, duly appeared in the first issue: it had been written many years earlier on 12 August 1946 and was a stylistically energetic example of what Scott was writing 'at a time when I was mad keen on everything Scots.'[73] This was a poem he had recently revised for use in a number of publications following his poetic renewal after 'Heart of Stone'. Scott clearly believed in this old poem of his, and in offering it to Tait he was by no means fobbing off a rival editor: nevertheless, one suspects that he was determined that a thoroughly Scottish Renaissance poem would appear in the first issue of *Scottish International*. On the other hand, one of the publications in which the poem also appeared was *Poet: An International Monthly*, edited from Madras: it would seem that the word 'international' was not quite such a red rag to Alex Scott as it was to some of his friends.[74] One suspects that his opposition was not quite so deep-seated and ideological as it was on the part of others. Edwin Morgan, when interviewed, did not recall Alex Scott as being clearly opposed to it, nor did Bob Tait regard him as one of their major opponents. That said, Tait's impression nevertheless was that:

> Alex's objections to us were pretty fundamental. We could do no right, or very little. He seemed, at least for a year or two, to go out of his way to give us a bad word (even when writing about something else) and, equally to go out of his way to give us the faintest praise even when we were, by his lights, at least giving houseroom to material he approved of.[75]

But however 'fundamental' Scott's objections seemed to Tait, it was Duncan Glen's impression that he came out against the new publication only after MacDiarmid did.[76] Nor was his opposition visceral like, say, Tom Scott's. By the autumn of 1969, when he was working on the page proofs of *Contemporary Scottish Verse*, he was perfectly capable of meeting Tait and resolving sensibly a minor problem of layout with regard to one of Tait's poems in the selection. (Equally, Grieve's opposition did not lead *him* to object to his eightieth birthday party being organised by the staff of *Scottish International*—by all accounts, a very good time was had by all.)[77]

Tait rightly acknowledges that Scott was capable of praising the journal when he found something in it he liked, as is borne out by the weekly articles he was writing in the *Scots Independent*. He never accepted, however, what Tait and his colleagues were trying to do. His column started on 13 January 1968, coinciding almost exactly with the first appearance, a fortnight later, of *Scottish International*. He devoted his fourth column, on 3 February, to the first issue, and seemed determined to criticise it. He complained about what seemed to him the inappropriate cover photograph (he couldn't see it as a joke) and for him 'the provocative title alone is hot potato enough to start fingers burning'. He complained that the contributors, all poets, were taking on a wide range of cultural topics on which (he thought) they wrote without qualifications and with unequal success: '[no article] enjoys any authority whatsoever. They are, essentially, amateur productions.' He acknowledged that the issue contained a range of verse but complained of 'two articles squirting venom on the Scottish Renaissance'. He thundered about the absence of any creative prose. In the last quarter of his review, he acknowledged a number of successes and virtues, but still ended on a sour note. It is difficult to judge how far he was writing from a position of determined, doctrinaire antagonism, and how far he was merely reacting to the pages he saw before him—a bit of both, one suspects. What is not in doubt, however, is the honest passion with which he attacked the production. He clearly felt that a strong statement was needed: as ever, the over-riding sense is of how much literature and culture in Scotland mattered to him. Yet this uneasy first article suggests that he was caught between the party standpoint of such as Grieve and Tom Scott, and his own honest recognition that the periodical contained worthwhile material. His main accusation against it was that its purpose seemed confused: it may well have been that it was his own position regarding it which was confused.

Over the next couple of years, succeeding issues of *Scottish International* were dissected as they appeared. Sometimes, he seemed to be softening, or coming to believe that the periodical was improving, but the criticisms did not stop and he never finally made his peace with it. Soon after his 'Around the Arts' column for *Scots Independent* was closed down, he penned the following on 23 July 1970:

> ***'Gratitude'***
> *(On ceasing to write a weekly column about the arts in Scotland)*
>
> Nae mair need
> To rax to read
> Thon *Scottish International*
> That's neither Scotch nor rational.[78]

If literary Scotland, as a whole, was clumsily negotiating a major turning point over *Scottish International*, the same might be said of Alexander Scott. Taken overall, his response was an aspect of his ambivalent attitude to the transformations of writing and culture from the mid-60s onwards. Essentially moulded in the immediate post-war era, he was both fascinated and repelled by the contemporary scene so vigorously flowering around him—partly feeling he should denounce it, and partly wanting to participate in it.

Scott remained true to the Scottish Renaissance for the remainder of his life, but the energy of the post-war phase of Renaissance makars gradually waned with the deaths of leading practitioners and the steady arrival of younger writers to whom the Renaissance was little more than history. So, to Tom Leonard and Tom McGrath, the urgency lay in: 'William Carlos Williams, Creely, Charles Olson, what we saw as exciting developments in mainly American poetry. The whole Lallans movement etc. was a cultural solar system away from that.'[79] Bob

Tait, too, recalls that his generation of writers simply disregarded the older ones, among whom, in any case, Alex Scott no longer seemed an insistent presence. Indeed, Tait thinks of him as 'the man who wasn't there'—as someone who had little or no presence in the circles in which Tait was moving.[80] His natural circle was an older one. Dunn and Leonard both pointed out to me just how many poets were born in Scotland around Alex Scott's birth year of 1920. (In comparison, Dunn feels part of a much smaller, or thinner, generation.)[81] In those post-war years, therefore, it had been easy for Scott to feel part of a substantial group of poets—a circle, moreover, that had at its centre the extraordinary personality of Grieve. Even in the late 1960s and early '70s, recalls Donald Campbell, there was a 'family atmosphere' among the writers to whom MacDiarmid was still important, thanks to the great man's charisma.[82]

But MacDiarmid died in 1978, and the 1970s saw others of Scott's generation of poets beginning to die off, as in the cases of Douglas Young and Sydney Goodsir Smith. On the other hand, Scottish literature's burgeoning as an academic subject in the '70s with its associated organisational developments brought Scott a differently focused circle of literary companions. In the early years of the new Glasgow department, too, academic matters claimed a higher proportion of his available energies than ever. Whatever the reason, his later years were less obviously dominated by the movement he had espoused in the 1940s. Even so, the last issues of *The Scottish Review: Arts and Environment* contain a discussion that quietly reflects the position between the generations late in Scott's life. Christopher Rush had reviewed Andrew Greig's collection *Surviving Passages*, lamenting how Greig, like others of Greig's generation, no longer reflected (it seemed to Rush) a local reality in their writing.[83] In the next issue, Greig responded, challenging Rush's assumption that this amounted to a major loss: he rejoiced in the freedom to participate in a worldwide literary exchange, and saw this is a distinction between his generation and the previous one:

> There is a very definite break between the whole tone and intent of the Scottish Renaissance generation together with the 'middle generation' that followed it, and that of the 'younger contemporary poets' that I think of as my generation.[84]

Scott clearly hated the idea that his 'middle' generation was being seen as the last with a Scottish Renaissance focus, and contributed an article of his own in which he denied that his own generation lacked interest in the wider world beyond Scotland. He also lamented that the speech and values of the Scottish Lowlands might not survive the onslaught of the English and American media: 'the Scots language—that once gave full expression to the Lowland Scottish ethos—is growing fainter and fainter, more restricted in vocabulary and less idiosyncratic in idiom, with each successive generation.'[85]

He himself, however, was no longer the dominant figure that he had been during the late 1960s. Thus, for example, he was provoked to fury by his omission from the list of supporters published in 1982 by the Scottish Poetry Library in its first leaflet: Tessa Ransford recalls the angry letter she received when she, new to the scene and not fully aware of his role in Scotland's literary developments of recent decades, failed to add his name to the list she had been given by colleagues in the library—a list that undoubtedly should have included him but which perhaps reflected, once more, some of the ongoing feuding of Scotland's literary world.[86] Widely representative of the creative, critical, publishing and academic dimensions of the Scottish scene, it included such old friends and colleagues as Norman MacCaig, Edwin Morgan, Derick Thomson, George Bruce and Maurice Lindsay. Scott understandably took his omission as an insult. But in any case, amongst the list's three dozen or so names, perhaps only Tom Scott's gestured towards the Lallans movement, which Alex Scott still strove to perpetuate. If the list reflected personal enmity, it also reflected the way history was moving as regards the twentieth-century Scottish Renaissance.

Chapter 6

Theatre

Among Alexander Scott's first literary efforts was a play, a dramatisation of the 'Admiral Benbow' chapters of *Treasure Island*, written under the stimulus of his first taste of live theatre when he was just twelve. It was performed before various classes at Kittybrewster Primary School.[1] Throughout his life he regarded himself as not solely a poet but also as a dramatist: in the 1950s drama was arguably his principal creative focus. His son Crombie believes that it was the failure of his dramatic career which was the primary cause of the depressed state, from the later 1950s, causing him to cease to write poetry for such a long time.[2] If so, the disappointment is certainly understandable, for there was a period when it seemed that a substantial career as playwright was opening before him. He was the author of at least eighteen plays for a variety of media. Three full-length works (*Right Royal, Tam o' Shanter's Tryst* and *Truth to Tell*) were staged by the Glasgow Citizens' Theatre in the 1950s, by casts that included such names as John Cairney, John Grieve, Fulton Mackay, Iain Cuthbertson, Alex McAvoy, Andrew Keir, Gudrun Ure, Molly Urquhart, Annette Crosbie, Ronald Fraser, Roddy MacMillan, Andy Stewart and Duncan Macrae. Alexander Gibson arranged the songs in *Right Royal*. Most of his plays were broadcast on radio and *Right Royal* (perhaps his greatest success) had a television production. The majority, however, are short works: even *Right Royal* and *Tam o' Shanter's Tryst* are expansions of shorter radio plays. They are, with only one exception, products of the late 1940s and the '50s; the exception is a final radio play from 1964, *The Monsters*.

There are two main reasons why Scott's plays are now unknown. For one thing, few were ever published, and of those that were most were short plays printed as pamphlets for acting purposes. *The Last Time I Saw Paris* was reprinted in *The Saltire Review* and *Gift to the Queen* appeared recently in *Scotlands*.[3] Most, however, exist as tattered broadcast scripts or typescripts in the possession of the Scott family, or in collections in the National Library of Scotland, in BBC archives and in the Scottish Theatre Archive. *Right Royal* appears to exist only as a tape of a radio broadcast, possessed by the family.

The other reason is that not only did Scott's play writing belong to the earlier decades of his career, but also his whole approach to drama belonged to a period of Scottish theatre which had decisively passed by the 1960s. Once again, Scott straddled historical change: hopes that he might participate in a theatrical Scottish Renaissance were dashed when that Scottish theatre scene moved in a direction of which he did not approve. Post-war programming which encouraged Scottish writers and plays reflecting Scottish life and traditions—and, of course, plays that were written in Scots—gave way to a more 'international' (that ominous word again) approach. And not only did new directors working in Scotland increasingly wish to look beyond Scottish material to drama from around the world but also, even closer to home, ideas about what constituted dramatic vitality were transformed by Osborne's *Look Back in Anger* (1956). Scott acknowledged as much when, in a talk entitled 'What kind of play now?', he grumbled about how, from the mid-1950s, the Citizens' management 'was more interested in following the movement which had begun at the Royal Court in London during the mid-fifties than in encouraging native drama'.[4]

The Glasgow Citizens' was the theatre with which Scott most closely identified. It was here that his three full-length plays were produced. From this distance in time, it is common to locate the decisive change in policy with the arrival of Giles Havergal in 1969, but Scott felt, a decade and more earlier, that things were already changing (from his point of view) for the worse. In 'What kind of play now?' he voiced his sense that the Scottish theatre had become far less favourable to writers of his persuasion than they had been in the late 1940s and early '50s. Equally strong in 'What kind of play now?', however, is a belief that theatre has always had a precarious place in Scottish life, but that the Citizens' under Bridie 'and for a few years after his too-early death in 1951' offered a brief period when the Scottish Renaissance could infuse Scotland's theatrical life and a Scottish national theatre company could begin to emerge. Scott dated the decline, as he saw it, from the mid-1950s:

> I hope that the production of *Right Royal* [in 1954] is only coincidental with the fact that since then the Scottish theatre has been in a condition of decline. The easy explanation for this is the advent of television, but other factors were at work too. So long as Bridie was alive, it didn't matter so much that many of the producers employed by the Citizens' were Sassenachs who ... knew nothing, or next to nothing, about Scottish cultural traditions and ways of life; for Bridie could advise them, and his prestige was such that his advice couldn't be ignored ... Within a few years of his death, however, Bridie's influence waned, and the theatre had a succession of producers and directors who, if they were English, had little knowledge of the Scottish drama and less interest, or who, if they were Scots, seemed afraid they might appear parochial if they encouraged native work.[5]

It may be that Scott was judging from too close a perspective, and with too many Renaissance axes to grind. Nevertheless, the assessment just quoted seems to have become his fixed view. His concern that the 'right' people should be in charge, especially at the Glasgow Citizens', is apparent as early as May 1954, in a letter to the secretary of the Scottish Sub-Committee of the League of Dramatists, Alec Robertson:

> Many of us here, including Roddy Macmillan, John Wilson, T. M. Watson, Alex Reid and myself, are highly perturbed about the latest turn of affairs at Glasgow Citizens', with the failure to renew Michael Langham's contract for next season after his brilliant series of production successes this spring, and with the directors' adamant stand on the matter of fortnightly repertory; and we feel that the League of Dramatists ought to have a special meeting to discuss the whole affair.[6]

(Robertson and his colleagues quickly realised that Scott, despite this peremptory intervention, was not actually a member of the League. Neither was he in 1957 when a similar exchange of letters took place. The impression given in the surviving letters on these matters is that Scott was rather sticking his nose in where he had no business, at least when his non-membership was taken into account. His anxiety regarding fundamental issues of theatre policy is, nevertheless, very clear: he felt utterly involved, whatever the legalities and niceties.)

Scott's belief—that the late 1950s saw the Citizens' suddenly turn away from the programming of new Scottish material which had marked the company's first decade and which had made it, of all Scotland's theatres at the time, the one most supportive of Scottish writing—is confirmed by theatre historians. As Cordelia Oliver has written:

> There is no doubt that ... a modest break in continuity did occur at Citizens' several years after the death of its founder. With the 1957 autumn season and through the late 1950s and early 1960s ... the input of specifically Scottish writing tailed off abruptly.[7]

More recent commentators such as Donald Campbell agree that the advent of television in the mid-1950s had a decisive effect on theatre in Scotland but are less inclined to insist on the relevance of ignorant Sassenachs and timorous Scots. As Campbell says:

> Before television, the theatre was regarded as a public facility, supported by regular playgoers certainly, but essentially an integral part of the general life of the community. After the arrival of television, theatre quickly assumed the role of a minority interest.[8]

Perhaps, though, the problem went even deeper, as Donald Smith suggests as he considers the larger social changes which took hold in the late 1950s: influenced by television as it was, the period was also a time in which homes were becoming more comfortable and people were staying in more.[9] Also, there was a great shift in populations to outlying housing schemes, with less proximity to city-centre theatres. And the great cultural shift from a national culture dominated by middle-class taste to one driven by a new working-class bias was setting in, with profound implications for all branches of entertainment:

> The Scottish theatres were exceptionally ill prepared for this climate of social revolution. In Britain as a whole, the initiative was passing from the middle-class theatre of the repertories to the expression of working-class experience. But in Scotland the subsidised theatres had eschewed working-class experience and cut themselves off from the popular theatre traditions, which might have offered new lines of development. The post-war Scottish playwrights were suddenly left high and dry in an apparently provincial regionalism, while, despite the rise of a new generation of acting talent, few Scottish directors were available to interpret the fresh situation in Scottish terms. Consequently, in addition to the long-running economic crisis and a forthcoming management crisis, theatre in Scotland was hit by an artistic crisis as well.
>
> In Glasgow, a decisive shift came in 1960–1 when, in the Arts Council's phrase, the Citizens' 'went experimental', producing Dürrenmatt, Giraudoux, Ionesco, Wesker's *Roots*, and *Breakdown* by Stewart Conn, one of the few Scottish playwrights to emerge during the 1960s.[10]

As noted above, however, a change had set in a few years earlier. If one compares the Citizens' programmes for 1953–4 (when Scott's first play for them, *Right Royal*, was staged) with that for 1957–8 (when his last, *Truth to Tell*, was presented), one finds that of the earlier season's twelve plays, eight are by Scottish authors or done into Scottish versions, whereas a few years later there were at most three out of seventeen. (These figures include, in each case, the famous Citizens' Christmas shows with their thirteen-letter titles.) Scott's conception of the Scottish drama he wanted to write fell victim to a profound change in theatrical and cultural circumstances: it was a major blow to him as an artist.

The following is a list of Scott's plays of which I am aware. The dates refer to the earliest indication of a play's existence I have been able to find, whether it be a date of production, or of printing, or given in some other reference. Except where indicated, all are either short single-act pieces or short radio plays lasting under an hour.

The Volcano (1947) [radio]
Prometheus 48 (1948) [stage; verse]
Sodger Frae the War Returns: A Ballad for Broadcasting (1949) [radio; verse]
Gift to the Queen (1950) [radio]
The Jerusalem Farers (1950) [radio; verse]

Uneasy Lies (1950) [radio]
Cutty Sark (1951) [radio]
The Last Time I Saw Paris (1951) [verse]
Untrue Thomas (1952) [radio and stage; verse]
Right Royal (1952) [full-length stage play based on *Uneasy Lies*]
The Deil's Awa (1953) [radio][11]
Shetland Yarn (1954) [stage]
Tam o' Shanter's Tryst (1955) [full-length stage play based on *Cutty Sark*]
Truth to Tell (1956) [full-length play; radio and stage]
The Monsters (1964) [radio]

In addition, the following are currently undated:

Bruce's Barber [radio, but in author's typescript only]
MacGregor Despite Them [typescript in private hands]
The Wanton Widow [ms. radio play][12]

Scott's main goal as a playwright was his attempt to help build a new Scottish theatrical tradition on the basis of the country's own literary and historical past. The majority of his plays use Scottish material or employ Scots dialogue either completely or to a marked extent. It was not that Scott was lacking in interest in plays from overseas, nor was he blind to greatness if it were not Scottish. Maurice Lindsay recalls, for example, that his friend was very keen on the plays of Ibsen,[13] and his many years of reviewing for radio arts programmes would not have happened had his mind been closed to everything that was not native. Yet his sense of the priorities for contemporary Scottish theatre remained firm: Scottish audiences needed, he insisted, Scottish material. Donald Campbell recalls how Scott believed (mistakenly, in Campbell's view) that there remained only one strand of a living Scottish dramatic tradition: music hall. Consequently, it was with that populist mode that revival, he thought, had to start.[14]

Most young people of Scott's generation were familiar with music-hall and pantomime, and Scott's association in the 1950s with the Glasgow Citizens' is likely to have convinced him that the Scottish stage was never more alive, or more enjoyed, than when a pantomime held sway: by all reports, the annual Christmas shows then put on by the Citizens' were something special. Furthermore, Scott's own theatrical involvements had been in school revues and student shows, and it seems possible that his conception of successful theatre was derived from the immediate heartiness of response such episodic and laughter-orientated productions generate. The student revue, at least as practised by the undergraduates of Aberdeen University, is a ragbag of songs, dances and sketches, a music-hall formula to which is added a strong, pervasive strand of dialect humour and a 'sophisticated' layer of self-conscious, ironic cultural knowingness—a description that begins to outline quite a few of Scott's plays, especially the three longer ones. Newspaper reviews of the Citizens' productions regularly compared the plays to pantomimes and student revues.

Scott's plays, therefore, with few exceptions, are characterised by episodic construction, broad and vigorous humour, and a bookishness which, thinks Campbell, is their principal limitation. What we do not find is a full-length, tightly organised exploration of a small group of characters in a single situation; far less do we find anything resembling a full-length tragedy. Above all, he avoids giving us realistic renderings of contemporary life. His strengths were in comedy, in fantasy and in brevity. Which is not to say that his plays lack seriousness. Indeed, looking back on his career as a dramatist, he would insist on considerable seriousness of intention. Thus, he wrote to George Bruce:

> I must stop writing comic plays—even after sixty years of Shaw and thirty of Bridie, only one critic in a hundred seems to have grasped the idea that it's possible to write comedy with a serious intention.[15]

In 1967 he defended himself and other dramatists against Bruce who, in a *Radio Times* article, had had the temerity to be dismissive of Scottish plays of the 1950s. While to many, Scott's loyalty to the Renaissance seemed to put him at odds with the achievements of twentieth-century drama elsewhere, he was still of the Renaissance mind that to be thoroughly Scottish in one's writing is to place oneself in the international vanguard:

> It seems to me that the best plays of Kemp and Maclellan and Reid are neither domestic comedies or histories, but costume fantasies—in this differing not a whit from the currently-fashionable Brecht—which often anticipate the theatre of the absurd ... *Right Royal* is an indigenous example of the theatre of the absurd, written long before such exercises became tediously fashionable.[16]

It was with *Right Royal*, expanded from *Uneasy Lies*, that he had his greatest success with theatre audiences. Not only that, but in 1952 it also won the Scottish award for a full-length play in one of the several Festival of Britain literary competitions in which Scott was successful. This is a tale of the efforts of King Dod III of Fife to fool Eric Bignose, prince of the Saxons who have recently taken over the Lothians, into thinking that Fife could defend itself against a Saxon invasion. *Right Royal* is a droll comic concoction which fuses a rough-and-ready picture of Scottish history of the period of Columba with a fusillade of modern conversational Scots richly endowed with cheerful anachronisms (Dod's right-hand man, the archdruid Ake, is contemplating putting in for 'a vacancy in Aiberdeen', the army of Fife consists of 'twa-score generals on the retired list, three corporals and a man', etc.). There is a nugget of seriousness, signalled by the new Christian teaching from Iona, which wins over Dod's daughter and (fortunately for the defenceless Dod) Eric Bignose himself. Beyond that, one discerns the theme of old rottenness being swept away and supplanted by youth, vigour and better-founded values. Furthermore, it was originally conceived less than six years after the end of the Second World War (and in a world offering no guarantees against a Third) and is a modest assertion of the wisdom of peaceful transitions and resolutions, a plea for the sensible resolution of international tensions and conflict. In a sense, it is a play about deterrence.

Yet this underlying seriousness is largely swamped by the sheer fun of the thing: even without the later expansion of the role in *Right Royal*, or the genius of Macrae who played the part in that later version, Dod is already a fine creation, a likeable Ebenezer Balfour, an old Scottish twister of limited horizons yet with a lively alertness to any threats to his own well-being.

The play was premiered on 3 May 1954 and performed to full houses, helped by much encouraging newspaper coverage. A radio production followed, on 27 August 1955, and BBC interest in the play continued with a television production on 12 December 1958. In each of these productions, Macrae played the lead. Thereafter, it was included in Iain Cuthbertson's experimental Scottish season at Perth Theatre, opening on 1 November 1967.

Tam o' Shanter's Tryst, the second of Scott's full-length plays, carried with it his highest hopes—which, in the event, were painfully dashed. Revisiting one of the best-known of all canonical Scottish texts, it was his most elaborate attempt to create a Scottish Renaissance play. His first treatment of the idea, the radio comedy *Cutty Sark* (broadcast 23 January 1951), had been a modest joke at the expense of the quick-witted but strictly moralistic wife and the gormless, lecherous husband. These are Burns' original stock figures, it is true, but in the poem the focus is on narrative, atmosphere and tonal complexity. In Scott's play, the characters, in all their cartoon-like simplicity, are centre-stage. Tam has fled home to his cottage, followed by Annie/Nannie and Auld Nick whose claim on Tam's soul following his weak-willed indulgence in a kiss from Nannie is eventually thwarted not so much by Kate's legalistic argument (marriage means that husband and wife are one flesh, and Nick has no right to hers) but by the Devil's realisation that the lascivious husband and the puritan wife will continue to give each other at least as much hell as he could possibly muster down below. Once again, serious (if standard) perceptions about the strength of the marriage bond and the tendency of men to stray are all but overlaid by the joking, and by the unremitting pace. On radio, it must have been a slight but entertaining half-hour comedy, its message of the tolerance and mutual respect required by marriage almost drowned by its frantic comic vigour.

For the theatre, this enclosed little jest was expanded by the addition of two preceding acts set in Kirk Alloway churchyard, and by some minor additions to the existing play. The most drastic innovation was the inclusion of songs, which made the proceedings the closest of all Scott's plays to the ideal of Scottish drama based on music hall. In the two new acts, local effect (song, situation, jest) takes precedence over narrative: Scott was assuming the audience's knowledge of Burns' story just as a writer of pantomime relies on the audience knowing the essence of Jack and the Beanstalk. If anything, also, the Scots in the theatre version is both more copious and more vigorous. Both versions of the play, furthermore, have something of the quality of the student revue, impudently playing with the revered classic text in the spirit of 'What *really* happened to Tam that night?'

Despite Scott's hopes, however, the run began badly on 17 January 1955: several mishaps in the comic action and staging meant that the performance looked under-rehearsed. (In addition to much singing, there was a certain amount of dancing, fairly elaborate visual effects and also 'flying effects by Eugene's Flying Ballet'.) At the close of the first performance, a dejected Scott addressed the audience, absolving the stage performers for the mishaps. In private, he blamed the director for not devoting enough time and effort to the preparations. Cath Scott remembers leaving him, next morning, still in bed, surrounded by negative newspaper reviews and hiding his head under the blankets. The memory remained bitter, although reviews during the ensuing performances suggest that the production settled down within a week or so.

There were few complaints about the production, which was generally liked: most of the hesitations had to do with the quality of the script, which seemed to many to be thin, flat and stretching the original idea too far. (Further disappointment lay ahead. He was contracted by the BBC to write a television version of *Tam o' Shanter's Tryst* and by December 1959 was hard at work on it. The BBC took cold feet, however, and after an escalating dispute about the legal position, which lasted throughout 1960, decided not to go ahead. Scott's revision included the writing of twelve new songs, and although the Corporation offered to recompense him for this he stuck out as long as he could for an actual production. Eventually, he had to give in.)[17]

The year following the staging of *Tam o' Shanter's Tryst*, however, brought Scott's most intellectually ambitious comedy, *Truth To Tell*.[18] This was first broadcast on the radio, on 22 October 1956, before being staged at the Citizens' in a run beginning on 14 April 1958. (It had originally been intended to stage it the previous autumn.) In a note 'On the interpretation of the play' prefixed to the typescript, Scott spells out his meaning: 'The theme of the play is the impact of beauty and intelligence upon society, the way in which society seeks to control—and even suppress—such unusual manifestations—and its ultimate failure to do so.'

Truth To Tell opens with the death of Socrates—except that the unworldly truth-speaker is sprung from his Athenian prison thanks to Plato's resourceful substitutions of opium for hemlock and of a slave corpse for the drugged philosopher. Taken to Carthage, Socrates immediately lands himself in more trouble through his persistent asking of naïve but uncomfortable questions. In the Carthaginian jail he encounters the slave-girl Aretê: 'A luscious little twenty-year old whose luxuriant bosom, curvaceous hips and lissom thighs are revealed rather than concealed by the scantiness of her apparel, a flimsy silk brassiere and a pair of gauze trousers.' (Press response to the Citizens' production suggests that Annette Crosbie was much appreciated in this part.) Thereafter, Beauty and Intelligence, united in their fates, are shipwrecked on the 'queendom' of Caledonia in which women have the upper hand and men are physically and mentally enslaved by the prevailing belief-system. The two new arrivals (predictably) bring about a revolution but thereafter are still regarded as too dangerous to be allowed their freedom. Imprisoned yet again, this time in a sacred cave, they defy expectations by not withering and dying: rather, they produce a healthy brood of offspring to plague the world even more.

Unlike the two earlier plays, this one would appear to have as its starting-point its theme rather than a character or a situation. Nevertheless, it begins with a typical Scott undergraduate whimsy: what if Socrates' famous death didn't happen, and he landed up in Scotland instead? Typical, too, is the surface liveliness and broad comedy. Scott was aware, though, that it could easily be presented as a romp and insists, in his note, that: 'the play is a comedy, not a farce, and should be played "straight".' Nevertheless, press comment showed no signs of responding to its ideas; rather, it divided into those critics who didn't think it funny, and those who quite enjoyed its comedy. It is in conversational English. There is no obvious reason why Scott should have chosen to write about the incompatibility between Society on the one hand, and Beauty and Intelligence on the other. The play derives, simply, from the modern artist's sense of alienation from the world around him.

It is a revealing play, in a way, for it underscores Scott's instinct to satirise the world he lives in—that is, to tell the truth about it as he sees it. Personal as the play may be, however, real seriousness of theme (and emotion) is swamped by crudely fantastic invention and by striving for laughs. The gap between the play's theme as expressed in the note, and the allegorical simplicity of the action, is too large. The play is the projection of a belief rather than a dramatic articulation of human behaviour. Nevertheless, Scott put much of himself, and of his energy, into it and its mixed, lukewarm reception was deeply disappointing. Not that it was a complete flop: in the letter to George Bruce of 23 April 1958, he was able to write: 'At the Citizens', *Truth to Tell* seems to be amusing the customers.'

Right Royal, Scott's most popular play, received an award from the Scottish Committee of the Arts Council. The same body, in 1951, awarded him first prize for Scots verse-drama for *The Last Time I Saw Paris*. (It also awarded him first prize for Scots lyrics in the same year.) A few years later, in 1954, *Shetland Yarn* won the Scottish Community Drama Association's One-Act Playwriting Competition. They also gave him an award for *Right Royal*. Despite his success with *Right Royal* and his strong links with the Glasgow Citizens' in the 1950s, however, it was in the one-act form that Scott produced his most convincing dramas. As a playwright, his strengths lay in witty dialogue and in the projection of individualised dramatic ideas or situations. What he did not seem to be willing, or able, to do was to invent extended emotional narratives, or to explore complex or unfolding emotional or moral sequences. He achieved length by the invention of striking outward event. Unity of effect, therefore, was best achieved in short, single actions. Furthermore, his principal outlet for his plays, the Scottish Home Service, was particularly welcoming to the shorter form. Of his short plays, only *Prometheus 48*, *The Last Time I Saw Paris* and *Shetland Yarn* seem not to have been broadcast: most were written for radio in the first place. Of the three full-length plays, only *Truth to Tell* was not an expansion of an earlier, short, radio drama. The one-acter was his natural dramatic form.

His first play to be staged (classroom pirates apart) was his short two-hander, *Prometheus 48*, written for the Aberdeen student show of 1948, Vincent Park's *Hooray for What.*[19] It is the effort of a clever and modern young man, and is a verse play, in English, in which Prometheus and Zeus are transformed into a scientist, who refuses to put his knowledge and gifts at the service of a totalitarian power, and a jailer who is the voice of a threatening communism. The Soviet Union would not explode its first atomic bomb until August 1949, but the impending sense of the world's danger when it achieved that goal was clearly strong in the preceding months. Scott's Prometheus is executed when he fails to divulge the secrets of his past work on uranium 235. Finally alone on stage, however, Prometheus' corpse stirs and he delivers his final soliloquy:

> I am the mind of man, and I am immortal,
> Though in my life I have died a million deaths ...

It must have been a strange element in the second half of a student musical revue, but Park and his colleagues felt it was something special, and arranged for its immediate publication by the Students' Representative Council. It is a serious effort, a product of its time, and written with a consciousness not just of Greek legend but also perhaps of both Shelley and of Lewis Grassic Gibbon's *Grey Granite*.

The theme of imminent world destruction appears to have been much on his mind, because it was given further dramatic treatment in *The Volcano* (broadcast 23 April 1948—the same week as the student show), in which a scientist tries to warn that the city of 'Inverdune' is about to be destroyed in a volcanic eruption.[20] Scott called this a 'parable play', and the blindness and cynicism which is the near-universal response to warnings of impending Armageddon undoubtedly refer to the world's difficult adjustment to the new threat of the post-war years.

Science fiction was something that had always appealed to him and to which he would return. However, at the end of the 1940s, his Scottish Renaissance impulse took over and he began to write performance works to further that cause. *Sodger Frae the War Returns* was his first attempt, but more of a breakthrough was achieved with *Gift to the Queen*.[21] Scott himself denied any doctrinaire intention, but the play gave scope to the nationalistic writer he had recently become, as 'What kind of play now' makes clear:

> I'm not aware of there having been any doctrinaire purpose in the scripting of *Gift to the Queen* in Scots. The play concerned the misadventures of my poetical namesake, the sixteenth-century makar Alexander Scott, and Scots was his natural medium.
>
> It appeared to be mine, too. At least, in writing this play in Scots I experienced an astonishing sense of release, the expression of elements of my personality which I had never been able to find phrases for in English; and I went on to write other pieces in Scots on traditional native themes.

The impecunious Alexander Scott (the play's hero, that is, as distinct from the hard-up young lecturer) decides to curry favour with the recently arrived Mary Queen of Scots by writing her a poem as a gift. Pushing himself forward thus to attract the attention of the great and powerful, he instantly becomes entangled in power and personality struggles of which he had known nothing, and finds himself a pawn in the larger tensions of history. He comes out on top, however, thanks to his chameleon-like creative ability and moral suppleness.

It is the first of several dramatic treatments of the nature of the poet and of the poet's relationships with others, and is one of Scott's most pleasing plays, its securely judged pace and structure deftly combining a lightly sketched but plausible rendering of sixteenth-century Scotland with a cross-hatching of knowing anachronism and self-reference. The closing announcer is asked by Scott to 'remind listeners that any resemblance between himself and his famous namesake is purely coincidental', but his treatment of his central poet-character both as a disconcerting truth-teller and as an unappreciated (and usually unrewarded) trifler normally ignored by the powerful and ambitious reflects his own amused awareness of the paradoxical status of all poets (and literary academics?). And the perception of Scotland as a harsh literary environment—the burden of so many modern Scottish texts—is only the deepest of the gentle anachronisms which lift the play above a merely period status. The criticisms of Edinburgh's commercial outlook, and of the insecure parochialism of its citizens' preference for the foreign over the native, was clearly intended to strike a chord in the opening years of the Edinburgh International Festival: 'They think it shows they arena provincial, if they mak a sang about [Mary's] foreign fashions: shows they're—weel—ye micht say, *international* in their outlook ...'

The Last Time I Saw Paris is one of the most memorable of Scott's plethora of jesting and punning titles.[22] It was the name of a hit song of the 1940s (recorded in 1941): the famous film with Elizabeth Taylor and Van Heflin did not appear until 1954, three years after Scott's play won its award. At first glance, it seems a play wholly lacking in seriousness. Rather, it is one of those works in which Scott takes pleasure in imagining the 'real' shenanigans behind some mythic tale. The prototype is the poem 'Sir Patrick Spens: The True Tale' of 1946. There, he had admitted that 'the ballants sing anither story,/But ilka sang's a swick'. He now applies the same principle to the original ballad singer, Homer, in this tale of how the Trojan War 'really' got started—not through outrage at the loss of the fairest woman in the world, but through commercial rivalry and petty blundering and subterfuge. None of the famed heroes—nor yet the heroine—is heroic: ten years of strife are engendered by a bedroom farce and human smallness.

Although the play can be taken (and no doubt was) as merely a loquacious and witty romp, there is seriousness here, perhaps even bitterness. It is striking how many of the earliest plays deal with war and rumours of war. As we have seen, two are conscious of the nuclear threat and the ideological conflicts at the root of that danger. *The Last Time I Saw Paris* and *Uneasy Lies/Right Royal* focus on armed conflict between peoples. The dramatised ballad for radio, *Sodger Frae the War Returns*, speaks for itself. *The Jerusalem Farers* deals with the Viking crusade to the Holy Land and acknowledges the cruelty and waste of war. All are distanced, in obvious ways, from the war Scott had fought, though they all seem to acknowledge its shadow. The degree of distance—comic, historical or both—which Scott always introduces tells its own story, however.

But if, during the war, the Scottish Renaissance had provided Scott with an alternative reality, it also began to dominate his plays of the 1950s. *Gift to the Queen* and *Cutty Sark* show him getting down directly to the business of building a Scottish Renaissance drama, and *Untrue Thomas* even dispenses with jests as it joins that endeavour.[23] Its seriousness lies not just in its lack of comedy but also in the degree of self-identification to be felt within it. Not only did Scott write here about the conflict between the poet's roles as committed artist and as family man, but he also dedicated it to his wife 'who did not despair of the rhymer'. As will be discussed in a later chapter, this conflict was all too real in the Scott household. The play hints, too, at marital infidelity, a possibility also to be discussed later, though one might as well say here and now that the present writer has no scandalous secrets to disclose. It is perfectly possible that the only real-life infidelity which ruptured family harmony and which is embodied here by the rapacious Queen of Elfland was Scott's constant pursuit of his muse—a real enough figure to his wife and sons. As regards the play's effectiveness, one acknowledges its tautness, its eerie evocation of Thomas' unlooked-for return after seven years and (as always) the confidence of the Scots writing. Going deeper, it is possible to see the heart of the play, Thomas's modish twentieth-century explanation of his seven-year absence in terms of a breakdown caused by the horror of involvement in the awfulness of human existence, as hinting at Scott's own deepest response to the war-torn world he had been living in. In the play, his escape from this into a world of art:

I scapit awa frae my hate o my ain hert's secrets
And walked anither warld nor wyceness kens,
Whar aa was shape and rhythm, hue and sang,
The hills gaed up in music, seas were drums ...

An evocation, perhaps, of the escapist plunge into poetic commitment which the war seemed to have instigated and which he had been pursuing with intensity since the guns fell silent in 1945—for the previous seven years, in fact. But if the play allowed him to look at himself with penetrating honesty, it also explored the difficulties of living with someone like himself and faces up to the possibility that there *is* no living with the likes of him. There is a real dilemma being explored here but the danger is that the play may seem to be no more than a pious attempt to make minor drama by extrapolating from—and so venerating—another classic corner of Scotland's literary past.

There are more marital complications in *The Deil's Awa* but this is pure comedy, made up of traditional folk-tale motifs: a search for seriousness within it would kill this half-hour of Scottish Home Service laughter, though no doubt Scott took the traditions seriously enough.[24] Set in the early eighteenth century, an Edinburgh-born farmer's wife, with social pretensions reaching above her origins, is tempted to dally (in her husband's Tam o'Shanter-like absence) with the local dominie, attracted by his person and his cultivation. Her style is cramped, however, by the presence in the adjacent barn of an itinerant student, grudgingly accommodated, and also by the unexpected return of her husband which necessitates the hiding of the dominie in a meal kist. From there to the predictable rumbustious climax is an easy step. The play offered an innocent 1950s Scotland half an hour of easy listening, the potential seriousness of the theme of marital disharmony even further banished than in Burns' great narrative poem.

And one might be tempted to say the same of *Shetland Yarn*, except that it contains the disquieting presence of real warfare not so very far off stage.[25] Set in Yell, in Shetland, in 1588, the destruction of the Armada is central to this 'yarn'. The men of the village having been summoned to Kirkwall to deal with an element of the Spanish fleet, the women are deciding that their fortnight's absence must mean that disaster has overcome them and their mating instinct is immediately focused on Pedro, a Spanish sailor shipwrecked on their doorstep. Yet another light farce ensues, except that Pedro's standing as an enemy combatant is never forgotten, especially when the men return to tell of a battle in Kirkwall, which has been undeniably bloody. One is tempted to see this play as crystallising so much of Scott's approach to writing in these post-war years: behind a surface treating, both comically and satirically, the follies and failings of men and women lurks a consciousness of war, disturbing in its menace.

Fears and war consciousness were much nearer the surface in *The Monsters*, which appeared after a hiatus in his drama output which matches quite closely the similar gap in his poetry.[26] And just as the resumption of his poetic flow was started by a return to one of his earliest poetic themes, his home city of Aberdeen, so *The Monsters* strongly echoed his earliest adult attempts at drama, with its bitter mistrust of politicians and their power over science and scientists (as in *Prometheus 48* and *The Volcano*) especially in the context of nuclear annihilation. It is a modest but accomplished radio drama, sharing with *Journey into Space*, that fondly remembered radio serial of the 1950s, a technological innocence which would not survive the era of manned space flight, which was just beginning. (Gagarin and Shepherd first flew in space in 1961.) It shares with *Journey into Space*, also, the idea that the planets may harbour beings of vast, unknown and threatening powers, especially psychological ones. Even more influential, perhaps, was Nigel Kneale's television serial *The Quatermass Experiment* (1953).

The story unfolds, however, not in deep space but in the mission control room and the government offices of a Britain which has sent a two-man expedition to Venus with which contact had been lost on a sixth and last orbit of the planet and which is overdue by six months from the time that air and supplies would have run out. Now, suddenly, it is returning, and the politicians and military men assume that Venusians have captured the ship and are using it to trick their way to Earth in the manner of the Trojan Horse. Military logic over-rides all wider considerations, but all attempts to blast the threat out of the skies mysteriously fail. When the ship lands, the two beings who step out are ambushed and killed: the radio audience is coerced into sharing the horror-filled expectations of the earthly characters that monsters will emerge. Which is indeed how those on the spot finally see them. But it turns out that the mysterious (and now dead) beings are the original spacemen whose circuit of Venus had resulted in the utter transformation of religious ecstasy: they had been transfigured and lifted to a saintly plane. As the play ends, their bodies begin to stir in the morgue.

The closing announcement is: 'You have been listening to *The Monsters*, a myth for radio by Alexander Scott' and the play's effectiveness does indeed lie in its ability to entertain at the level of science-fiction-horror while at the same time dramatising the mind-set which had resulted in mutually assured destruction and also in its suggestion, in the last frantic few minutes of the action, of something of the nature and mystery of religious experience. The over-arching burden of the play is the limitations, and self-destructiveness, of political action based purely upon fear and total mistrust, but this very secular message is enlarged by its sense of the unknown.

But if the play gestures towards the numinous, it also benefits from a particularly firm grounding in a reality: the pivotal phase of the action is the unfolding failure of missiles to stop the ship's approach, and Scott's handling of this military phase of the story is marked by an inwardness with the language and the thinking of officers in the field. And not only does the play, in its brief compass, prove surprisingly multi-layered but it also unfolds as an expertly controlled narrative. He was able to tell George Bruce that it had gone down well, and it seems to have stimulated him to a re-engagement with the genre which prompted his suggesting a radio talk on J. T. Macintosh, the Aberdonian writer of science fiction, a suggestion that developed into one 'putting forward the idea that our myths should be found in the pages of science fiction.'[27]

The letter to Alan Bold of 19 February 1979 makes it clear that even in the later part of his life Scott regarded his plays as an essential part of his total achievement. Donald Campbell, who did not get to know him until the 1970s but who found his support and friendship of decisive importance in his own career, found him still very concerned with drama. Campbell's own theatrical background and successful career as a dramatist meant that he and Scott had the stage as an important mutual interest. Campbell shares with the present writer, however, the view that Scott was at his best in the short, one-act form, though I am inclined to see this as arising not solely from a failure to generate ideas demanding full-length treatment but also as a reflection of Scott's special instinct for the medium of radio.[28] Something about that purely aural medium stimulated him with a sureness which the physicality of the theatre did not.

It may be that Campbell puts his finger upon it when he says that Scott saw a play primarily as a piece of literature and only secondarily as something to be put on in a theatre. Campbell knows that Scott thought of himself as a man of the theatre but does not really believe that he was: his theatrical background (as we have seen) was purely in the amateur arena and he was never a true 'rogue and vagabond' of the theatrical profession. He never ceased to be the man of letters or to think of a play as, at base, a book. Campbell claims that Scott did not fully understand some fundamental truths of the professional theatre: for example, theatrical 'success' is not merely a case of having a play mounted by, say, the Glasgow Citizens' (as Scott was inclined to think) but comes after that with some wholly unlooked-for audience response, or with the transfer of a production to London. Nor, says Campbell, is acting a matter of impersonation or pretence (again, as Scott seemed to believe) but is really a matter of 'truth' and 'conviction'. Drama seldom involves histrionics or heightened delivery: it can often come from underplaying in a manner with which Scott had little sympathy. And yet, surprisingly, in his plays he shied away from the big dramatic moment. Perhaps most seriously of all, thinks Campbell, Scott seems not to have understood that the fundamental job of the playwright is to give opportunities to actors. It could be argued that Scott did that, to the fullest extent, only once, in his creation of King Dod in *Right Royal*, which Macrae declared to be 'a smasher of a part'.[29]

If radio drama may be seen as more nearly akin to storytelling—to public narration—than to the flesh-and-blood encounter between actor and audience, then we may understand a little better Scott's limited and somewhat specialised success as a dramatist. A radio play is arguably nearer to a book or short story than a full-blooded theatre experience would normally be. Scott seems to have perceived poems, novels and plays of all kinds as belonging to one world; they really belong to two, as undergraduates in a library struggling to imagine the theatrical life of a play-text know only too well. Furthermore, Scott's own theatrical experience was not merely amateur, as Campbell points out, but derived mainly from the revue and the student sketch. It is from that medium, with its emphasis on brevity, singleness of dramatic idea and the grabbing of immediate laughs, that Scott's concept of drama emerged—a tendency that found theoretical justification in his belief that music hall is the only surviving form of Scottish theatrical life. In the world of *Look Back In Anger*, it was a concept of theatre that was unlikely to survive very long.

Yet Scott was correct in regarding his plays as an integral part of his output: they deserve better than the oblivion in which they languish and more extensive study than they have received here. It is not simply a matter of doing justice to an obscure but worthy body of work, or even of perhaps providing amateur theatrical groups with some additions to their repertoire. Scott's plays highlight both a dimension of the history of broadcasting in Scotland, and also a major turning point in the story of the nation's theatrical life as a whole.

Chapter 7

Broadcasting to the Nation

In the absence of recording equipment—or of systematic policies for recording or archiving programmes—broadcasting is an ephemeral medium. The survival of programmes, once broadcast, can be a very hit-or-miss affair, as periodic pleas by the BBC for the use of old private tapes regularly illustrates. So it is no surprise to find that Alexander Scott's career as a broadcaster (like his career as a dramatist) is now largely forgotten. Nor would it appear to be possible to reconstruct that career in detail. It is clear, however, from evidence surviving in BBC archives, from Scott's poetry notebooks and from the recollections of his contemporaries, that Scott was a frequent and regular broadcaster and that, moreover, he used the broadcasting media in Scotland as an important outlet for his creative work. Some of his closest friends and professional contacts were in BBC Scotland—above all, George Bruce. And several interviewees have commented how, at parties hosted by the Scotts from the 1950s onwards, creative personalities (especially actors and producers) from the world of Scottish broadcasting were much in evidence.

In his broadcasting heyday (roughly, the 1950s and '60s) Scott's unmistakable voice was a feature of Scottish radio. Indeed, as mentioned elsewhere, Scott was thought of, by the young Tom Leonard and his friends, not so much as an immediately relevant poet but rather as a regular contributor to 'a stuffy old programme with old men in it'. Trevor Royle valued Scott as 'a natural broadcaster'.[1] On at least one notable occasion, broadcasting played a decisive part in his creative career, when the BBC television commission for 'Heart of Stone' brought years of poetic infertility to an end.

Radio in particular was the focus of much of Scott's activity for several decades. It was a medium he seems to have loved, and in which he was very pro-active not only as a poet but also as a reviewer, dramatist and indeed as an academic. He is perceived by some university colleagues, in fact, as having had much of the journalist in him. Perhaps radio programmes, with their comparatively short deadlines and their audiences stretching far beyond university specialists, offered him a more congenial medium for his criticism than did the more traditional, and perhaps more constraining, types of printed academic output. It is by no means certain, however, that he himself paid much attention to fine distinctions of academic publication: to him, what was said was usually more important than where it was said. This was not an attitude, however, which helped him when questions arose of promotion to senior rank.

While Scott understandably regretted the frustrating wartime delay in getting on with his life, he was fortunate that the end of his undergraduate days coincided with the great national burst of energy which post-war reconstruction drew from British society. One of the many areas that enjoyed an immense boost from the drive to create a brave new world was broadcasting: the post-war BBC benefited from fresh planning and commitment. As Asa Briggs and W. H. McDowell have shown, it was one of the British institutions the future shape of which was reviewed and planned for even before the war ceased.[2] The result was a period of reorganisation and development which enabled innovation and the exercise of talent on a scale greatly in excess of anything possible in the pre-war period.

A crucial development was the creation of a new pattern of radio broadcasting, with regional services now complementing the fresh structure of London-based programmes. So, in addition to the Home Service, the Light Programme and the Third Programme, networks such as the Scottish Home Service were established across Britain to cater for the perceived demand for a measure of local autonomy and the ability to reflect regional life. The post-war Scottish operation was a particularly vigorous one, and the circumstances that prevailed in the decade after the war resulted in a Scottish broadcasting environment that encouraged innovation and high standards. It has become a cliché to call the period a 'golden age of Scottish broadcasting'. As McDowell says:

> With fewer lines of authority in Scotland compared to London, radio producers in Scotland experienced a greater sense of freedom and authority. Their authority derived to a significant extent from their specialist knowledge in specific subjects. For example, George Bruce stated that he was appointed as programme assistant in December 1946 because of his knowledge of Scottish literature.[3]

The health of Scottish radio broadcasting, however, was not due solely to the internal arrangements of the Scottish Home Service. The developed BBC, at national level, created an environment in which quality was valued. Thus, Scottish programme producers had a higher proportion of their output taken for broadcasting on the Third Programme than did their counterparts in any of the other UK regions. The Scottish Home Service was on the lookout for new and talented contributors in the fields of talks, reviewing and drama. It also sought to reflect all that was new and best in the post-war Arts scene. No wonder that Alexander Scott found it an environment in which he was instantly at home.

It would seem that the first time that any material of Scott's was broadcast was 15 October 1945, when his poem 'Homage to Grey Granite' was read on the Scottish Home Service.[4] He was still in uniform, but back in Aberdeen and desperate to resume his undergraduate course and his life as a writer. He would also have been glad of the fee of two guineas. This first broadcast of one of his poems was swiftly followed by at least four others in 1946, and by an extract of thirty-three lines from his version of the Anglo-Saxon poem 'The Seafarer' on 18 March 1947, followed on 29 October by a reading of the whole poem. It was clearly to these readings that George Bruce was alluding in a letter to Scott written at the time of Bruce's retiral from the BBC, an occasion marked by a dinner in his honour organised by Scott and Maurice Lindsay, and also by an article on Bruce which Scott had contributed to the *Radio Times*. In his letter of thanks, Bruce wrote:

> We were a long time together in the endeavour of broadcasting. I never forgot the occasion of reading your poem made out of The Seafarer. All that Charles Murray could never do for me you did at a stroke in that single effort.[5]

According to BBC archive material, the two readings from 'Seaman's Sang', in March and October 1947, were the fifth and sixth occasions on which poems by Scott were read on the radio: as he completed his undergraduate degree, Scott was already becoming used to broadcasting. Analysis of his meticulously kept record of his poems and their publication history suggests that the late 1940s was one of the periods when his poems were most frequently broadcast, several being read (often, it would seem, by himself) each year between 1946 and 1950. After 1950, however, his poetry was read on air much less frequently—only occasionally, it would seem, in the early 1950s and not at all in the later 1950s and early '60s. This later period, of course, coincides with his worst period of inability to write verse. Radio readings were more frequent, once more, in the early 1970s, on both Radios 3 and 4, by which time television was the dominant medium. Eight of his poems are recorded as having been read on BBC television in 1974, and twenty-one in 1977, which suggests that, whereas in the early years he was contributing individual poems to regular Arts magazine programmes, in the 1970s he was the subject, rather, of occasional substantial items or perhaps even complete programmes. This latter format was used most extensively of all in a programme he recorded for his friend Michael Grieve, then working for Scottish Television in Glasgow. With Grieve's help and support, the ailing Scott recorded a programme, broadcast on 14 June 1988, in which he read twenty-six of his own poems—a number of them, admittedly, being from the 'Scotched' collection of tiny epigrams.

The reading of his own work, however, was only the tiniest part of Scott's broadcasting. There is an early BBC memo from George Bruce, dated 26 February 1947, requesting payment for Scott 'who is to take part in the above contribution from Aberdeen'.[6] This refers to his performance in a short 'crime sketch' for a programme entitled *Monday Night at Eight*. He must have performed satisfactorily, for in 1948 he participated in a memorable radio production of

Lewis Grassic Gibbon's *Sunset Song*, playing John Guthrie. In a later letter, he said that playing this role was 'one of the great experiences of my artistic life.'[7] Less solemnly, he would joke with his family that this role, that of a domineering father-figure, was a bit of typecasting.

There do not seem to have been many other occasions when he acted on radio, but his abilities seem to have been known in BBC circles for a long time. In June 1966, for example, arrangements were being made for Scott to prepare the script for an item on Grassic Gibbon for *Woman's Hour*, with Effie Morrison reading Chris Guthrie's words. The producer, Matthew Spicer, was having difficulty finding an appropriate actor to read Robert Colquohoun's sermon, which brings *Sunset Song* to an end, until Morrison, according to Spicer, suggested Scott himself 'because you are "a very fine actor".'[8] Scott relished reading 'the minister's marvellous concluding speech'. Nevertheless, he was clearly regarded as appropriate for only a certain kind of regional role, his hard voice and vigorously masculine delivery ruling him out for other parts. Even George Bruce, while recognising Scott as the best person (better, even, than Edwin Muir) to answer a talk previously given by Iain Hamilton in which Hamilton had attacked contemporary Lallans verse, had to admit 'that Scott's principal limitation is his rather hard, unpleasant voice.'[9] Earlier, Bruce, discussing with Maurice Lindsay an item on William Thom planned for one of the early programmes in the series *Scottish Life and Letters*, wrote:

> I agree with you entirely about Alec Scott's harshness. I just don't think he is the person to read Thom. Indeed I strongly recommend either John Mearns or A. M. Shinnie, both of whom have pleasant Aberdeenshire voices and both have an ear for that simple pleasing kind of poetry.[10]

On 23 April 1948, there was broadcast *The Volcano*, the first of his plays for radio. He wrote it speculatively, without having a prior BBC commission. As the Corporation's Ena Quade wrote in a memo: 'Mr Scott is not a professional writer', a view that would doubtless have irked him, even though the play was written during his first year of university lecturing, in Edinburgh.[11] Thereafter, a number of plays for radio were written and broadcast over the next fourteen years, the period when he was striving to establish himself as a dramatist. They are discussed along with the rest of his drama, though it is worth pointing out here that *Right Royal*, which had had such a success in the theatre, seems to have been found equally effective as a play for broadcasting, for it was given productions both on radio (27 August 1955) and later on television (20 October 1958).

The year 1948 also saw the beginning of Scott's long career as essayist, commentator and reviewer on Scottish radio. On 29 September he read a seven-minute review of volumes of poems by Sir Alexander Gray and George Campbell Hay, the first of innumerable broadcasts of the same kind. (To Hay would be dedicated Scott's second collection of verse, the *Selected Poems* of 1950.) It was as a reviewer and author of talks on literary and cultural matters that he made his most substantial contribution to radio, broadcasting three or four times a year from 1947 onwards, until well into the 1960s at least. Although his principal reasons for devoting so much energy to broadcasting were his desire to have his own poems aired and to spread the word about the revitalised vision of Scottish literature (of all periods) which the Renaissance had brought about, he was also in it for the money, especially in those early years of modest university pay and a growing family. Thus, in November 1948, he was quibbling with the BBC over the payment offered for a reading of 'Haar in Princes Street': Maurice Lindsay had alerted him to the fact that it would be going out not just on the Scottish Home Service but also on the Overseas Service, so that the suggested four guineas should arguably have been twelve.[12]

Despite the pressures of those first years of teaching in Edinburgh and Glasgow, Scott contributed talks, and ideas for talks, from the beginning. A couple of months after the review of Gray and Hay he wrote to producer Robin Richardson asking to be able to review Hamish Henderson's *Elegies for the Dead in Cyrenaica*: 'When I saw this book in manuscript, I considered it to be one of the few truly significant examples of "war poetry" that the last war has produced.'[13] In June 1949 a twenty-minute script of his on George Douglas Brown was used for a schools broadcast. That same month he volunteered to review W. S. Graham's new book of verse. A few months later, he was writing to Robin Richardson volunteering to review Lindsay's *At the Wood's Edge* and was also writing to another talks producer, Alistair Dunnett, suggesting a talk on the recently deceased Edgar Rice Burroughs:

> linking up Burroughs' Tarzan stories with the medieval beast fable as written by Chaucer and Robert Henryson (among others), and drawing a parallel between his stories about Mars with the tales of wonder so popular among the folk of the Middle Ages.

Scott thought this would be 'both popular and of some value from the point of view of literary criticism'—a formula which inspired much of his broadcast talks.[14] Scott completed a script on Burroughs by mid-April 1950, but in the end Dunnett could not fit it into the planned slot. (An essay on precisely this topic eventually appeared in the winter 1955 issue of the *Saltire Review*.)

Broadcasts were live, of course, and when a programme was scheduled to go out from Edinburgh (as often happened) Scott had to make an overnight stay: 'Could you, from your end, fix me up with a hotel near Broadcasting House—licensed if possible—for the night of the broadcast?' This letter begins with yet another argument about a fee.[15] Whatever the arguments, however, Scott was clearly taking every opportunity to air not only his creative work but also his response to the unfolding Scottish literary scene and his interpretation of Scotland's literary past. Programmes such as *Arts Review* and *Scottish Life and Letters* allowed him to do all three. Indeed, he became a general-purpose reviewer of Scottish cultural events, as for example on 3 February 1952, when he not only led a discussion on Maurice Lindsay's collection *Ode for St Andrews Night* (which he did not like) but also participated in discussing a Glasgow concert by the Scottish National Orchestra and an exhibition of paintings by Walter Sickert in Edinburgh. He was prepared to review performances of opera, such as Verdi's *Luisa Miller* in April 1960. As late as 1969 he was reviewing the Czech director Juraj Jakubisko's debut movie, *The Crucial Years*. Regular major arts events, such as the Edinburgh Festival and the Pitlochry Festival Theatre's annual programme, involved him in much broadcasting, and in frequent travelling around Scotland. The BBC clearly enabled him to keep alive that broad engagement with the diversity of Scotland's cultural range that he had first shown during his journalistic work on *North-East Review*.

Equally clear, however, as one surveys the material in the archives of the BBC and in the Maurice Lindsay Collection in Edinburgh University, is Scott's love of the medium itself. At times, he seems simply to have wanted to be on the radio:

> I've read Speirs' book on Chaucer, and I'll certainly review it if you want me to—though personally I'd much rather talk about a contemporary Scottish writer like Andrew Young than a 14th-century English one. But you're the boss. Let me know which one you want, and give me a date for the script.[16]

And he was not only compliant and willing, but very pro-active. He was constantly putting forward ideas for programmes, and programme series. This forwardness began early, as can be seen from the correspondence between Bruce and Lindsay in 1948, while they were developing the idea for what became *Scottish Life and Letters*. As Bruce wrote to Lindsay: 'Alex Scott has already proposed to me a different series—ten minutes of poetry twice a week in which one or two poems would be presented with comment.'[17] At this period Scott was just completing his first term teaching at Glasgow.

Scott was equally keen to develop his ideas about other Scottish writers. So, for example, the second half of 1950 saw him contributing a talk (in September) on 'Fergusson's contribution to Scottish literature' and, in November introducing 'an anthology of Stevenson's verse' in which he presented Stevenson as 'the first of the moderns' thanks to his 'eclectic approach to using Scots.'[18] A decade later, while preparing a talk on S. R. Crockett, Scott wrote to Bruce:

> I think I'll take the line that Crockett's real, individual talent was for broad, farcical humour, but this was overlaid by his concern to cater for the popular taste for romantic adventure on the one hand and tender love-tales on the other.[19]

A year later still (5 November 1961), he offered a talk on Muriel Spark as a product of Edinburgh, a point which he believed had not been made up to that time: he thought it would 'break new ground'. In 1965, he offered a piece on James Macgregor, an Aberdeen-born writer of science fiction who wrote under the name 'J. T. Macintosh' and who had graduated in 1947 with Scott, Thomson and Keir. A fortnight later he proposed expanding the Macgregor talk to include comments on Mitchison's *Memoirs of a Spacewoman* with a yet further expansion to cover the whole topic of Scottish science fiction.[20] Scott's instinct to communicate in a mode which was simultaneously popular and academic is clear in all these ideas—and, indeed, the two were linked, more often than not, by a third impulse: to confirm, elucidate and celebrate the great literary revival of which he felt himself to be part. Nowhere was this clearer than in the long letter he wrote to Bruce, urging that he be given the opportunity to make the case for Eric Linklater: 'the most consistently, and most undeservedly, underrated of all the writers who at one time or another have been associated with what I prefer to call the "Scottish Resistance" rather than the "Renaissance" movement.'[21] Later in the letter, his ideas expanded as he considered:

> the fascinating fact that poets and novelists and dramatists who appeared to stand on the same ground during the period circa 1925–35 in Scotland have taken off from there in radically different directions. I hope I am right in thinking there are the makings of a significant series here. Perhaps 'the Scottish Resistance Movement—Struggles and Surrenders' might be considered as a convenient blanket title.

'A significant series'—not a 'significant book' or 'significant article'. Three weeks later (28 March), this idea had developed into a projected radio series on neglected novelists: Mitchison, Linklater, Gunn and Jenkins.

As one would expect, the poets who lay particularly close to his heart in the 1950s, Soutar and MacDiarmid, were also the subjects of radio projects. So, on 11 October 1953, he broadcast a forty-five-minute feature on Soutar, 'The mortal maker', which was followed on 29 April 1954 by an adaptation, for the Third Programme, of *A Drunk Man Looks at the Thistle*, which he was able to feel had been particularly successful. In it, he reduced MacDiarmid's poem (2,685 lines) to 1,266 lines and arranged it so that it could be read by four readers—Scott was always mindful of the practicalities of broadcasting.[22]

Scott did not see radio solely as a substitute for the lecture theatre or the academic article—or for the poetry journal. Its immediacy and flexibility also made it an effective medium for debate and controversy, tending to mute the asperity which could occasionally surface in his comments in other media. So, on 14 October 1949, his pre-recorded reply to a previous talk by Sir Alexander Gray in which Gray had made the case for Kailyard poetry, was broadcast in *Scottish Life and Letters*. It took the form of a 'letter' to Gray, couched with all the respect a twenty-eight-year-old tyro academic owed to a senior writer and scholar. It is a well-judged rebuttal, and it acknowledged the appeal of Kailyard writing but denied it the final accolade—greatness. And in so doing, it revealed what the young Scott regarded as constituting greatness in poetry:

> But greatness? Hardly a hint of it. No urgent, compelling rhythms; no striking, original imagery—often, indeed, no images at all, not even the traditional ones, just rhymed statement after rhymed statement; and, greatest defect of all, no passion. Enough and to spare of pathos and regret, and a good measure of irony and off-taking wit, but no cries of exultation and agony, no outbursts of delight and despair.[23]

A few days later, Bruce wrote to Lindsay:

> I think Alexander Scott's postscript was excellent. Sir Alexander Gray has written me to say he agrees with nearly everything Alexander Scott said. A most happy ending to the great debate.[24]

Equally cordial and thoroughly argued, no doubt, was Scott's response, early in 1962, to a talk Walter Keir had given claiming that Scotland had produced no good writing in English. Egged on in part, no doubt, by thoughts of his own English poems, Scott requested the opportunity to reply, reminding Bruce of the value of Gunn's novels, the work of 'the dramatists' (doubtless, including himself), and Bruce's own published poems.[25] But this defence of Scottish writing in English can be set alongside that response he had made in the seven-minute talk on the Third Programme, 'In defence of Lallans', on 15 September 1954, which answered (as mentioned on p. 153) a broadcast in which Iain Hamilton had criticised Lallans and the 'fabricated' Scots poetry being published by MacDiarmid's younger contemporaries.

Alexander Scott was a man whose career, in all its variety, was driven primarily by his instinct to give full scope to the talents he discovered within himself. The opposite of a ruthless careerist (though he possessed an abundant awareness of his own skills and merits), he threw himself fully into whatever sphere opened up before him, his drive for self-fulfilment supplanting any instinct towards self-advancement. He was ambitious, but lacked focus and calculation. Broadcasting was one such sphere which completely engaged his talents. It was his good fortune to find himself in the right place at the right time: his abilities were just what were required at a time when radio broadcasting in Scotland was thriving as never before or since. He was at home in the broadcasting studio, because its demands for a combination of authoritativeness and accessibility were just what he had to offer.

Chapter 8

Meetings, Minutes, Agendas

Committee work is seldom the subject of gripping narrative. Nevertheless, the policy initiated by the Scottish Arts Council (SAC) in the mid-1960s, to nurture literature in Scotland by encouraging new writing and by making accessible as wide a range as possible of worthwhile older literature, was an important turning point contributing significantly to the creation of today's lively Scottish literary scene. It also had the unexpected benefit of enriching beyond all conceivable prophecy Alexander Scott's broader professional life and of transforming him from a solitary satellite occupying an orbit of little influence into a major planet in the Scottish literary heaven. In other words, he was able to play a central part in igniting the renewed interest in Scottish writing to which we have grown accustomed today. And in personal terms, the flurry of activity initiated by the SAC created for Scott a version of the ideal academic community, supportive of his own particular interests and values, with which Glasgow University on the whole had not provided him.

These broad developments, of course, were not just due to one man, or to any particular group or initiative. Political developments and the emotions lying behind them inevitably played their part. Conversely, the increasing liveliness of Scotland's literary life in the 1970s and '80s must have contributed in turn to the stirring national self-awareness. In any case, it was a process in which Scott participated vigorously and idealistically. In exploring his part in it, some of the larger story is uncovered. And while his involvement was worthwhile in itself, one finds, too, that his increasing immersion in cultural committee work seems to have brought him its own reward. As his pupil Douglas Gifford says, it 'brought him in from the cold.'[1] Scott's efforts on behalf of Scottish writing and culture, during countless meetings of various earnest bodies, constitute a paradoxically distinctive and valuable part of his achievement.

In February 1965, Lord Goodman, chairman of the Arts Council of Great Britain, published his White Paper *A Policy for the Arts*. Among its other innovations, this had the important result of bringing literature as a whole into the Arts Council's remit; hitherto, it had concerned itself only with poetry. Both the Arts Council and its Scottish Committee set up literature panels to take on this new challenge. At the second meeting (6 May 1966) of the Edinburgh-based Literature and Play Panel: 'there was much discussion on helping to bring into print, and preserve in print, worthwhile Scottish books, fiction or non-fiction.'[2] At about the same time, a confidential report, 'Aid to literature—progress report', was presented to the panel by Alisdair Skinner, the Literature and Drama Assistant. This is an honest and trenchant survey of the current state of Scottish publishing, with all its considerable limitations. The way forward, nevertheless, seemed to be to find a sympathetic and efficient Scottish publisher who might undertake, in conjunction with the Arts Council's Scottish Committee, a series of high-quality paperbacks of Scottish books past and present. At first, the likeliest firm appeared to be Collins, the last major family-owned Scottish publisher prominent in Britain as a whole, but after some promising initial exchanges Collins pulled out early in 1967. Nevertheless, the SAC (as it had by now become) continued its efforts to create a commercially sustainable series of paperbacks making Scottish literature easily and permanently available. This goal became the over-riding one for the Literature Committee of the SAC during the rest of the 1960s and into the 1970s, until they found in the Edinburgh publishers Canongate the ideal partner.

The creation of a publishing outlet for Scottish writing, however, was far from being the only activity to which the new SAC Literature Committee addressed itself. The first time Alexander Scott is mentioned in its documents, for example, is when he is listed as one of the 'nominators' for a literature prize in 1967. At the same time, in June of that year the Literature Committee formulated a proposal for a writing fellowship to be jointly funded by the SAC and the University of Edinburgh. When the agreed candidate, Norman MacCaig, took up the post in the autumn it was the first of a series of important fellowships of this type held within Scottish universities.

With initiatives such as these, the SAC began intervening substantially in the literary life of Scotland outside the university departments of literature and substantially shaped an environment in which Scott, with others, would play a prominent and at times controversial part. Scott's first major involvement with the SAC, his role as 'nominator' for the literature prize apart, came in September 1967 when he was invited on to a new panel set up 'to deal with problems concerning the publication of Scottish books—it would be called "The Scottish Book Council".'[3] His remit would be 'to advise on Scottish literature': suddenly his specialism, which had hitherto confined him to a position of obscurity within Glasgow University, was resulting in his views being sought, his opinion being valued and his energies being allowed to influence, directly and substantially, Scotland's literary activity. And at the same September meeting he was also included in an 'advisory panel on the recording of Scottish literature'. This last was chaired by Douglas Young and had its first meeting on 10 November 1967, when Scott, according to the minutes, waded in at the outset with information about how Glasgow schools were developing Scottish studies, thereby creating a possible market for the long-playing records the committee hoped to generate.

From the documents relating to the Recordings Panel before it was wound up in March 1969, it seems that Scott was among the most enthusiastic of its members. Indeed, he continued to work towards the goal of creating a library of recorded verse even after the panel ceased to exist. Thus, the Literature Committee eventually received a report from Douglas Eadie (the SAC literature assistant) describing a breakthrough in the arrangements for a series of records. No progress had been made previously, due to:

> the difficulty of finding a company willing or satisfactorily able to undertake the production and distribution of records of the work of Scottish poets. This situation has now changed, and two reputable companies are eager to initiate a series of such records. Acknowledgements are due here to the perseverance of Alexander Scott and the Universities Committee on Scottish Literature to which he is secretary.'[4]

This points to an even more important SAC initiative.

On 26 April 1968, there met at the instigation of the SAC a group of academics from departments of literature around the Scottish universities, all with a prominent interest in Scottish literature. They included Thomas Crawford (Aberdeen), Prof. T. A. Dunn (Stirling), T. Douglas Gifford (Strathclyde), Prof. John MacQueen (Edinburgh), J. F. Ross (Glasgow), Alexander Scott (Glasgow) and Donald Low (St Andrews). Apologies were received from Edwin Morgan (Glasgow) and Robert Carnie (Dundee). For the SAC, Ronald Mavor and Alisdair Skinner were present and the Literature Committee's convenor, Douglas Young, chaired the meeting. It had been called:

> at the suggestion of the Council's Scottish Book Panel to investigate the possibility of creating a more co-ordinated policy in the teaching of Scottish Literature in Scottish Universities and a better market there for certain out-of-print Scottish classics.

In the minutes of the discussion, Scott's contribution is once more prominent. The group moved towards a measure of co-ordination of teaching programmes so as to justify new editions of classic texts and to create 'a pool of books from which several departments might select texts for study in their larger classes, preferably over more than one year'. And then the communitarian impulse *really* took off:

> Professor Dunn pointed out the need for an independent committee not only to discuss the question of out-of-print texts, but also other aspects of liaison between the different university English departments. After discussion, it was agreed to form a Scottish Universities Liaison Committee, with Professor Dunn and Mr Alexander Scott in the capacities of Chairman and Secretary respectively.

From this formalised grouping of university teachers of Scottish Literature there grew, a year or two later, the yet more all-embracing Association for Scottish Literary Studies (ASLS), which took in teachers, school inspectors, librarians, language specialists and interested members of the general public, and which initiated a range of publishing and educational activities for all levels of Scottish literary education. In time, the Universities Committee on Scottish Literature withered away, its role having been taken over and greatly expanded by ASLS, which for long, now, has been a respected and valuable presence in the arena of Scottish literary education and publishing. Throughout, it has been supported by the SAC with which it has always worked closely.

Scott found himself at the centre of an exciting suite of developments, which bade fair to help realise his idealistic dreams for writing in Scotland. His position as the most long-standing academic in Scotland devoting his time entirely to the teaching of Scottish literature, combined with his recent re-emergence as an actively publishing poet (with, above all, *Cantrips* in 1968), made him the obvious choice for inclusion in any body concerned with the Scottish literary scene. Thus, for example, he was one of three (with Norman MacCaig and Alistair Mair) suggested for yet another SAC panel on 5 May 1969, this time 'to advise on those writers living in Scotland whose work would be most likely to improve, or be sustained, if they were given a bursary, whether or not these writers had in fact been sponsored'.

From this nexus of bodies and committees emerged the first major publishing series to attempt to supply the need for modern paperback editions of important Scottish writing past and present. After the firm of Collins fell by the wayside, an alternative publisher for a 'Scottish Library Series' was found in Calder & Boyars. John Calder already had a reputation as the daring and innovative publisher of experimental writers who made up, between them, much of the artistic avant-garde in the 1950s and '60s: his list included works by (among many others) Samuel Beckett and Alain Robbe-Grillet, Ivan Illich, John Cage and Hubert Selby, jun. Calder was alert to the excitement and commercial possibilities in the nascent burgeoning of Scottish literary publishing. His dealings were more immediately with the Universities Committee on Scottish Literature rather than directly with the SAC, which has always operated through firms it has encouraged and supported rather than publishing on its own account. So it was that the Scottish Library Series was initiated in 1968, after negotiation with the Universities Committee, though with the SAC keeping an extremely close eye on these arrangements, not just out of fatherly interest but because it would be heavily involved in the financing of each volume. Scott had been appointed general editor, with ambitious plans for the swift emergence of a substantial number of volumes, at the rate of three per year. The negotiation of subsidies for the individual volumes seems to have been fraught from the start, however, and Scott found himself having to act as negotiator between (at various times) the publisher, the SAC, the Universities Committee, and the individual volume editors. In just over a year, the cracks were already beginning to show and to be reflected in SAC Literature Committee minutes:

> The Literature Assistant [Douglas Eadie] explained that the difficulty here was Mr. Calder's assumption, which had gradually emerged through correspondence, that the Council was committed to subsidising each book in the Scottish Library Series at a rate of 40% of production costs.
>
> It was agreed that it should be made clear to Mr. Calder that the Council would decide the amount of subsidy on each title as production costs were submitted, rather than on any fixed basis, and that any advance on subsidy to cover editors' fees should be considered as part of the whole subsidy.[5]

Nor were the emergent difficulties solely to do with subsidy: the planned first three volumes were slow in appearing, with everyone at the Scottish end blaming the publisher. By the autumn of 1970, the SAC was taking a fresh look at their arrangements for the publication of the books they wished to make available. For the SAC Literature Committee meeting of 17 September 1970, Douglas Eadie tabled a substantial and systematic two-part paper entitled 'The Scottish Arts Council and publishing', which included an invitation to his SAC colleagues to consider an alternative publisher. Eadie's survey of the alternatives was not exactly encouraging, however. Of the remaining long-established Scottish publishing houses, he claimed, only Collins had a good name among booksellers. He had initial doubts, too, about the recently formed Scottish Academic Press, and summed up as follows:

> All in all, inept marketing, eccentric editorial judgement, and therefore the ability to attract only writers who have not been able to place their books with a London publisher, characterise the existing Scottish publishing scene, which is in any case a sea fraught with the reefs and shallows of personality and attitude.

Eadie's successor as literature assistant, Trevor Royle, shared his hesitations about Calder & Boyars, and on 16 March 1971 the SAC Literature Committee decided to approach Routledge & Kegan Paul with a view to their taking over the series.

Despite growing SAC impatience with Calder & Boyars, Scott continued for some time to act as middle man, as he was committed to getting out the initial planned volumes (committed, that is, both to the editors personally and to each project as worthwhile in itself), and a number of titles in the series appeared over the next fifteen years. Within weeks of his taking on the role of general editor in October 1968, he had to employ skills of patient diplomacy with which, given his reputation for bluff aggressiveness and shortness of fuse, he is not usually credited. Manuscripts essential to the editing process were allegedly held up in the publisher's office, promised contracts took ages to appear, publisher and editors (in a chicken-and-egg situation) demanded from each other basic information regarding lines-per-page and volume size. A dispute arose regarding the royalty to be paid to Robert McLellan for the new edition of his play *Jamie the Saxt* so that Scott even offered to transfer his 1% general editor's royalty on the volume to the author so that things could move forward.[6] And the planned timetable of three volumes per year from 1969 onwards slipped badly right from the outset.

The dream of a new series to transform the availability of Scottish university texts proved uphill from the start. Nevertheless, a number of important and (thirty years on) still useful volumes appeared in this, the first major attempt to create a modern library of well-presented Scottish material. What Scott and his editors achieved was very worthwhile, and lessons were rapidly learned for the immediate future. And although it came to be felt in Scotland that working with John Calder could be difficult, the series benefited from the gusto and, indeed, the optimism which he initially brought to it.

By the time Sydney Goodsir Smith's play *The Wallace* was issued in 1985, however, Scott had long since ceased to be involved in Calder's series. Their parting of the ways was caused by an earlier Goodsir Smith volume, the *Collected Poems* of 1975. Scott's name still appeared in it as General Editor of the series, but John Calder's recent published account correctly conveys the emotional force of Scott's repudiation of the volume.[7] What is less to be relied on is his explanation for Scott's outrage and also his ascribing to Scott of a malevolent vendetta which produced tangible results. I have no doubt that Calder based his narrative on what he remembers about what happened and what he was told, and that it was written in good faith. The record and the recollections of others, however, suggest that his account requires correction. Here is how Calder puts it:

> The Chairman of the Literature Panel of the Scottish Arts Council was Alexander Scott, a poet and an academic, who had earlier compiled with Norman MacCaig a large anthology of *Contemporary Scottish Verse*, for my Scottish Library Series. Scott was annoyed with us for having picked Tom Scott instead of himself, to edit and see through the press the *Collected Poems* of Sydney Goodsir Smith, which happened in 1975, and he wanted to stop us getting any more grants out of revenge. When Hamish Hamilton applied for a much larger subsidy [for a collection of short stories by Elspeth Davie] than we had requested, they received it instantly.
>
> ...
>
> Sidney [*sic*] Goodsir Smith died while his *Collected Poems* were still in proof. He had made many changes, above all simplifying his Scots dialect poems to make many of them easier to read by non-Scottish readers. I asked Hazel, his widow to recommend someone who could

> finish the proof-reading who was sufficiently familiar with his work, and she named Tom Scott. This made Alexander Scott, who felt that it should have been him, a bitter enemy. He attacked the edition when it was published as corrupt, blamed me for changing the spelling and anglicising many of the poems, and would not accept that this had been done by Sidney himself or in some cases indicated by him to me or to Hazel or others. One result was losing Scottish Arts Council support, especially in the case of Elspeth Davie, as has been told. Alex Scott continued sniping at me up to his death.[8]

The implication that Scott abused a position of power and influence to pursue a private 'revenge' is a serious one, which must be considered in some detail. There is little doubt that he was piqued at not being asked to complete the work on his close friend's collected poems. (In fact, Tom Scott was equally another of Goodsir Smith's close friends and, according to Smith's widow, her husband could never understand why the two Scotts couldn't get on.)[9] It was no doubt true, too, that just before his death Smith was preparing a version of his poems which had been anglicised for wider comprehension, as Calder says. To some critics, Tom Scott seems to have lacked some essential skills as a textual editor and the prevailing view amongst academics concerned with the matter is that the volume which emerged is textually poor. As Duncan Glen says, Scott was 'absolutely right' about the quality of the proof-reading in the volume. (One notices, for example, that 'MacDiarmid'—as so often by this stage in his life, the founder of the twentieth-century Scottish Renaissance had been asked to contribute an introduction—is mis-spelled on the title page itself.) The essential issue here, however, is the question of Alexander Scott's 'revenge'.

Despite Calder's claim, Scott was never 'the chairman of the Literature Panel of the Scottish Arts Council'. As we have seen, he had been a member of various SAC committees from 1967 onwards. and by the mid-1970s his voice was a prominent one in Scottish literary circles, both academic and non-academic. Nevertheless, so far as one can tell from written records and also from the clear recollections of Trevor Royle, the SAC's 1970s literature director, Scott was never in a position to influence decisions regarding subsidies for John Calder's proposed publications.[10] In a private communication to me, however, Calder insists that: 'I stick to what I said, which was confirmed by others at the time.'[11] One suspects that what may have happened was that Scott, denouncing the volume at every opportunity (in print and in conversation), helped substantially to bring about the widespread realisation of its deficiencies. No doubt his friends and contacts in the SAC rapidly came to know his views, as did just about everyone else concerned with literature in Scotland at the time.

SAC annual reports outline the following picture. By 1975, the year in which the Goodsir Smith *Collected Poems* was published, Scott would appear to have been absent from all SAC panels and committees for several years. (His secretaryships of the Universities Committee and of ASLS must have taken up much of his 'spare' time from the early 1970s onwards, as did the creation of the new department at Glasgow in 1971.) On 27 June 1975, however, he joined the SAC Literature Committee; this was the first time he had been on that important SAC body, and this had come about through the instigation of Trevor Royle, who both suggested his name and persuaded Scott to allow it to go forward. (Scott had believed initially that his name would not be acceptable to the Literature Committee.)[12] The chairman of the committee, by this stage, was the novelist Neil Paterson.

Meanwhile, on 7 January 1975 (several months before Scott joined the SAC Literature Committee), there had met a new sub-committee of the SAC Literature Committee in the form of a Grants to Publishers Committee.[13] This had taken over from the Literature Committee the responsibility for deciding on the applications for subsidy submitted by publishers. From the time of its creation, the Grants to Publishers Committee made *all* the decisions in this area, passing on its recommendations to the main Literature Committee for ratification. The Literature Committee, in practice, never overturned any recommendation from the Grants to Publishers Committee. As simply one of several ordinary members of the Literature Committee (along with Professor Tommy Dunn, Professor Derick Thomson, James Allan Ford and Mrs Mary Klopper, a local authority representative), Scott was in no position to enable his private feelings about Calder to enforce the overturning of decisions regarding subsidy which had been taken elsewhere. Furthermore, he was a member of the Literature Committee for only two years. And when he left it after 1976 he was never again a member of any SAC committee, although his involvement with other organisations such as ASLS ensured that he kept in close personal touch with those who were.

With regard to the rejection of Calder's application for a grant to publish Elspeth Davie's collection of short stories, this was a decision taken at the first meeting of the Grants to Publishers Committee (7 January 1975), six months *before* Scott joined the Literature Committee and well before the Goodsir Smith edition was published later in that year. This last was also granted a subsidy at the same meeting of 7 January to enable Tom Scott to complete work on it.[14] There is obviously no way in which Scott's eventual judgement upon that volume could have influenced the January decision on the Davie proposal, and the reasons why that decision was taken had nothing to do with him. John Calder's other claim—that his general loss of SAC support was the 'result' of Alexander Scott's attacks on the Goodsir Smith volume—seems over-simple when one remembers that the SAC was already beginning to look for an alternative publisher by 1970 and also when one notices that at least two much later volumes published by Calder's firm, Robert McLellan's *Collected Plays* (1981) and Goodsir Smith's *The Wallace* (1985), both acknowledge SAC support. Calder's extended difficulties with the SAC arose out of a difference of perception between them as to the purposes of council funding.

Calder & Boyars was far from being the only publisher with which the Universities Committee had contact: the surviving minutes of their meetings are evidence of an astonishingly energetic urge to explore all possible channels whereby Scottish literary material could be made available.[15] It was almost as if they were trying to create a new academic subject from scratch: the sporadic (though frequent) teaching of Scottish literature, which had been going on across Scotland for several generations, was suddenly replaced by a near-frenzy of co-operative striving. In addition to belonging to different university departments across the country, the committee members found themselves in what increasingly resembled a secondary, federal department, which claimed much of their allegiance and which they nurtured and supported with as much care as they did the institutions which paid their wages.

It was a moment of intense collaboration which probably would not have been possible in more recent decades, when government funding policies for the universities have tied significant monies to often narrowly defined research outputs, thereby forcing academics to concentrate their energies, frequently to the exclusion of other academic-related activities, on personal research and publication in the hope of keeping their own home departments in a state of financial well-being and good academic repute. Collaboration in the form that produced the Universities Committee and the ASLS has been replaced by a new and enforced competitiveness. When academic collaboration occurs nowadays, it has to be in the form of efficiency-generating collaborative degrees and teaching programmes concocted between specific academic units, and whereas the members of the Universities Committee got together for the good of the subject, contemporary collaboration is usually for the sake of attracting more overseas students and their fees, or for enabling departments to maintain or increase their 'attractiveness' and hence their undergraduate numbers in the face of the imperialist depredations of their competitors. In the new millennium, university teachers are once more heavily focused on their own departments and their research ratings: as one ex-president of ASLS recently said to another (i.e. myself), lamenting that neither of us had been at a meeting of ASLS Council for ages: 'However did we find the time?' Thirty years ago, however, most of the active university teachers of Scottish literature resident in Scotland gladly found the time to attend upwards of half a dozen meetings per year (and sometimes many more) of these new bodies and their offshoots, and to do the often laborious work (organisational or academic) which that involvement implied.

The range of what was being planned was prodigious: many new editions and reprints of Scottish works from all periods, a new and authoritative multi-volume history of Scottish literature, an international register of activity in Scottish literary studies, a discursive annual survey of work published in the field, the creation of a library of sound recordings of poets reading their own poetry, major international conferences, the nurturing of the study of Scottish literature in schools, and the creation of the new association which became ASLS. And at the heart of this fervour of trans-university endeavour was Alexander Scott, not merely the minute taker and meeting arranger, but the University Committee's principal negotiator with other organisations and publishers, the general editor of the new series of publications which the Committee was sponsoring, and the joint editor of the first (and certainly not least successful, as John Calder himself acknowledges) of the series' volumes, the anthology *Contemporary Scottish Verse 1959–1969*.

The ASLS was founded at a meeting in SAC premises on 31 August 1970.[16] For the purposes of the meeting, at which a draft constitution prepared by the Editorial Committee of the Universities Committee on Scottish Literature was agreed and an interim body of officers elected, Scott acted as secretary. He was not one of the first ASLS office bearers, but joined the Editorial Board along with M. P. MacDiarmid, John MacQueen, Donald Low and Thomas Crawford. The minutes of those early meetings suggest, however, that he was one of the most actively involved in discussion, and one of the most pro-active of council members, from the very beginning. Furthermore, the ASLS's first annual volume was Hogg's *The Three Perils of Man*, to be edited by Douglas Gifford, at that point engaged on a doctoral thesis on Hogg with Scott as his supervisor. And when, in January 1972, neither the president nor vice-president was able to be present, the council meeting was chaired by Scott. In 1974 he became ASLS secretary, and two years later was elected president, a position he held for three years. Thereafter he remained a powerful presence in the ASLS and made a significant late contribution to its development when he helped found its creative writing annual, *New Writing Scotland*, as its joint editor during its first four years.

Scott's involvement in these two bodies placed him near the heart of what for a while was a major dynamic movement helping to shape Scottish literary activity in the 1960s and '70s. In these committees he was a dominant presence, constantly speaking out in a decisive, downright manner. As Trevor Royle says, he would often say what needed saying; at other times, admittedly, he would give vent to his prejudices and dislikes. Neil Paterson, chairing the SAC Literature Committee in 1975, had been worried that Scott's reputation for argumentativeness would make him an uncomfortable presence on the group, but he was pleasantly surprised.

Royle describes Scott's contribution as 'very constructive'. For example, he took the unusual step of requesting that a particular matter be placed on the agenda for the September 1975 meeting—normally, the agenda was centrally decided beforehand within the SAC. Scott, finding at his first meeting that special awards of £1,000 were occasionally given out to individuals (in this case, David Murison of the *Scottish National Dictionary*) who had made a specially distinctive contribution to the literary life of Scotland, immediately proposed for the next meeting that Duncan Glen, who since the 1960s had single-handedly been publishing *Akros* and a whole host of related books and pamphlets, be given a similar award. When the matter was debated, it was seen to have merit and was agreed.

Royle's second example refers to the way Scott effected, in October 1975, a major extension to the already successful SAC Writers in Schools scheme, whereby practising writers spoke to school children about writing and about their own work. Scott proposed that the scheme be extended to cover universities, hospitals, clubs, etc. As a result, the greatly extended scheme is still one of the most successful initiatives of its kind. As Royle says, Scott had a great 'feel' for what can be done to popularise literature; he was certainly one of the most active and popular writers to participate in the scheme. When Scott left the SAC Literature Committee after the normal spell of two years, it was felt that his presence had been greatly worthwhile.[17]

Royle's picture of an individual and forthright contribution accords with my own recollections of Scott's input at meetings of the Universities Committee and of the council of ASLS and its various subordinate boards. Whether or not he was acting (as he often did) as a chairman or secretary, Scott's presence was palpable and his contribution almost invariably constructive. There was admittedly always the air about him of *primus inter pares*, and Tom Crawford, while highly appreciative of all the work he saw Scott doing, also felt that self-promotion was an element in the motivational mix.[18] This, if true, was hardly surprising in the context of the new lease of academic life which these Arts Council-generated bodies bestowed upon Scott, heightening his engagement with his subject. Crawford stresses, in fact, Scott's committee work as a major part of his life's contribution, as does Scott's successor as head of the Glasgow department of Scottish Literature, Roderick Lyall.[19] Lyall describes what the Universities Committee achieved as 'crucial' and stresses the centrality of Scott's grasping, in the 1960s, of the way in which Arts Council involvement through the support and encouragement of publishers would be necessary for the creation of the student texts without which the subject could not properly take off. Lyall describes Scott as 'much more of a cultural activist than an academic'—a bias which, given the circumstances of the time, made him very important indeed. The demands and opportunities of the late 1960s and '70s enabled Scott to function with great effectiveness at the intersection of cultural activism and academia, a role for which temperament and experience had fitted him extremely well.

If the Universities Committee and ASLS had been the only organisations in which Scott participated prominently, his record as a cultural promoter and organiser would have been a notable one. As it was, at various times he also participated, with his habitual salience, in the running of such bodies as the Saltire Society, the Advisory Council for the Arts in Scotland (AdCAS) and the Scots Language Society. He participated in the activities of Scottish PEN (the international writers' organisation) and was on the Scottish Advisory Committee of the British Council in the period 1977–9. He was also highly supportive of such ventures as the Scotsoun series of taped readings.

Of these other bodies, it was perhaps in the Scots Language Society (SLS), or the Lallans Society as it was originally known, that he made the most individual contribution. It was through this body that the poet Ellie MacDonald got to know him: she joined it around 1974 when Scott was already its preses (president).[20] She started a branch in Dundee, which Scott and his wife came through to inaugurate. This, says MacDonald, was typical of him: he was a very 'hands-on' preses who was willing to go to any lengths to further the society's aims. (A year into the existence of the Dundee branch, for example, he returned to give another reading with a view to doing all he could to make it succeed. 'It was important to him', says MacDonald.) Equally typical of him, also, was the fact that he was 'nearly always' preses: it was a group that he dominated naturally. Duncan Glen recalls an occasion when Scott, casually late for a committee meeting of the SLS, eventually turned up and, ignoring the fact that others were for the moment well in command of the proceedings, instantly assumed the chair and gathered all the reins into his own hand.[21] Despite his high-handedness, he was (in MacDonald's eyes at least) 'an excellent preses of SLS': she believes that no one has done it better because 'no one else had *such* belief in what it was all about'. His dominance had nothing to do with his position as an academic, however—rather, his status derived from his poetry. Admittedly, the other poets and writers who were much in evidence in the SLS would not have been impressed by academic credentials, but one also senses that (unlike the Universities Committee and ASLS) this was one of the activities—and one particularly close to his heart—which made up that great swathe of his life and priorities lying outside, though contiguous with, his academic day job.

When different viewpoints emerged, his position was predictably decisive. One division within the society, for example, was between members who were simply interested in the Scots language as used in everyday contexts, as opposed to that dominant group (which obviously included Scott) for whom the issue of Scots as a literary language was ever uppermost. Another dispute was over whether or not the society should allow itself to adopt an overtly political aspect. There were those for whom the cultural issues were inseparable from political activity, of however mild a sort. The issue came to a head over whether or not the SLS should take a float in a procession of political protest in Edinburgh—Scott was adamant that they should not, but others disagreed so violently that they resigned. Scott, however, 'was having none of it' and the fact that others left rather than him underlined his dominance of the committee.[22]

His prominence on such a range of committees, and his willingness to undertake whatever consequent spadework was asked of him, is testimony to the completeness of his commitment to the goal of restoring the languages and literature of Scotland to what he believed to be their rightful place in the life of the nation. He would undoubtedly have been willing to use this last phrase himself, yet it was characteristic of him that the incipient nationalism contained within it chimes with his outlook in only the broadest and vaguest sense. The person who held out so firmly against a SLS float was, as Maurice Lindsay thought, 'the least political person I've ever met'.[23]

Chapter 9

Poetry

It is not possible, in the present study, to provide a full and systematic examination of Alexander Scott's poetry. Yet it is now our principal reason for remembering him at all, and it may be possible here to suggest lines of future discussion. Admittedly, elucidation of his poems does not depend on biography, nor on the reader achieving a rapport with a very private poetic sensibility. Indeed, it is one of the most obvious features of his poems that they are lucid and accessible (some Scots vocabulary apart) even on one's first encounter with them. During Scott's lifetime, his poetry gave pleasure to readers who knew little or nothing about him beyond the fact that he was a prominent academic in the field of Scottish literature. Yet inevitably, the subject matter of his poems, and the trends perceptible in them, can be related to his experience of life.

In 'Coronach', the poem that is generally acknowledged as his finest poetic response to his war experiences, he imagines his dead comrades sanctioning, indeed urging, his vocation as a poet:

> Sing til the warld we loo'd
> (For aa that its brichtness lee'd)
> And tell hou the sudden nicht
> Cam doun and made us nocht.[1]

The role being bequeathed to him is part lover or wooer (the world is a beautiful but treacherous woman) and part unit commander (whose sad duty it is to write to the loved ones of his dead men). And the doubleness of the role he finds himself playing is a function, in turn, of the doubleness of the world itself, for in the beauty of life lies the origin of his devotion, while its murderous perfidy provides the occasion for his tight-lipped, gruff and soldierly manliness. The poet in him reconciles the two, here and in his work as a whole: the poet it is who perceives that the distance between the world's loveliness and its falsity and brutality is as little as that between 'loo'd' and 'lee'd', 'nicht' and 'nocht'—and makes a poem about it. This is one of the patterns of his life and work—a hard and unideal reality intrudes upon the world of his private hopes and dreams; the solitary aestheticism which had become the goal of his youth is thwarted by the brutality in all our lives. His poetry, in all its variety, is the utterance of a man caught between intoxication with experience, and recoil from it.

From his earliest schoolboy efforts, his poetry embodies a capacity for intense self-scrutiny. His privateness, sometimes verging on self-centredness and selfishness, resulted in a flow of early poems largely taken up with his own immature emotional response to the world which was unfolding around him. Maturity, in the shape of a developed style which was tougher, far less self-involved and more emotionally tight-lipped, greatly reduced the confessional mode of his early verse even when it did not eradicate it entirely. It is the difference between, for example:

> Willow, do you weep for me?
> Dry thy tears, then, willow-tree.
> Lo, as I walked here by the river,
> My heart with sorrow sore did quiver,
> For dark were the waters, and dark was the sky,
> And by the sedged banks the reared rushes were dry
> And sickly yellow, and brightness was fled,
> And all spring's glorious colours seemed dead,
> Until I saw your green head bent above
> The dark-foaming waters: and all my deep love
> Of glowing hues was born again,
> And banished away from my heart was pain ...[2]

which was written in 1939, and the following poem, which is dated 8 August 1943:

> Adam from a prone position
> Mourned his miserable condition.
> Saw no solution, found no way out,
> Though he had dreamt of a different lay-out.
>
> Eve did not share his dreams at all
> But watched the mirror on the wall,
> Woke the children Cain and Abel
> And laid the breakfast on the table.[3]

The initial tenderness, self-scrutiny and depth of feeling were not banished, however, as 'Coronach' shows. Nor was a vital response to the world's hardships a characteristic of his later style only: in the earlier poem above, the willow's head, though bowed, rises above the dark turbulence beneath, and the image gives the poet strength. Poetic maturity, however, did involve the creation of a style in which emotion is constrained by the weight of experience, and romantic excess made impossible by the gruffness and peasant common sense of his new post-war persona, that of a man experienced in what life can deal out—and also that of someone committed to MacDiarmid's tough-minded Renaissance. Once Scott had found his essential mature manner, these were the two major contexts within which he wrote his poems: an ongoing self-awareness and self-scrutiny as he monitored his responses to life's beauty and ugliness—and his commitment to the Scottish Renaissance movement.

It is clearly possible, therefore, to think about the great wartime transition in Scott's poetry in terms of those grand opposites—innocence and experience. Another equally grand pair may also be helpful—male and female. G. S. Fraser associated the control of feeling, the muting of emotional expression, 'poetic workmanship', distancing, wit and irony with the 'male element in poetry', as opposed to a female, Dionysian, 'wild primitive orgiastic dance'.[4] Readers of Scott's poems often feel a prominent masculinity in them—in the voice, in the attitudes and in the stress on craftsmanship and emotional distancing. And all this is in the starkest contrast with the apparently uncontrolled romantic aestheticism of that superabundant flow of juvenile verse.

Scott switched, in 1943, from being an extremely 'female' poet to being a startlingly 'masculine' one. In one way, his adoption of Scots gave him a new masculine gruffness of poetic voice. Scots, furthermore, is a medium (as Douglas Dunn, for one, believes)[5] which is perhaps best suited to the employment of traditional Scottish verse forms and modes: if so, then Scott's instincts towards scholarship and craftsmanship had found their ideal vehicle. In addition, however, Scots might also be seen as enabling him to control emotion with a more masculine form of lyricism—in an unpublished note on 'Heart of Stone' he refers to 'the restraint inherent in the medium'.[6] The language became a means of reconciling the masculine and feminine sides of his poetic nature.

In many of Scott's comments over the years, the impression is given that what his 'commitment to the Scottish Renaissance movement' amounted to was a commitment simply to the continued use of Scots for poetic purposes. As has been noted, the years after the war was a time when he was 'mad keen on everything Scots'. J. Derrick McClure has given a modern account, which need not be repeated here, of Scott's use of the language in his poetry.[7] What might be added to his analysis is the simple observation that Scott used at least two styles of poetic Scots, though some of the poet's own accounts imply that he thought of only one type, which he called, with increasing frequency, 'aggrandised Scots'. For many of his poems, this seems a good term: the foundation on a spoken language is always palpable, but the extra poetic richness he habitually achieved was the result of such features as a broader range of vocabulary, and an extra emphasis on sound, than the spoken language ever displays. The result is a distinctly public mode, a performed verse, mannered and projected, felt as a guise—a persona of a type that is not an invariable consequence of the adoption of Lallans, which other poets can often use much more conversationally, much more privately. Compare a specimen of this style of Scott's with characteristic extracts from the writing of two of his contemporaries. Here is his 'Skull Sang':

Gangan my gait, I walk or rin,
And yirth ablow me aye is banes,
I set my fit on my guidsir's skull,
Albeid his bluid is in my veins.
I set my fit on my guidsir's skull
That liggs sae laich i the mools aneth
As I traivel the road that spans the warld
And leads me on til my ain death.

Compare with that MacDiarmid's 'Dandelion', more conversationally relaxed, the focus less on the language and more purely on the images and ideas:

I saw my brain as the sun micht see
        A dandelion ba'
And think it was its ain
        Pale image that it saw.

I saw my brain as the sun micht see
        A dandelion ba'
— And noo like a starry sky
        My thochts owre a' thing blaw.

Or with Sydney Goodsir Smith's 'Late', which is musical and mannered also, but less aggressively masculine in its sound—and its sound less insisted upon—than Scott's:

Sweet hairt, I lay in bed last nicht
Alane and yet with ye
Alane I lay but no my lane
For the lane bed was full of ye.

Aa kens there's whiles a silly truth
Sets in the drunkard's ee —
Here nou's a forest-bleezan truth
Frae the hairt o the barley bree:
Its flame inflames the tither flame
As ye, and me ...

We ken the flame inflames the flame
As the wind brings in the sea —
Ken, tae, that fire consumes itsel
— As ye, and me.

The consonantal vigour of 'Skull Sang' is typical of a sense of language which uniquely marks Scott's handling of Lallans, especially in the first half of his poetic maturity. It is a style that turns even the most intimate of poems into a public utterance, distancing the poet from the subject matter and the emotion associated with it, especially when it is combined, as it often is, with a prominent stanzaic structure, as in 'To Mourn Jayne Mansfield'. When both the subject matter, and the occasion of the poem, are themselves deeply public as in 'Heart of Stone', then the style booms out, especially when Scott himself reads the poem (as on the Scotsoun recording). Scott took the term 'makar' very seriously indeed, and insists (as it were) that the reader be aware of the craftsmanship of each poem. The result is a poetry that keeps the poet, as a private person, at a distance, even when the subject matter seems intensely personal, as in 'Continent o Venus', or in that utterance from the depths of possible clinical depression, 'Mirk Midnicht':

> The fire burns laich,
> The clock creeps roun frae twal,
> And I maun dwall
> Alane, and dreich.
>
> In dule this nicht
> The dowie hours ere daw
> Gae hirplan slaw
> To sink frae sicht ...

Unlike most of the other poems, this one is not dated in the notebooks, but Scott located it between 'From You, My Love' and 'Prehistoric Playmate' in the *Selected Poems* of 1975—in other words, right on the transition between the end of his post-war phase in the late 1950s, and the beginning of his mid-60s recrudescence. A letter to Alan Riddell suggests that it was one of the poems produced when he returned to writing in the mid-1960s, rather than reflecting the onset of the failure of poetic inspiration in the late 1950s (as I had previously tended to think).[8] It is surely an account of something Scott had experienced, but I now see it as a recollection rather than as an immediate overflow of anguish. With its idiosyncratic form (each stanza enclosed and trapped in its circular and inescapable rhyme pattern; each one a struggle to something like fullness in the second line, only to fall back to the minimal movement of two stresses in lines three and four), it is as crafted a poem as any of his others. Distance and control lurk, also, in its echoes of *In Memoriam* and of Coleridge's 'Frost at Midnight' and 'Dejection'.

Scott's handling of Scots, however, is not invariably bookish, bardic and heightened. In many poems, especially from the mid-1960s onwards, the colloquial and non-aggrandised take over. This is most obvious of all in the 'Scotched' sequence with its slangy conversationalism, but Leonard's 'thi langwij a thi guhtr' comes close, too, in (for example) 'Gentlemen Prefer Blondes', 'Doun Wi Dirt!' and 'Paradise Tint':

Said Adam til Eve,
'Ye've gart me grieve.'
Said Eve til Adam,
'Aipples, I've had 'em!'

Said Adam til Nick,
'Ye snake! Ye swick!'
Said Nick til Adam,
'Me—or the madam?' ...

It is noticeable, however, that poems like these containing utterly informal Scots tend to be particularly stylised in terms of structure, as if a tightly constraining stanza pattern were necessary to keep the verbal looseness in check. When Scott uses colloquial Scots, the reader is always very aware that its role is that of a thoroughly reductive idiom, with nothing of Leonard's, or Kelman's, social and cultural agendas to take account of. In these poems, the colloquial voice itself is satirised, and viewed ironically. And that sense of a temporary impoverishment of language, of a decline from a higher verbal standard, points us to another implication of Scott's Renaissance commitment.

Although he used Scots in so many poems because the language came naturally to him and expressed something important of himself, Scott also used it to provide a cultural reference point. The voice of his aggrandised Scots combines an outlook of peasant common sense with a judgmental perspective based on Scottish tradition. In other words, in his Scots poems the world is viewed from the standpoint of the putative independent cultural life which Scotland (in the Renaissance analysis) once had and ought to have again—and viewed also with the downrightness which emerges from Scotland's democratic instincts. The contemporary Scotland in which Scott and his friends were fighting on behalf of their movement was clearly radically different from the Scotland they presumed they would have been living in had the country remained culturally independent. The gap generates many of Scott's poems. His role as a Lallans poet, therefore, was both to help provide a body of Scots poems for a future tradition, and to criticise the present for its insufficiency.

The satiric tendency of his verse is particularly marked from the mid-1960s onwards, when the gaudy freedoms of the period confronted his own middle-aged distance from the follies and tolerance of youth. At the same time, however, one detects a contrary impulse behind his 'pop poems', namely a desire to join the psychedelic generation even while he beats them. (Both senses of 'beat'—to strike and to outdo —are relevant here.) Thus, to take one of the earliest of these, 'Prehistoric Playmate', his disapproval of the nude photographs of Ursula Andress published in the April 1965 issue of *Playboy*, timed to coincide with her new stardom in that year's Hammer film treatment of Rider Haggard's *She*, cannot be entirely disentangled from his male fascination with the prospect of her nakedness. The poem's implication that Scott was, for his generation, comparatively *au fait* with the more sexually free manifestations of 1960s culture is confirmed by his covering comment to George Bruce when sending him 'Prehistoric Playmate' for possible inclusion in the first *Scottish Poetry* anthology. 'Playmate' would appear to have been not yet universally familiar in its Hefnerian sense (despite the fact that the magazine had been in existence for a dozen years):

> Perhaps I should explain that the title, 'Prehistoric Playmate', derives from the fact that the nudes which appear in *Playboy* magazine are described as 'playmates'. The poem is, of course, a satire on pornography—but I trust it's something more, too.[9]

(If the sexuality of the poem suggests that Scott was experiencing something of a resurgence of the sexual energies and fascinations of youth, the fact that he sent it to Bruce on the same day that he completed it suggests that the undergraduate eagerness he had shown in the late 1940s to be published as frequently and immediately as possible had also returned.)

Despite the trendiness of its subject matter, however, the poem takes a stance rooted in Scottish literary tradition. It combines (as does 'Tam o' Shanter', for example) a voice and personality of earthy and reductive commonness—'A bargain (at fowr-and-thruppence the timeless tit)'—with an educated sophistication of mind and awareness: the poet is clearly familiar with, and susceptible to, 'Haggard's dwaiblie dwaum o the East'. The essential criticism in the poem is of the way a trashy present degrades the heritage of the past—admittedly, not a specifically Scottish heritage in this case, but it is the application of 'aggrandised' Scots to judgmental cultural attitudes which matters here. Even so, the stature of the English novel which the photographs degrade is also seen as limited—it is, after all, a 'dwaiblie dwaum'.

The two sides of Scott's Lallans persona are given separate voice in the contrasted pair of poems which make up 'To Mourn Jayne Mansfield'. 'Sair Sonnet' draws strength, in its twentieth-century Renaissance manner, from the world of the makars: it seems to echo distantly Henryson's 'Testament of Cresseid', not so much in direct verbal similarities as in the rich sounds and stately movement and pace—and also in its combining of a sympathetic (and sexual) personal response with a blunt brutality while contemplating the death of a society's iconic beauty, a figure of sexual promiscuity and pathetic vulnerability. Compare:

> Lo, fair ladyis! Cresseid of Troyis toun,
> Sumtyme countit the flour of womanheid,
> Under this stane, lait lipper, lyis deid.
>
> ('The Testament of Cresseid' ll.607–9)

with Scott's:

Faan is thon powe that crouned her fairheid's flouer,
Hackit awa as gin by the heidsman's aix —
Our lust the blade has killed thon bonnie hure,
Puir quine! that aince had reigned the Queen o Glaiks.

There is a whiff of satire in applying this echo of Renaissance majesty to a lurid modern life and brutal death, but on balance Scott appears to be genuinely mourning the dead starlet. Nevertheless, he also appears to be hoping that some of the work of mourning the woman—of cherishing her despite her faults—will be done by the distant echo of Henrysonian humanity. Not all readers find his moral bluntness, or his clear awareness of her bodily attractions, sufficiently counterweighted by such considerations. And the bodily attractions loom even larger in 'Hollywood in Hades', a joke apparently designed as a common man's unfeeling response to the death, a harsh jest fitted to the outlook of cruder-minded users of the Scots language. The satire can perhaps be seen as directed against the mentality of those who find humour and arousal in the association of death with Mansfield's much displayed body. The trouble is that the irony is far from inescapable, and the superficial scholarliness of the references (Hades, Charon's barque, etc.) suggests that the bookish poet himself shares the joke, rather than keeping distant from it.

In the letter to Riddell mentioned on p. 175, Scott refers to his currently writing 'a series of satires on the contemporary exploitation of sex'. This implies a more controlled approach than the poems show with any clarity, and plays down the characteristic spontaneity of his inspiration. In fact, Scott had difficulty in controlling the tone of, and enabling the reader to feel comfortable in, these poems apparently disapproving of the sexy freedoms of the 1960s scene. Consider one of his longer poems in this group. 'Deir Deid Dancer', on Isadora Duncan, concerns a scandalous female artist of an earlier age, but the stimulus for the poem came from a television programme, 'Isadora Duncan: The Biggest Dancer in the World', by that quintessential 1960s creator Ken Russell. The poem wears its Scottish Renaissance credentials on its sleeve with its quotation from *A Drunk Man Looks at the Thistle*, but its Scots mode is self-consciously colloquial rather than elevated or aggrandised:

The Reids rinnan short o the ready,
She sailed til the States wi her steady,
She jigged to win gowd frae the Yankees,
'A Communist ploy!' cried the swankies …

When Scott submitted the poem (as he seems to have done with every poem he was writing at this time) to his friends, the editors of the *Scottish Poetry* anthologies, Edwin Morgan in particular hated it. In the correspondence between the editors, Morgan's various comments articulate an extreme reaction:

> The mechanical pile driver thump of Deir Deid Dancer remains with me.
>
> Deir Deid Dancer. This has energy and some invention. It lacks flexibility. It ends with the same mechanical robustness as at its opening. It deaves my lugs. Not sureabout [sic] my vote. Prefer 'Supermakar Story' ...
>
> DEAR DEID DANCER.—A strong No for this! This poem really irritated me. Admitted, Isadora lived a sort of tragic-comic life not without moments that can be seen as ludicrous; but I don't think she was vulgar as the poem is vulgar. Yesenin, too, is a very different character from the one portrayed here. It is the blotto/auto touch which shows the crudity of the piece. It takes a Byron, who has panache and an underlying seriousness, to get away with things like that. Don't you get SO TIRED of this Scotch habit of PULLING THINGS DOWN? He seems to think the last verse atones for all.[10]

It is true that the poem was dashed off in enthusiastic haste the day following the broadcast, and one can feel Scott's intoxication with the abundant stream of words, images, rhymes and stanzas that were flowing from his pen. Other critics see this poem as one of his best performances. McClure, for example, describes it as:

> one of the most riotous poems in modern Scottish literature, with demotic and slang expressions together with words from the more undignified reaches of traditional Scots being 'sent up' together in a truly glorious cascade of crazy rhymes

—rhymes which include, for McClure also, 'blotto/auto'.[11] Both critics are responding to a poem that operates by immersing the reader, rather than by stimulating to fine judgement: McClure likes this approach, Morgan did not. The problem is, I suggest, that Scott (in his joy at finding the inspiration flowing) has indeed concentrated on the visceral rather than on the finer perceptions. It is certainly possible to enjoy, with McClure, the linguistic torrent—and to regard the insistent rhymes and rhythms as an essential part of the effect rather than as a sign of mechanical deadness. On the other hand, one is indeed left wondering, with Morgan, what (if anything) we are supposed to think of the Isadora the poem sketches, and wondering also if Scott had thought much about it. The last stanza alone does indeed seem intended, belatedly, to guide us. It may be that the flagrant flippancy of the tone is an attempt to catch Russell's irreverent style (though I have only the dimmest of recollections of the film myself); it may be also, as I think is the case in many of these poems, that the crudeness of response as embodied in the colloquialism is itself an object of satiric attack. Anyone who had not seen the film, or who knew nothing of Isadora's story, would find much of the detail of the poem baffling: in a sense, the subject is not so much Isadora as the voice and persona which the words create, and to which two distinguished commentators react so differently. The film, and its subject, is the chance excuse for the creation of a mainly verbal experience. It may be that the essential criticism to be made is that Scott allows style to take the place of substance.

A poem of the length of 'Dear Deid Dancer' requires a structure that is not only stanzaic but also moral: such an extended utterance is incoherent without a foundation in attitude. On the other hand, one reason why the briefest of the Scots satires, the poems of the 'Scotched' sequence, are so widely felt as successful is that, along with Scott's punning habit of mind, their very lack of a precisely articulated ironic focus becomes not a weakness but a strength. Is Scott attacking deeds, or merely habits of mind? Is he attacking the imperfections of others, or does he include himself? Their brevity is full of possibility, and their ambiguities often make them seem larger poems than their word counts imply—yet that very brevity is essential to their delightfulness. Their basic stance is another instance of 'pulling things down', but their national self-denigration is given the most acceptable form possible in the shape of a brief and witty joke. The object of the satire varies from poem to poem. In some, it is simply an attitude of mind which is laughed at:

> *Scotch Pessimism*
> Nae
> Gless.

In others, it is both a complex attitude of mind and a way of behaving:

> *Scotch Passion*
> Forgot
> Mysel.

In others again, a cultural hinterland, explanatory of Scottish idiosyncrasy and bleakness, is pointed to:

> *Scotch Optimism*
> Through a gless,
> Darkly.

This last, with its multiple layers meaningfully interacting, is an example of Scott's pun-making instincts yielding particular poetic gold. Others succeed through the jesting wildness of the punch-line, title and poem clashing explosively in style and context:

> *Scotch Equality*
> Kaa the feet frae
> Thon big bastard.

If there is an over-riding satirical point shared by this surprisingly varied sequence, it is the smallness of the visible Scottish mentality. And that is as solidly a Renaissance critique of contemporary Scotland as one will find: it is a criticism that goes right back to the beginnings of MacDiarmid's cultural revolution—and indeed, in itself, the 'present-day-Scots-are-a-hopeless-lot' attitude underlying the sequence might have exasperated the reader through its clichéd familiarity, in something of the spirit of Morgan's response to 'Deir Deid Dancer'. As it is, the joke is a form that works especially well when it triggers a simple shared assumption or attitude, and in these poems Scott had stumbled upon a particularly effective way of re-expressing the Renaissance judgement on twentieth-century Scotland.

It would be all too easy, however, to imply that Scott's commitment to MacDiarmid's Renaissance resulted in pure negativity—that is, in nothing more than a critical, judgemental attitude to the Scotland he had to live in. As pointed out above, however, he used Scots also because he found that it was a medium in which he was naturally successful. He had discovered that he himself needed it and he naturally believed, with his Renaissance colleagues, that Scottish people as a whole need the language to express their mind-set. Thus there was no question of satire being the only reason for using it: he believed it important that Scots be firmly established as a permanent and central Scottish poetic language. Consequently, he used it in a variety of ways.

The standpoint of Renaissance critique of contemporary Scotland merges, therefore, with his more uniquely personal consciousness of the gulf between a dreamed-of ideal existence and his all-too-vivid sense of the brutal reality of human experience. As already indicated, he first perceived the gulf, with maximum clarity, in the wartime transition from Aberdonian academia to his confrontation with violence and human evil at its most extreme. If he wrote little about the war during the post-war years because, as he pointed out to Alan Bold, he had written about it so much while it was going on, it still left its mark on his writing, in occasional direct glimpses (as in 'Twa Images' from 1949, or 'Front Line' from 1972) but, more pervasively and subtly, in poems which, in a variety of ways, reflect the clash of hard reality with dream or idyll. An example is 'Greek Summer 74', his poem on that year's historic events in the eastern Mediterranean which finally toppled the Greek colonels and created the partition of Cyprus—and which coincided with his own family holiday in Greece.

> Our private paradise
> falls to be part of the world …

Hitler's war had torn apart his childhood haven of Aberdeen; now Greece, the substitute-haven which replaced Aberdeen in his later years, was similarly (if less extremely) blasted.

Not that he wanted to exist merely in his own idyllic world and avoid engagement with reality. Indeed, an engagement with reality is one of his over-riding characteristics as a poet. Moreover, he is realistic both about the world at large and about his own responses to it. Many of his most successful poems are those in which he combines a disillusioned detachment with a heartfelt involvement. In 'Coronach', for example, he opens (as Douglas Dunn points out to me) with an unexpected truculence, an honest, hardened selfishness, a note of thrawn-ness. But part of that honesty is the recognition that his heart is 'thowless'—'useless, spiritless', as he himself glossed the word—in his stubborn self-absorption, a deadness which happily gives way when the appropriate lament bursts through as he finally engages with the dead.

'Heart of Stone', to take another example, gives voice to his love for the city that had been a lodestone for his hopes and emotions during wartime and his early decades of family, poetic and professional life; at the same time it sees the city in all its faults and limitations. Nor is this simply a matter of counterpointing paragraphs of praise with paragraphs of blame. Ultimately, he sees the city as simultaneously bewitching and forbidding, glorious and enticing in its drab greyness and unyielding stoniness. The paradox is in the title, the English of which has puzzled many readers of a poem which seems otherwise to be such a sturdy affirmation of Scottish Renaissance literary Scots. But if the initial English 'heart of stone' seems to point (on balance) to the city's unappealing stoniness of heart, the concluding 'hert o stane' (with its sideways shift into Scots from the bleak standard English phrase) portrays the city, rather, as an outward embodiment of a life at the centre of stone's essence—a soft and nourishing vitality at the core of the 'living rock'. The poem makes the short journey from the English title to the final Scots phrase, and once more a slight shift of sound carries worlds of meaning, the Scots bringing out the ambiguity which was always there in the English phrase.

This pivotal poem was one of his major creative efforts, in which he invested hugely. In it, the Aberdeen of his youthful past and of his adult present combine in a paradoxical balance of affection and criticism. The slightly brittle stance—both loving and outraged—helps convey the (paradoxical) emotional appeal of the city's hardness. It was a poem that came from deep within, the culmination (as he well realised) of decades of trying to write adequately about the place. This explains what photographer Alan Daiches found when he began attempting to 'collaborate' with Scott on the work: it transpired that Scott was not open to the kind of shared exploration which Daiches had so enjoyed while working on the first poems in the television series, those with Sydney Goodsir Smith and Robert McLellan. Unlike them, Scott seemed to see Daiches as there simply to illustrate what was significant to himself: where the earlier writers had re-explored their locations together with Daiches, Scott merely conducted him to the spots which he regarded as important. Admittedly, he then left Daiches to take the pictures, but the photographer had the distinct impression that Scott was drawing primarily on his own memories, and that the poem was already (in some sense) well on the way.[12] On the other hand, in the paragraph about

'Heart of Stone' found amongst Scott's papers, he implied that the visit with Daiches did indeed enable him to look at Aberdeen afresh.

> I went up to Aberdeen with the photographer Alan Daiches, and in showing him those aspects of the town which had special significance for me I was able to look at them again as if I were seeing them for the first—as well as the umpteenth—time. Even so, several months went by before I set pen to paper, while I waited for the subconscious to sift through my many and various impressions of the city and produce the single image which would be both a summation and a starting-point. That image emerged as the gull whose gray plumage matches the predominant aspect of the granite city and the sky above it and the sea around its shore ...

Reality's paradoxes prompt Scott to a paradoxical handling of language: contrasts of feeling charge a poem with poetic life. As a man and as a poet, Scott lived at points of conjunction—whaur extremes meet, one might say. For example, as he entered manhood he had to be an infantry officer responding fully to the demands of the 'real world' at its most brutal, while maintaining a literary life of private creativity and comment. Writing home from the war for the *North-East Review*, he produced a flow of 'reports' which veered across the boundary between journalistic essays and fiction. Throughout his professional life, he was both a creative writer and an academic, never quite disentangling the claims or values of each. His literary broadcasts were partly Reithian addresses to a popular audience, partly academic publishing (in his own eyes, at least). As a dramatist, he aspired to popular success with modern audiences but sought it by striving to create plays drawing directly upon traditional Scottish themes and material: instead of simply giving his dramatic instincts their head, he wrote his plays from the perspective of the literary historian and cultural nationalist. As regards his family and social lives, he was both intensely gregarious and intensely isolated, a loner who needed the circles (his immediate family, and his friends among Scotland's writers and academics) which gave him support but which he instinctively sought to dominate.

These oppositions have their counterparts in his poetry. He wrote poems in both Scots and English from the 1940s onwards, maintaining a commitment to the latter even in the teeth of his own ideological commitment to fundamental Renaissance ideals, and also despite the general view (of which he was aware but with which he was always reluctant to agree) that he was at his best in Scots. Desiring to build on specifically Scottish literary traditions and mistrustful of poetic developments in other parts of the English-speaking world, he nevertheless sought to create a modern poetry which reflected the contemporary world of Scotland—but the result was writing that increasingly failed to engage the attention of the younger writers whose world that was. His poetic gaze was directed both inward and outward: many poems explore and celebrate intensely private feelings and experiences while others react to the most outward features of his time and place. He can be both a thoroughly confessional poet, and a satirist.

Underlying much of this, however, is a recurring interplay between past and present: the present is compared implicitly with Scotland's past traditions, the trials and imperfections of his present experience are contrasted with youthful happiness. Every now and then, also, the past in the shape of war memories fleetingly intrudes. If 'Coronach' and 'Heart of Stone'—both pivotal poems which look back at a past as a means to springboard into a future—seem to be possible illustrations yet again, then so also are various poems from throughout his mature career. Even that first published poem, 'At Summer's End', juxtaposes the bygone summer of youthful freedom and promise with the autumn of brutal reality and the world's cynical manipulation—the coming winter is a 'grim-visaged soldier'. A very different poem, his first mature effort in Scots, 'Untrue Tammas', juxtaposes the sordid, mundane world of everyday reality—the world in which Tammas is addressing his cynical neighbours—with the ideal world he has known in the past and on whose reality he insists. He speaks of a world of wonder and of creativity, where mundane circumstances do not stand between the poet and his ability to write. Again, past and future pivot on the present, and Tammas turns his back once more on prosaic reality to return to the land of comfort and ideal self-fulfilment. (Another reading of this surprisingly ambiguous poem is offered in chapter 2.)

Many of his poems can be thought of as depictions of present-day manners falling-off from a traditional ideal. Thus, 'Sodger Frae the War Returns', in its curious way, judges the corruption of the present (the selfishness and opportunism of the faithless girlfriend, experienced no doubt by many returning soldiers) with the outrage of the heroic warrior—'heroic' at least in that he has put himself in danger's way. As surprisingly often in Scott, the relevant context is an ancient, even classical, one—the experience of the demobbed soldier discovering that his lass hasn't hung around for him is implicitly contrasted with the centuries-old notion that love is the warrior's peacetime reward. How seriously should we read this poem? Can we raise the invited cheer over that 'skelp ower the face' without a qualm?—we hae a problem here.

Less problematic than 'Sodger Frae the War Returns' is 'Sir Patrick Spens: The True Tale', the first of several works in which Scott, in a mood of comic satire, purports to tell the 'truth' behind some hallowed literary legend. *The Last Time I Saw Paris*, *Tam o' Shanter's Tryst*, *Truth to Tell* and *Bruce's Barber* are examples from among the plays. It is easy to read these works as anti-heroic, a modern down-to-earth realism cutting the posturing of the past down to size. Yet they work at least as well when taken the other way: their voice of mischievous satire is perhaps a limited one, incapable of responding to the grandeur of the material it debunks. While Scott would always deny that he himself had been a hero, there is evidence that he could be seriously interested in heroism as a subject for contemplation. In his letter to Sir Herbert Grierson, on winning the Grierson prize in 1946, he had claimed that: 'ever since reading Hemingway's *For Whom the Bell Tolls* I have been fascinated by the problem of modern heroism'. He had gone on to say that on the battlefield the type of heroism he had observed most often was of the reluctant, enduring kind rather than the fearlessly eager sort beloved of the press.[13] And he begins an 'introductory note' to one of his copies of the play *Bruce's Barber* (n.d.) thus:

> This play has been written in order to illustrate the fact that heroic actions, although they are usually initiated and led by persons of heroic character, frequently involve quite unheroic people, who may find themselves playing vital roles in circumstances quite outside their usual experience and capacity. While the presence of such people does not diminish the greatness of the heroic action, it introduces a strain of common-sensical comedy into situations which otherwise might seem almost too histrionic in their grandeur.

The slightness of 'Sir Patrick Spens: The True Tale' might seem far removed from such high-flown considerations, yet its dating in the notebooks suggests, if nothing else does, that Scott's complex sense of modern heroism is an appropriate context in which to view it. It is dated 6 June 1946, an anniversary of D-Day which also saw the recording of 'Coronach' itself, as well as 'Sang for a Flodden', one of his translations from Anglo-Saxon—and the one most directly concerned with the heroism of those who can withstand 'the wecht o war'. Indeed, 'Sang for a Flodden' carries its own comment on the present from the heroic past, though not necessarily a negative one: Scott has clearly seen with his own eyes (and also experienced within himself?) both the cowardice and the heroic endurance which the translation celebrates.

But if, in this cluster of poems, the judgement of the past upon the present is far from simply negative, elsewhere the present shows up badly in the comparison. 'Evensong', from just over a week later, describes a Wordsworthian loss of intensity in his response to nature in comparison to what his youthful self would have felt. The clue, once more, is in the imagery:

> Such moments once, a dazzle of revelation,
> Would dagger the heart defenceless. Now I listened
> Without a wound, accepting the song I was given ...

Have his feelings been numbed, as a result of the violence he has survived? In comparison with his past self, he is now a survivor and observer, rather than the emotionally defenceless youth of his schoolboy ecstasies. A much better-known poem, 'Haar in Princes Street', confronts the lost, directionless, fog-bound souls of the present with implicit denunciation by Scotland's past achievers:

> The past on pedestals, girnan frae ilka feature,
>   Wi granite frouns

They glower at the present's feckless loons,
Its gangrels tint i the haar that fankles the future.

A similar contrasting of a dreich post-war Scottish urban scene with a more appealing past (this time, of Eden itself) is found in 'Blues for *The Blue Lagoon* (Rain in Sauchiehall Street)', which is discussed on p. 191.

A particularly witty example of the poetry of past and present is that thoughtful and good-humoured late poem 'A Gey Flash Gordon', which brings together many of Scott's favourite preoccupations in a Scots of colloquial informality. Like so many of his poems, it is apparently an unexpected poetic response to the daily happenings of life: the poet and his wife are at the annual struggle to get the Christmas cards in the post when a television repeat of the 1930s serial *Flash Gordon: Space Soldiers* not only distracts him but also sets his imagination doubly going—and looking back. Partly it is the re-encounter with this crude and childish entertainment of his boyhood which brings back the past, and partly it is his ever-punning mind which makes of the name 'Flash Gordon' a joke which only a slick-minded north-east Scot is liable to come up with. And the joke summons up both his own wartime exploits, and the whole world crisis of the 1930s and '40s, in neat contrast to his present middle-aged domesticity and the comfortable security of his married life. What pleases about the poem is the ingenuity with which such disparate elements are brought into confident relationship, and the only-half-serious musings about the parallels between the simplistic Flash Gordon story and modern history. Even more, however, it offers (from an utterly unpredictable perspective) a picture of a happy and mature married life, the dangers and the childish tastes of the past serving primarily to underscore the satisfying domesticity of the present. And although in no way part of the poem, there is an added piquancy in one's awareness that the year following this happily grumbled-about Christmas will bring the first news of the emphysema which would dominate, and shorten, the rest of his life.

'Grace Ungraced' is a sadder poem and was Scott's last of any length although still written seven years before he died. It was both a spontaneous response to the television screen and a reaction to the world he had got to know during more than sixty years. The death and funeral of Grace Kelly in September 1982 coincided almost to the day with the destruction by Lebanese Christian militia of the Shatila refugee camp: both were prominent in the television news. 'Grace Ungraced' is as clear an example as any of Scott's juxtaposing past and present, and also the world's beauty and its horror. Kelly's enchanting beauty in her last film, *High Society* (from 1956—apparently shown on television as a tribute at the time of her funeral) has less power over the poet than his memories of *The Swan* (also 1956): once again, his recollections of a female star provide him with an image of the ideal from the past, juxtaposed not only with her present mortality but also with the far more shocking mortality occurring in Lebanon. Even this last, however, may be taking some of its vividness from Scott's own memories: while television accounts of the massacre were sufficiently stark to account for the fleeting impressions of the final twenty-six lines, one remembers that he too had encountered violence of the kind he describes:

> — flames flender
> bullets blatter
> habberan habberan habberan habberan
>
> feerochs o fire

Once again, the poem is an intensely personal encounter with two extremes of what the world has to offer. And furthermore, it neatly illustrates the two extremes of his poetic Scots, both the richly aggrandised Lallans (its resources of sound fully drawn upon, its perpetually unexpected vocabulary carrying the reader through a wondrous landscape of sound and image) and the demotic Scots of the final section. Kelly's death at least seems part of a fit scheme of things; the Lebanese massacre is far less easy to enfold in a dignified lament, although the return of the aggrandised style, determinedly alliterative, makes a failed attempt:

> In laith Lebanon,
> killed i the cause o coorse Christians,
> laired wi a lauch for lament.

As this attempt to reassert the extended alliteration of the earlier part of the poem shows, in the face of such awfulness it is not so much the musical and imagistic resources of Scots which crumble as the ability to make any coherent statement whatever. Only fragments of sentences, only phrases, become possible. Finally, in the poem's last two lines, something resembling a proper sentence re-emerges and the poet seems to pull himself together once more. Scott's craftsmanship had suffered no diminution, even at this late stage in his career.

If the wartime years saw two major turning points in Scott's poetic development (the embracing of a 'modern' style, and the commitment to the Scottish Renaissance movement) there was an equally important, though outwardly less obvious, turning point fifteen years later—less obvious despite the fact that it was marked by a poetic silence of many years. Scott's surviving family attribute the personal and poetic crisis of the late 1950s and early '60s to his disappointment over his failing career as a dramatist. But that is perhaps a somewhat too narrow way of looking at it. Alongside the purely personal disappointment there must have been an even more disturbing realisation, namely that the Scottish Renaissance, apparently the way of the future during the immediate decade after 1945, was not so certain to triumph as the 1960s revolution emerged and gathered pace. In the immediate aftermath of his First-Class Honours degree, he had been able to write to Maurice Lindsay that: 'at present I am dealing with the article for [*Scottish*] *Life and Letters*, taking as theme the move by most of the younger Scottish poets from English to Scots.'[14] Now, with the loss of theatrical opportunity for the kind of Scottish Renaissance plays he wanted to write, he may well have begun to realise that there was something more behind it than merely the perversity of theatrical management. The times were a-changing and he no longer stood, as a Renaissance poet, in the same relationship with his putative readership. In the late 1940s and early '50s, he had been writing poems in Scots for a Scotland which, he believed, was (or soon would be) receptive to them. Suddenly, the huge shift in theatrical taste revealed that the Scotland of the emergent 1960s was beginning to deny the Scottish Renaissance, and turning its back on the post-war moods which had nourished his early mature creativity. This went to the heart of Scott's sense of himself as a writer.

It is possible, I think, to feel the difference in the poems produced in the two phases, at least if one surveys the *Collected Poems*. Before the later 1950s, Scott had been standing (as it were) alongside his Scottish-Renaissance-persuaded readership as he explored his experience through his poetry. From the mid-1960s onwards, on the other hand, that reader's sympathy was less to be taken for granted and consequently the confrontational and satiric possibilities of his Scots persona became more prominent. As we have seen, the times themselves—the public culture of the 1960s—became for him an issue, and a subject of poetic criticism, whereas in the earlier period the poems (as one reads them) seem to have come to him from farther away, as it were, from a region where thought, feeling and the Scots language naturally co-exist. There is a creative unexpectedness of thought and observation, an openness to the possibilities of the interaction of language and the world, which is what one looks for in successful poetry but which is perhaps harder to find in Scott's poems of the later period. Might the following two poems, superficially similar in subject matter, embody something of the contrast?

Birds in Winter

Winter the warld, albeid the winnock-pane
  Has flouers o frost as bricht as spring's.
The clouds the sea-maws scour are kirkyaird stane,
Gray and cauld and lourd on skaichan wings.

The peerie birds in ilka naukit tree,
  Quaet they sit as cones o fir.
Langsyne they skimmed the lift, stravaigin free,
But grippit in winter's neive they canna stir.

They canna stir. The sea-maws up and doun
  Gang owre and owre and owre the sky.
The peeries wait for death wi never a soun,
The sea-maws rax for life wi never a cry.

[20 February 1947]

Cauld Glory

The lift blae, the laich sun
a louran bluidshot ee,
the cranreuch poutheran perished grun
and sclentan frae ilka tree
in winternichts o steely starns
that stound the harns.

The girss weirs icy threads,
its flouers hae frost as seeds,
ilk leaf gane bare and broun
til scartan Time
is glenteran white as a bride's goun,
sae wapped in a rauchen o rime.
[28 December 1976]

The earlier poem seems to me mysterious in comparison with the more straightforward descriptiveness of the other. 'Birds in Winter' conveys a mind in motion, an observing eye exploring the visible scene, and an utterance in which the Scots has a natural inevitability. 'Cauld Glory', in comparison, is a more rigid poem, and one in which the sounds and the distinctiveness of the Scots have their own purposefulness. Inward and personal as 'Birds in Winter' certainly is, it assumes a reader ready to share with the poet the observations, thoughts and utterance which constitute the poem. In 'Cauld Glory', the reader is confronted—perhaps even challenged—by a language as much as by an observed scene. This brings its own pleasure, of course, but one feels that the scene has been observed, *then* the poem has been made. Is it simply hindsight that makes one feel that there is a self-conscious literariness about the aggrandised Scots we encounter in it?

Both phases contain a great variety of poems, and generalisation is difficult. Yet the period between 1945 and 1957 contains more poems with the haunting quality of 'Birds in Winter': 'Coronach' of course, 'Deathsang', 'Haar in Princes Street', 'Continent o Venus', 'Deathsang for an Auld Man Young', 'The Bricht Bird', 'Blues for *The Blue Lagoon*', 'Twa Images', 'Love is a Garth', 'Reid River', 'Dinna Greet' spring quickly to mind. In the later period, not only does satire loom ever larger but also many more of the poems bend in the stylistic wind and use the conversational Scots discussed earlier. When the theme demands it, Scott will still resort to full aggrandisement, as in 'Mak It New' (which greets what he hopes will be a new generation of makars) and in the poems in memory of Douglas Young, Goodsir Smith and MacDiarmid. On the other hand, poems in English seem to have a greater prominence once more. The shift of Scott's sense of himself as a prominent member of an all-conquering Makars Club to being a poetic Last of the Mohicans was one of the drivers which shaped his poetic career.

Which style was uppermost as he returned to poetic fecundity with 'Heart of Stone'? At first glance the poem is the freshest of starts, and one that reconnects completely with his inspiration and preferred language medium of the late 1940s. Yet for all its vigorous reassertion of his youthful poetic values, it may also be felt as a gesture of defiance, as it celebrates stony endurance in the face of the destructive elements. Granite-like and ornately prominent in his output, it seems in retrospect to be a monument in memory of a lost age in his personal development.

Another driver shaping Scott's career, of course, was his position as an academic. It is one of the assumptions of this book that, at least to some extent, the activities of poet and academic, in Scott's life, were in opposition to each other. There are certainly grounds for thinking that his commitment to participating, in all sorts of ways, in the larger literary life of Scotland acted to the detriment of his academic career. It also seems reasonable to consider, on the other hand, to what extent, if any, his academic teaching and research helped, hindered or in any way influenced his writing of poetry. In a recent study, Robert Crawford has made the case for seeing, as one of the marked features of poetry in modern times, the close association of the academic and the creative. He explores the creative possibilities of the interaction between the two activities, while he himself and his colleague Douglas Dunn are particularly good examples of how it is possible to be, simultaneously, a major poet and a leading academic.

> My argument is that sometimes awkward, but often fruitful links between academia and poetry condition how the figure of the poet has developed in English-language societies since the mid-eighteenth century.[15]

His book acknowledges however, as it must, that there has also been a tradition of antagonism between the worlds of the poet and the academic: the academic drive to judgement and to analysis (at times, perhaps, seeming to use works of the imagination as the excuse for yet more fine-spun displays of cleverness) can easily be seen as something very different from the spontaneous, if thoughtful and intelligent, response that a work of literature appears to ask of a reader. In more practical terms, too, there is no automatic easy fit between the activities of the poet and the academic. While the poet, more often than not earning next to nothing from writing, will sometimes be envious of the usually much better (and more reliably) rewarded commentator on his or her work, it is not always the case that writers given substantial posts in university departments take easily to all the requirements—especially the administrative and assessment requirements—of the position. Douglas Dunn has commented helpfully to me on the practical experience of being a poet with a full-time university position, confirming one's suspicions that one does indeed have to be able to lead two lives to succeed—inevitably, Messrs Jekyll and Hyde were invoked in the discussion, but the image confirms that one has to be both fully a poet and fully an academic.[16] At least one or two of my interviewees (though not Dunn) had a sense that, deep within, Scott was more of the former than the latter. Dunn, moreover, sympathised with Scott in his periods of difficulty in writing at all, and suspects that it can be all too easy for a poet immersed in teaching and research to begin to think of his or her own poetry from an academic standpoint, and be inhibited as a result.

How far, then, is Scott's poetry bound up with his academic thought and work? The answer is, I think, comparatively little. (Some of his plays, on the other hand, seem to have sprung from his academic reading, in particular *Gift to the Queen* and *The Wanton Widow*, about Alexander Scott I and William Dunbar respectively.) A handful of poems, admittedly, have an air of the academy about them. More constant throughout his writing career, but especially in its later stages with the holidays in Mediterranean locations, is his use of classical references. His completion of his undergraduate studies coincided with what is perhaps his most stylistically 'modern' (and so, bookish) poem 'The White Devil' (with its motto from Webster and its sprinkling of references which he feels require footnotes) as well as with his renderings into Scots of Anglo-Saxon poems which he was encountering on his course. Further 'translations', from Derick Thomson's Gaelic, come soon after. The period of his more general teaching of literature, at Edinburgh, coincides with 'The Gowk in *Lear*'. His most footnoted poem, 'Supermakar Story', however, is a parody of the academicism of its satiric target rather than an academic performance in its own right. Beyond this, there are frequent references in his poems to Scottish poets and texts, as one would expect: in this, his academic and Renaissance concerns overlapped. More hidden resemblances to poems from the past also lurk, as in the relationship between 'Benbecula Bear' and Burns' 'To a Louse'.

'Blues for *The Blue Lagoon*' in particular, however, is written with a heavily academic persona, without a hint of satire: its middle section begins with a quotation from T. S. Eliot and responds to the 1949 film in a self-consciously intellectualising way, reading its story as a version of the Fall. It contains more literary references than just about any other of his poems. It is as if the young university lecturer felt a little uneasy about going off to see such a titillating piece of popular cinema and felt that he had to intellectualise it before justifying the whole thing with a poem. It is one of the most important of his poems dealing with the fall from the ideal to reality, from innocence and happiness to the grimy actuality of twentieth-century adult experience. Whether or not he felt guilty about taking an afternoon off to see the film (the second line suggests an afternoon showing), Scott produced a poem that at first glance seems broadly satirical—the first of his major poems about the superficiality of the cinema—but which on examination turns out to be somewhat more personal. For not only does he bring a flashing display of his literary knowledge to bear on the risqué subject-matter, but he also introduces himself in the last line of the first section:

Dowie the croud,
Buttoned coats to haud the rain awa
And faces buttoned ticht fornent their wae—
'Better they grat their grief,' the makar cried.

So the poem develops into yet another treatment of his recurring theme, the loss of Eden, with the toughness of the post-war environment a fitting instance, yet again, of the world's essential nature as he now sees it.

All in all, however, this scarcely amounts to the poetry of academe one might perhaps have expected from such a prominent poet–academic. Scott compartmentalised to a surprising extent. Just as students and colleagues could be surprised that he did not bring his great breadth of reading to bear on the content of his lectures, so readers of his poems encounter poetry from which an overt intellectualism is largely banished. While he was greatly concerned with the condition of contemporary poetry in Scotland, and indeed with the condition of the contemporary world, those concerns did not lead him to apprehend his world in any specially intellectual or philosophical way. It is as if he encountered his age through the television screen rather than through the library. Indeed, he seems to have positively despised approaches to poetry that he regarded as 'academic'. Here, for example, is an extract from a letter to Maurice Lindsay from G. S. Fraser:

> I am in a rather melancholy mood about my reputation as a poet. In a kind of huge encyclopedia of living poets, published by an American firm, of which I got a free copy because I wrote a few contributions myself, Alexander Scott, whom I have never met, but whom you probably know, because he teaches in Glasgow, says I never wrote a good poem after about 1943—all the rest is 'sentimental' or in the worst sense 'academic'.[17]

In a further letter, Fraser returns to the theme:

> I don't know why Alex Scott dislikes me so much. I have never met him (not that I am such a hateful person, if you did meet me). I am just as typically Scottish as he is ...[18]

If Scott did indeed positively dislike Fraser without ever meeting him, we can only conjecture that the feeling arose as a result of the differences in their two careers, when in a superficial sense at least they had started out in parallel circumstances: both bookish products of Aberdeen in the inter-war years. Scott was certainly conscious of him early on: in the letter to Maurice Lindsay from 1947, he says: 'I believe G. S. Fraser has now also turned to Lallans and if you have any of his work that I could use I should be glad to have it, as I haven't seen any Lallans verse of his in print.'[19] But Fraser developed rapidly into a prolific and authoritative commentator on the contemporary British literary scene, someone to whom a vast and detailed intimacy with (apparently) everything recently written in English seemed part of the fibre of his being. He lived and throve in the centre of an established intellectual world, while Scott strove (with others) to build an independent northern bailiwick. Even before he became a paid-up academic in 1959, Fraser produced in the much-thumbed *The Modern Writer and his World* an academically respected account of current trends. Fraser was a Scottish man of letters who did not commit to Scotland but whose 'world' was British and international as opposed to Scott's more local focus. Scott could take a disdainful view of Scottish literati who lived, and thought, furth of Scotland. He and Fraser were clearly chalk and cheese. And if we take Fraser's poetry as characteristic of what Scott thought of as 'academic', then that would appear to mean 'meditatively personal', 'avoiding extremes of emotion', 'lucidly articulate in English', 'safely civilised', etc. Fraser also seems to have been aware of the great differences between his poetry and that of his fellow-Aberdonian, but was capable of viewing the matter generously. In a letter to Scott, Edwin Morgan reported the following:

> Something to pass on to you: George Fraser in a recent letter had a P.S. saying 'If you ever see Alex Scott tell him that I read poems about Aberdeen, including his long one in Scots or about a third of it, recently at Aberdeen Grammar School and took care to say—what is true—what an infinitely finer and stronger poet he is than I am.'
>
> So—let that start off your week for you![20]

Poet–academics such as Fraser, Morgan and Thomson must have appeared to Scott to have achieved the double life with an ease which he knew he was himself far from attaining, both with respect to the increasingly troubling fitfulness of his poetic inspiration and also as regards his struggles to achieve his academic aspirations (both for himself and for his subject). And just as he failed to bring off the academic book on 'the modern Scottish writer and his world', which he and others had every right to expect on the basis of his personal immersion in that world, so he avoided infusing his poetic practice with any of the qualities he chose to regard as 'academic'. One wonders, therefore, if his refusal to allow the 'academic' and the 'poetic' to meet in his poetry worked to its detriment?

It did, in that his approach left him thirled to a particular moment and a particular movement. The process which was apparent by his later years has continued: Scottish writing has moved off in a direction that he largely rejected (largely, though not entirely: Cath Scott recalls, for example, that her husband had a high estimate of the talent of the young Robert Crawford) with the result that he is increasingly ignored by a younger generation as Edwin Morgan is not. In the first years of the new millennium, he is largely forgotten. He is now (merely) part of Scotland's literary history. Nevertheless, the part he played in spreading a knowledge and love of Scotland's literary heritage should be better known. Even more, his poems can still give pleasure and command respect, as is acknowledged by the many contemporaries of his to whom I have recently spoken, and as I have also found in presenting his poems to a younger generation of students. His unique combination of individuality, accessibility, wit and passion can still speak to readers today. The present book is an attempt to encourage present and future readers to engage with him.

Chapter 10

Meeting the Makar

To return, finally, to the man: as much could be written again to supplement the sketch of Alexander Scott offered by the preceding pages. The interviews I have conducted, and the documentation I have consulted, contain innumerable flashes which reveal him. And yet were it possible to combine them all into one readable statement, it would still be no more than a gesture towards pinning down his individuality. In any case, while Scott the private man is an important memory to his family, friends and colleagues, his claim on the attention of a reader is based upon his contribution to the world of his time and that is what this study is concerned with. Furthermore, he is still a powerful presence in the lives of his immediate family, and there is no need to make all of their recollections public property. Not that there any dark secrets from a family life which while imperfect and sometimes strained had at its centre what sounds like an immense amount of love.

It is remarkable, however, how vividly Scott is still alive in the memories not just of his family but of all those who variously encountered him. Whatever their spheres of interest, Scott became a permanent part of their world. I confess that I expected to find many more traces of lingering resentment after all those feuds, all that bitterness and disappointment in his academic career, all those blunt words in reviews, all that speaking of his mind, all those bossy interventions. As it happens, I have spoken to no one who, having worked with him closely over a sustained period, disliked him. Most of my interviewees look back on their dealings with him with positive pleasure; even those who crossed swords with him found that they could get on with him and warm to him. Admittedly, some who encountered him more briefly or superficially were put off by him: he could seem intimidating or exasperating, or possessed of too short a fuse. Many others, however, warmed to his charm—a word used by several.

Many saw, or suspected, a contrast between the outer and the inner man. What Trevor Royle calls his 'roughy-toughy' exterior masked, he believes, a 'softie underneath'.[1] That exterior often consisted of an aggressive manner, and a tendency to see things in starkly black-and-white terms. His bluntness and directness could be startling, and his general manner domineering. Yet one could accept his honesty for what it was, and see it as reflecting his essential innocence (another word used more than once) and his passion for the things he valued and believed in. Even those at the receiving end of his ire could usually detect a trace of principle in his stance, along with all the personal involvement. Not that he was constantly angry—far from it. The abiding memory of Scott, for many, will be of a most agreeable companion, a cheerful drinker, a colleague who, if he dominated every committee or group of which he was part, would enliven it with his jokes, wit and downrightness. Yet the inner and outer contrast was always there, and while all acknowledge the 'hardness' of the exterior several detected a fragility within, a fragility which his family naturally knew better than anyone else.

The gap between the inner and outer man was substantial, however, and several interviewees remember him as one who did not open up readily to others. Rod Lyall says that he seldom let others 'through the guard', while Edwin Morgan recalls his clear reticence as regards certain fundamental aspects of his experience, such as the war, and sexual matters.[2] Morgan was always a little surprised that Scott never commented on the issue of Morgan's sexuality, and is one of those tempted to ascribe Scott's reticence to his Aberdonian origins. Others such as Ellie MacDonald, who also sought to comment on Scott's regional associations, link them to what they saw as his 'old-fashioned' qualities—a certain puritanism in his response to human behaviour, a traditionalism in his views of right and wrong.[3] David Hewitt recalls that he had a strong sense of rectitude and that he would disapprove when colleagues 'mucked around'.[4] There was a stiffness in both the inner and the outer man, which helped give him his powerful, distinctive presence. Sometimes, however, the outer stiffness and the inner softness could combine, to good effect: his military and gentlemanly qualities teamed with his inward sensitivity to enable him to deal with younger friends, colleagues and students in strongly supportive, if paternalistic, ways. Rod Lyall, Douglas Gifford, David Hewitt and Tom Leonard all found themselves benefiting from his fatherly instincts.

The impression made by the 'outer man' was partly the result of his appearance. Nature endowed him with height, with very strong and striking facial features, and with luxuriant hair which, if anything, was even more impressive when it turned silver. And just as he never succumbed to baldness, neither did he become portly as the years advanced. He always wore heavy-rimmed glasses. The result was that he could often look forbidding, as Douglas Kynoch admits.[5] Bob Tait's private phrase for this towering demeanour was 'Wuthering Heights in specs'.[6] His voice, too, was naturally loud, slightly grating and strongly accented: full of character but far from mellifluous (as can be heard in several Scotsoun recordings). And he was always smartly dressed in a well-cut suit—I cannot remember him in anything else, the formality of the suit helping maintain the impact of his hard demeanour. He was undoubtedly vain of his appearance: as Hewitt says: 'Alex knew that, whatever the company, he was always the best-looking chap there.' Douglas Gifford, too, acknowledges a 'sexiness' about him, and both Cath and Crombie Scott have told me of how he would sometimes be propositioned in the street, by strangers of both sexes.[7] At parties, young women would flirt with him. On the other hand, he was always extremely jealous if anyone looked as if they were flirting with Cath.

Did he ever succumb to temptation? It is perhaps not surprising that very occasionally rumours of unfaithfulness would arise. Friends were aware of Cath Scott's occasional nervousness that her husband's natural appeal might lead to complications, but she herself was the one amongst all my interviewees who spoke most fully on this subject. She recalled how, at one point, rumours were indeed put about and traced by her husband to the wife of a fellow-poet: Scott indicated to this source, via a third party, that he was prepared to go to law to scotch the tales which were beginning to circulate. Friends and working colleagues, among those who knew Scott better than most, are confident however that there was never any major episode of unfaithfulness, thanks both to his clear devotion to his wife and also to that 'old-fashioned rectitude' which was part of his makeup. I have discovered no infidelities. That said, all his writings, published and unpublished, juvenile and mature, make clear that Scott took a lively interest in sex. Indeed, the conjunction of sexual energy and puritan instinct was one of his defining tensions, as his student autobiography in particular makes clear. Despite the interest in him of some members of the *North-East Review* circle, and also of the occasional male stranger in later life, he was always strongly heterosexual in his orientation.

Many of the poems suggest a healthy and hearty enthusiasm for sex, as does so much of the unpublished autobiographical material dealing with his young days. His plays, too, frequently invite us to a cheerful enjoyment of sexiness and flirtatiousness. If he himself did not habitually stray towards female attractiveness, his eye certainly did, and he was not ashamed to acknowledge it. It may be that his personal revival in the mid-1960s included a measure of renewed libido, with which his discovery of the joys of Mediterranean holidaying was bound up. At least two Glasgow University colleagues commented to me on their surprise at the sexual element with which Scott would colour his tales as he passed round his holiday snaps. The period of the mid- and late-1960s contains, in fact, various signs of a greater openness in him, for a while, on matters of sex—'for a while', because it looks like a phase that ran somewhat counter to that deeper reticence about sex which Crombie Scott believes was his father's essential nature, inherited from Magdalena Scott's reticent and 'proper' attitude to such matters. The son feels that his father could not escape the Calvinism of his upbringing, even though he tried to.

He adored his wife, and she him, but he could be a hard man to live with. As Cath Scott says: 'Alex got a hell of a lot of his own way!' Just as his academic career was arguably compromised by his devotion to writing, so, at times, was his family life. His wife and sons found themselves living not just with him but with (Crombie's expression in particular) 'his muse'. And when she was unkind, they all knew it. It was particularly unfortunate for the adolescent boys that their years of transition coincided with the worst period of poetic dearth. All three were only too aware of living with a poet, and with one they regarded as having exceptional talent. His literary stature, achieved and implied, was part of their lives, as was his war-hero status: it was as if he towered over them more than physically. If friends and colleagues were aware of his privateness and his unwillingness to open up, so too his family would often find that his preoccupations would set him apart from them. Cath Scott looks back to the Mediterranean holidays, above all, as the times when Alex was at his best as a relaxed companion. Crombie Scott cherishes the memory of those not-too-frequent or extensive times when he felt that he and his father got particularly close.

And yet Alex was no detached intellectual attracted solely by the esoteric. Indeed, he had a great liking for aspects of popular culture. Take the 1960s (and '70s), for example. If one goes by the poems alone, it is easy to feel that Alex viewed the psychedelic culture of the time with a jaundiced, middle-aged eye. And so he did to some extent, but the 'pop poems' convey also a cheerful fascination with the 1960s world, a fascination that friends and family confirm. Crombie Scott recalls that his father rather liked much of what was going on, at least in a superficial way. He watched *Top of the Pops*, with a particular (predictable?) enthusiasm for the dancing of Pan's People. Elton John became his favourite pop singer, according to Donald Campbell, who also remembers Alex's willingness to adopt the latest sartorial trends (bell-bottom trousers, 'flower-power' ties, long flowing hair).[8] There was a powerful populist streak in Alex, and a particular interest in various aspects of popular culture. He had a special fondness for Hollywood movies (both of the romantic and lurid kinds) of the 1930s and 1940s, while another survival of the pleasures of his youth was his continuing love of the Bunter stories of Frank Richards, first encountered in *The Magnet* in the 1930s. These last had been part of the inspiration of his great juvenile breakthrough into creative writing, and in his last years it was his intention to repay the debt (as it were) by writing a critical book on Richards, to which end he purchased reprinted volumes of the Bunter stories. Unfortunately, nothing came of this. Popular science fiction films continued to attract him. Crombie recalls, too, the weekly rush of himself, Ewan and their father to get to the *Eagle* comic, and Dan Dare, first. Alex's pleasure in the superficialities of 1960s trends, however, did not go so far as to embrace the more controversial aspects of that cultural revolution, and the puritan in him disapproved of sexual licence and also of drug taking, though he strove to be liberal and tolerant. Nor did he approve of the more freedom-taking innovations in the literature of the period, such as 'concrete' poetry (as we have seen) or the lyrics of Bob Dylan which Alex regarded as lacking 'craft'.[9]

Finally, however, one returns to his honesty. Most of those who came in contact with him realised that his bluntness, which could be uncomfortable and undiplomatic, was a positive thing. He would speak the truth as he saw it, with an occasional naivety which did not always stand him in good stead but which many, on reflection, realised was a strength. But if bluntness was salient in the outer man, the inner man had a vulnerability which was far from immediately obvious. Those who sensed it, however, usually saw it as part of his appeal. His physical and charismatic prominence, matched with his downrightness, made him an easy target for mimics and for the occasional snide comment. He was involved in too many squabbles. Yet it has become clear to me that the great majority of those who think back on him (as I have asked so many to do) find that they recall him as someone they are extremely glad to have known. Alex himself, however, does not seem to have cared much about how people were going to remember him. What he worried about was how people were going to remember his poetry.

Alex had started smoking when he was a schoolboy and never seems to have been able to stop. Unsurprisingly, his consumption shot up during his war service: Cath Scott recalls that the ration of 110 cigarettes a week was never enough and that she would send him extra ones. No one seems to have doubted that the emphysema, diagnosed in 1977, was bound up with his smoking. He was encouraged to stop—the rest of his family did, to help him—but to no avail. Crombie Scott thinks, however, that his father did at least smoke far less after 1977. For much of the 1980s, he was a semi-invalid. Cath Scott retired early from teaching, to look after him. It was a difficult period for both of them, with Cath finding life increasingly quiet and lonely. They talked about this, however, and she started going to weekly painting classes which helped considerably. It is not clear when Alex knew about his cancer: it seems to have been diagnosed only a matter of three months before his death, but Cath says that she 'knew' much earlier than that, and Crombie thinks that his father did, as well.

The last years before his death saw spells in hospital, and an increasing inability to get out and about. His family agree that his alcoholic consumption increased markedly during this period. He was finally admitted to Stobhill Hospital in Glasgow, where he died on 14 September 1989, surrounded by his family. He was cremated at Maryhill Crematorium; the eulogy was spoken by Maurice Lindsay. His ashes were scattered by his widow in the O'Dell Memorial Garden in King's College, Old Aberdeen, on 2 December 1989.

Crombie knew about his father's cancer only six weeks before he died. During the final spell in hospital, father and elder son grew closer than ever before. Among the last things Alex said to him was: 'In life, you have to take terrible blows'. Crombie does not know what this specifically referred to, but he found it 'chilling'. He recalls, too, how Alex found that the only things he now wanted to read were sea-faring novels by Patrick O'Brian. Travel formed a large part of these final conversations, especially journeys to Greece and the Mediterranean. And so, when the final moments came, it was Crombie who pressed into his father's hand a drachma, to pay the ferryman.

Notes

Notes to the Introduction

1 Whyte (2004), p. 3.
2 Interview with Trevor Royle (8 January 2003).
3 Dunn (1992), p. xxxvii.
4 Herdman (1999).

Notes to Chapter 1

1 Scott, A. (1979), p. 89.
2 National Library of Scotland (NLS) Acc 12236/9.
3 NLS Acc 12236/9, p. 53.
4 NLS Acc 12236/9, p. 152.
5 Scott, A. (1979), pp. 89–90.
6 Scott, A. (1979), p. 90.
7 Scott, A. (1979), p. 100.
8 Interview with William Robertson (14 February 2003).
9 Scott, A. (1979), p. 91.
10 Interviews with Catherine Scott (15 November 2002) and Crombie Scott (9 January 2003).
11 NLS Acc 12236/9, p. 48.
12 NLS Acc 12236/9, p. 57.
13 Scott, A. (1979), p. 93.
14 NLS Acc 12236/12–23.
15 NLS Acc 12236/9, p. 61.
16 NLS Acc 12236/9, p. 57.
17 NLS Acc 12236/9, p. 78.
18 Telephone conversation with the author (autumn 2002).
19 Scott, A. (1979), p. 91.
20 Interview with the author (9 January 2003).
21 NLS Acc 12236/9, p. 104.
22 Scott, A. (1979), p. 95.
23 NLS Acc 12236/10.
24 NLS Acc 12236/9, p. 203.
25 NLS Acc 12236/9, p. 286.
26 NLS Acc 12236/9, p. 123.
27 NLS Acc 12236/9, p. 122.
28 NLS Acc 12236/9, p. 390.
29 NLS Acc 12236/9, p. 357.
30 NLS Acc 12236/9, p. 342.
31 NLS Acc 12236/9, pp. 189–90.
32 NLS Acc 12236/9, p. 195.

33 NLS Acc 12236/9, p. 190.
34 Scott, A. (1979), p. 104.
35 NLS Acc 12236/9, p. 160.
36 NLS Acc 12236/9, p. 180.
37 NLS Acc 12236/9, p. 183.
38 NLS Acc 12236/9, p. 197.
39 NLS Acc 12236/9, p. 296.
40 NLS Acc 12236/9, p. 325.
41 NLS Acc 12236/9, p. 332.
42 NLS Acc 12236/9, pp. 336–7.
43 NLS Acc 12236/9, p. 343.
44 NLS Acc 12236/9, p. 342.
45 Unpublished poem (autumn 1941), NLS Acc 12236/6.
46 NLS Acc 12236/9, p. 347.
47 NLS Acc 12236/9, p. 346.
48 Scott, A. (1979), p. 103.
49 NLS Acc 12236/9, pp. 303–4.
50 Interview with Derick Thomson (7 November 2002).
51 NLS Acc 10374/5 (19 February 1979).
52 *Scots Independent*, 6 July 1968.
53 Interview with Derick Thomson (7 November 2002).
54 NLS Acc 4791/11.
55 Interview with Catherine Scott (29 November 2002).
56 Interview with Maurice Lindsay (10 September 2002).
57 NLS Ms 9334, ff.229–31.

Notes to Chapter 2

1 National Library of Scotland (NLS) Acc 12236/34.
2 Army Personnel Centre, Secretariat Division, Historical Disclosures.
3 Public Record Office (PRO), ref. WO171/1301; WO171/5198.
4 NLS Acc 10374/5 (19 February 1979).
5 Interview with Crombie Scott (9 January 2003).
6 Interview with William Robertson (14 February 2003).
7 NLS Acc 12236/34.
8 Whitaker and Whitaker (2000), p.99.
9 Interview with Donald Campbell (3 September 2004).
10 Hastings (2004), pp. 86–7.
11 Scott, A. (1979), p. 102.
12 NLS Acc 12236/9, p. 312.
13 Scott, A. (1979), p. 102.
14 NLS Acc 12236/32.
15 NLS Acc 12236/9, p. 216.
16 NLS Acc 12236/28, 30.
17 Scott, A. (1979), pp. 103–4.
18 NLS Acc 12236/33.
19 NLS Acc 12236/34.
20 NLS Acc 12236/34.
21 NLS Acc 10374/5 (11 June 1979).
22 NLS Acc 12236/34.
23 NLS Acc 12236/34.

24 Where no reference is given to a poem, it will be found in David Robb (ed.) (1994).
25 See Robb (1999), pp. 46–80.
26 NLS Acc 12236/30.
27 NLS Acc 10374/5 (11 June 1979); Acc 12236/34.
28 NLS Acc 12236/34.
29 NLS Acc 12236/34.
30 NLS Acc 12236/34.
31 Robb (1999).
32 NLS Acc 12236/34.

Notes to Chapter 3

1 Murray (2000), pp. 165–9.
2 Interview with Derick Thomson (7 November 2002).
3 Interview with Maurice Lindsay (10 September 2002).
4 National Library of Scotland (NLS) Acc 4791/11.
5 Interview with Edwin Morgan (5 September 2002).
6 Wright (1977), p. 82.
7 Scottish National Portrait Gallery, PG 2824.
8 Letter of 5 January 2003.
9 Interview with John MacQueen (9 October 2003).
10 NLS Acc 6419 box 38b (letter of 9 November 1948).
11 Glasgow University Calendar 1913–14.
12 Interview with A. A. M. Duncan (9 January 2003).
13 Moss, Munro and Trainor (2000), pp. 223–7.
14 Letter of 21 July 2003.
15 NLS Acc 8144/11.
16 Hook (1998), p. 173; and Crawford (1998), p. 229.
17 Written reply to questions (June 2003).
18 Interview with A. A. M. Duncan (9 January 2003).
19 Interview with John MacQueen (9 October 2003).
20 Moss, Munro, and Trainor (2000), p. 224.
21 Moss, Munro. and Trainor (2000), p. 225.
22 Letter of 5 November 2003.
23 Edinburgh University Library: Maurice Lindsay Papers. MS 2030/31/145–160.
24 Edinburgh University Library: Maurice Lindsay Papers. MS 2030/31/145–160.
25 NLS Acc 12236/7.
26 Reply of June 2003.
27 NLS Acc 12236/35.
28 NLS Acc 12236/35.
29 Interview with Crombie Scott (9 January 2003).
30 Interview with Robert MacDonald and Ronald Jack (15 November 2002).
31 Interview with T. Douglas Gifford (11 September 2003).
32 Interview with Roderick Lyall (24 January 2003).
33 NLS Acc 12236/Additional papers deposited December 2000.
34 Private conversation. (3 February 2004).
35 Written reply to questions (autumn 2003).
36 NLS Acc 12236/36.

Notes to Chapter 4

1 Interview with David Hewitt (16 June 2004).
2 Now, of course, single honours as well.
3 Interview with Roderick Lyall (24 January 2003).
4 Interview with A. M. M. Duncan (9 January 2003).
5 Written reply to questions (June 2003).
6 Interview with David Hewitt (16 June 2004).
7 Interview with John MacQueen (9 October 2003).
8 Information about staffing and about course content is available in the official calendars of the Scottish universities.
9 Interview with T. Douglas Gifford (11 September 2003).
10 Interview with Roderick Lyall (24 January 2003).
11 Letter to the author (25 July 2003).
12 Glasgow University Archives (GUA): Art 1/12 (6 November 1962).
13 GUA: Art 1/12 (4 February 1964).
14 National Library of Scotland (NLS) Acc 11535/2; letter of 13 November 1965.
15 NLS Acc 12236/8; letters from Kenneth Buthlay (25 January and 28 March 1966).
16 Personal conversation with Professor Campbell.
17 Interview with Edwin Morgan (5 September 2002).
18 Interview with A. A. M. Duncan (9 January 2003).
19 NLS Acc 11249; letter from Alexander Scott to Alastair Mackie (28 March 1971).
20 Written reply to questions (June 2003).
21 GUA: Principal Williams' Papers (folder marked 'Gayre Chair of Scottish Literature', letter of 10 December 1985).
22 Interview with David Hewitt (16 June 2004).
23 Interview with Roderick Lyall (24 January 2003).
24 Interview with Ronald D.S. Jack and Robert MacDonald (15 November 2002).
25 Interview with Roderick Lyall (24 January 2003).
26 Email communication (December 2003).
27 Interview with Tom Leonard (17 December 2003).
28 Interview with Jack Rillie (28 June 2003).
29 GUA: Principal Williams' Papers (P698/14, memo of 8 April 1976).
30 Personal conversation with G. Ross Roy (summer 1994).
31 GUA: Principal Williams' Papers (P698/14, memo of 28 January 1976).
32 GUA: Principal Williams' Papers (P28/13, letters of 14 December 1977 and 26 October 1978).
33 Interview with T. Douglas Gifford (11 September 2003).
34 GUA: Principal Williams' Papers (P28/13, letters of 25, 29 October and 9 November 1979).
35 GUA: Principal Williams' Papers (P28/13, letters of 12 and 22 November 1979); interview with A. A. M. Duncan (9 January 2003).
36 GUA: Principal Williams' Papers (P28/13, letter of 14 December 1979).
37 Interview with Roderick Lyall (24 January 2003).
38 GUA: Principal Williams' Papers (folder marked 'Gayre Chair of Scottish Literature', letter of 28 October 1980).
39 GUA: Principal Williams' Papers (folder marked 'Gayre Chair of Scottish Literature', letter of 7 January 1981).
40 Interview with Roderick Lyall (24 January 2003).
41 Interview with A. A. M. Duncan (9 January 2003).
42 GUA: Principal Williams' Papers (folder marked 'Gayre Chair of Scottish

Literature', letter of 15 January 1981).
43 Interview with Jack Rillie (28 June 2003).
44 Interview with A. A. M. Duncan (9 January 2003).
45 Scott, P. H. (2002), p. 276.
46 Lindsay (2001), pp. 209–10.
47 Interview with Tessa Ransford (12 November 2004).
48 Interview with Roderick Lyall (24 January 2003).
49 Interview with David Hewitt (16 June 2004).
50 Interview with Ronald D. S. Jack and Robert MacDonald (15 November 2002).
51 Interview with Roderick Lyall (24 January 2003).
52 Interview with Roderick Lyall (24 January 2003).
53 Interview with Trevor Royle (8 January 2003).
54 NLS Acc 12236/8; letters (n.d.) postmarked 5 October 1970 and 9 February 1973.
55 Interview with Trevor Royle (8 January 2003).
56 Interview with T. Douglas Gifford (11 September 2003).
57 Interview with Roderick Lyall (24 January 2003).
58 Butter (1966), p. 179.
59 Interview with Isobel Murray and Bob Tait (22 September 2003).
60 MacCallum (1996).
61 Scott, A. (ed.) (1952b); and MacQueen (1970).
62 Interviews with Duncan Glen (20 September 2002) and with Philip Hobsbaum (31 August 2004).
63 NLS Acc 12236/27.
64 Aitken (1961).
65 NLS Acc 8144/11 (letter of 11 December 1950).
66 NLS Acc 8144/11 (letter of 2 October 1950).
67 NLS Acc 8144/11 (letter of 14 July 1954).
68 Prüger (2001).
69 BBC Written Archives Centre (WAC) SC 103/58/1 (letter of 23 April 1956).
70 NLS Acc 10823 (letter of 21 July 1958).
71 WAC SC103/58/1 (letter of 23 April 1958).
72 WAC SC103/58/1 (letter of 20 January 1965).
73 NLS Acc 12236/8 (letter of 9 August 1967).
74 NLS Acc 12236. Additional papers deposited in 2000.
75 NLS Acc 12236. Additional papers deposited in 2000.
76 NLS Acc 11249 (letter of 4 September 1975).
77 NLS Acc 11249 (letter of 4 February 1977).
78 Interview with Duncan Glen (20 September 2002).
79 Aberdeen University Archives U.180.2.
80 NLS Acc 6374/1 (letter of 30 July 1970).

Notes to Chapter 5

1 The only complete run of the *North-East Review* known to me is held in Special Libraries and Archives, King's College, University of Aberdeen
2 National Library of Scotland (NLS) Acc 12236/9, p. 236.
3 NLS Acc 12236/28.
4 NLS Acc 12236/32.
5 NLS Acc 10374/5 (letter of 19 February 1979).
6 NLS Acc 11661.
7 NLS Acc 4791/15 (letter of 15 March 1966).

8 NLS Acc 6419/38b (letter of 9 November 1948).
9 NLS Acc 4791/14; 7440/1–2,5–6.
10 NLS Acc 7440/2 (letter of 3 April 1966).
11 Edinburgh University Special Collections: Maurice Lindsay Papers GEN 2030/31/145–60 (letter of 28 April 1972).
12 NLS Acc 6419/38b (letter of 9 November 1948).
13 NLS Acc 6419/38b (letters of 9 November 1948; 9 March and 20 April 1950).
14 Edinburgh University Special Collections: Maurice Lindsay Papers GEN 2030/25 (letters to the *Glasgow Herald*).
15 Edinburgh University Special Collections: Maurice Lindsay Papers GEN 2030/31/201–10 (letter of 5 October 1948).
16 Edinburgh University Special Collections: Maurice Lindsay Papers GEN 2030/31/257–312.
17 Edinburgh University Special Collections: Maurice Lindsay Papers GEN 2030/31/176–200.
18 BBC Written Archives Centre (WAC) SC 103/58/1 (letter of 30 January 1949).
19 Edinburgh University Special Collections: Maurice Lindsay Papers GEN 2030/31/1–11 (letter of 24 September 1948).
20 Grieve and Scott (1972), p. ix.
21 McClure (2000), p. 121. Interview with Maurice Lindsay (10 September 2002).
22 McClure (2000), p. 121.
23 NLS Acc 11808/19 (letter of 23 September 1982).
24 NLS Acc 12236/1 (letter of 17 July 1968).
25 Interviews with Duncan Glen (20 September 2002) and Maurice Lindsay (10 September 2002).
26 NLS Acc 11535/2 (letter of 13 December 1967).
27 NLS Acc 11535/2 (letters of 3 December 1969 and 18 January 1970).
28 NLS Acc 10374/5 (letter of 19 February 1979).
29 Dunn (1992), p. xxxvii.
30 NLS Acc 11249 (letter of 15 July 1980).
31 NLS Acc 11249 (letter of 22 November 1971).
32 NLS Acc 7440/2 (letter of 30 September 1966).
33 NLS Acc 12236/8 (letter of 2 April 1962).
34 NLS Acc 12236/8 (letters of 9 August 1967 and 21 April 1968).
35 NLS Acc 10802/36 (letter of 20 December 1972).
36 Interview with John MacQueen (9 October 2003).
37 NLS Acc 12236/7 (letter of 20 March 1966).
38 NLS Acc 12236/7 (letters of 8 January and 9 and 30 September 1965).
39 NLS Acc 12236/7 (letter of 3 August 1967).
40 Interview with Trevor Royle (8 January 2003).
41 Interview with John MacQueen (9 October 2003).
42 NLS Acc 4791/14/555 (letter of 4 May 1965).
43 NLS Acc 11661 (letter of 4 February 1970).
44 Interview with Trevor Royle (8 January 2003).
45 NLS Acc 10374/5 (letter of 11 June 1979).
46 Bold (1983).
47 NLS Acc 10374/5 (letter of 18 October 1983).
48 Interview with Thomas Crawford (30 September 2002).
49 Interview with Ellie MacDonald (8 September 2003).
50 NLS Acc 11808/19 (letter of 23 September 1982).

51 Glen (1964), p. 219.
52 Lindsay (1962), p. 7.
53 Lindsay (1983), p. 172.
54 NLS Acc 11535/2 (letter of 13 November 1965).
55 NLS Acc 4791/15 (letters of 22 and 25 March 1966).
56 NLS Acc 12236/3 (letter of 5 March 1968).
57 NLS Acc 12236/3 (letter of 8 August 1968).
58 Interview with Edwin Morgan (5 September 2002).
59 NLS Acc 12236/8 (letter of 24 March 1971).
60 NLS Dep 355/208.
61 Bob Tait: written answer to questions (September 2003).
62 Interview with Philip Hobsbaum (31 August 2004).
63 Bob Tait: written answer to questions (September 2003).
64 Interview with Edwin Morgan (5 September 2002).
65 NLS Acc 12236/7 (letter of 7 October 1967).
66 Herdman (1999), p. 28.
67 Interview with John MacQueen (9 October 2003).
68 Interview with John Herdman (13 January 2004).
69 NLS Acc 12236/3 (letters of 21 April and 15 May 1968).
70 NLS Acc 12236/7 (letter of 18 September 1967).
71 NLS Acc 12236/7 (letter of 7 October 1967).
72 NLS Acc 12236/8 (letter of 11 October 1967).
73 NLS Acc 4791/15 (letter of 15 March 1966).
74 Issue of November 1967.
75 Bob Tait: written answer to questions (September 2003).
76 Interview with Duncan Glen (20 September 2002).
77 Interview with Bob Tait (22 September 2003).
78 NLS Acc 12236/37.
79 Tom Leonard: written response to questions (autumn 2003).
80 Interview with Bob Tait (22 September 2003).
81 Interviews with Douglas Dunn (23 September 2003) and Tom Leonard (17 December 2003).
82 Interview with Donald Campbell (3 September 2004).
83 Rush (1983), pp. 43–8.
84 Greig (1983), p. 6.
85 Scott, A. (1984), p. 7.
86 Interview with Tessa Ransford (12 November 2004).

Notes to Chapter 6

1 National Library of Scotland (NLS) Acc 12236/9/74–7.
2 Interview with Crombie Scott (9 January 2003).
3 *The Saltire Review of Arts, Letters and Life* Col. 4, No. 12 (autumn 1957), pp. 23–36. *Scotlands* Vol. 5, No. 2 (1998), pp. 15–33.
4 Broadcast on *Scottish Life and Letters* on 26 May 1968. Typescript in private hands.
5 Broadcast on *Scottish Life and Letters* on 26 May 1968. Typescript in private hands.
6 NLS Ms 26318, f.21 (letter of 22 May 1954).
7 Oliver (1999), p. 23.
8 Campbell (1996), p. 137.

9 Smith (1998).
10 Smith (1998), p. 263.
11 Another version of this play, with the title 'The Lad o Pairts', is in typescript in NLS Acc 12236 Additional Papers (1).
12 NLS Acc 12236 Additional Papers (1).
13 Interview with Maurice Lindsay (10 September 2002).
14 Interview with Donald Campbell (3 September 2004).
15 BBC Written Archives Centre (WAC) SC 103/58/1 (letter of 23 April 1958).
16 WAC SC 103/58/1 (letter of 27 September 1967).
17 WAC Alexander Scott: Personal File 1 (1940–62) (letters of 4 January, 15 February and 29 May 1961).
18 NLS Acc 12236/55.
19 Family copy.
20 NLS Acc 12236/54.
21 NLS Acc 12236/57. Reprinted in *Scotlands* Vol. 5, No. 2 (1998), pp. 15–33.
22 NLS Acc 12236/53.
23 NLS Acc 12236/58,60.
24 NLS Acc 12236/52.
25 NLS Acc 12236/50.
26 NLS Acc 12236/63.
27 WAC SC 103/58/1 (letters of 20 January and 4 March 1965).
28 Interview with Donald Campbell (3 September 2004).
29 *Evening Citizen* (1 May 1954).

Notes to Chapter 7

1 Interview with Trevor Royle (8 January 2003).
2 Briggs (1979); McDowell (1992).
3 McDowell (1992), p. 88.
4 BBC Written Archives Centre (WAC). Alexander Scott personal file— File 1: 1940–62 (RCont 1).
5 National Library of Scotland (NLS) Acc 12236/1 (letter of 2 June 1970).
6 WAC SC 23/407/1, Alexander Scott file 1 (1947–63) (memo of 26 February 1947).
7 NLS Ms 26075, f.32 (letter of 7 June 1966).
8 WAC SC 103/58/1 (Lectures: Alexander Scott 1948–77) (letters of 20 and 22 June 1966).
9 WAC SC 23/407/1 (memo of 6 August 1954).
10 Edinburgh University Special Collections: Maurice Lindsay Papers GEN 2030/30/25–101 (letter of 29 April 1949).
11 WAC RCont 1 (letter of 25 March 1948).
12 WAC RCont 1 (letter of 28 November 1948).
13 WAC SC 103/58/1 (letter of 19 November 1948).
14 WAC SC 103/58/1 (letters of 9 June 1949 and 25 March 1950).
15 WAC SC 103/58/1 (letter of 10 April 1950).
16 WAC SC 103/58/1 (letter of 21 February 1951).
17 Edinburgh University Special Collections: Maurice Lindsay Papers GEN 2030/30/25–101 (letter of 21 December 1948).
18 WAC SC 23/407/1 (memo from George Bruce, 14 September 1950).
19 WAC SC 103/58/1 (letter of 28 August 1960).
20 WAC SC 103/58/1 (letters of 5 November 1961, and 20 January and 4 February 1965).

21 WAC SC 103/58/1 (letter of 2 March 1966).
22 WAC SC 23/407/1 (memo from George Bruce, 8 March 1954).
23 Edinburgh University Special Collections: Maurice Lindsay Papers GEN 2030/27.
24 Edinburgh University Special Collections: Maurice Lindsay Papers GEN 2030/30/25–101 (letter of 18 October 1949).
25 WAC SC 103/58/1 (letter of 12 February 1962).

Notes to Chapter 8

1 Interview with T. Douglas Gifford (11 September 2003).
2 National Library of Scotland (NLS) Dep.355/208. [Except where otherwise indicated, this collection is the source for the information regarding Scottish Arts Council (SAC) deliberations in this chapter.]
3 Minute of 11 September 1967.
4 Minute of 21 April 1970.
5 Minute of 20 November 1969.
6 Correspondence in the author's possession.
7 Calder (2001).
8 Calder (2001), pp. 380, 422.
9 Telephone conversation between Hazel Goodsir Smith and the author (December 2002).
10 Interview with Trevor Royle (8 January 2003).
11 Note to the author (16 December 2003).
12 Interview with Trevor Royle (8 January 2003).
13 Interview with Trevor Royle (8 January 2003). Minutes of the SAC Literature Committee (made available by Trevor Royle).
14 Interview with Trevor Royle (8 January 2003).
15 Copies in the author's possession.
16 Association for Scottish Literary Studies Council minutes, in the author's possession.
17 Interview with Trevor Royle (8 January 2003).
18 Interview with Thomas Crawford (30 September 2002).
19 Interview with Roderick Lyall (24 January 2003).
20 Interview with Ellie MacDonald (8 September 2003).
21 Interview with Duncan Glen (20 September 2002).
22 Interview with Ellie MacDonald (8 September 2003).
23 Interview with Maurice Lindsay (10 September 2002).

Notes to Chapter 9

1 Robb (1994). All poems not otherwise footnoted will be found in this edition.
2 National Library of Scotland (NLS) Acc 12236/31 poem 125. [In thc notebooks, the poems are numbered consecutively through his life.]
3 NLS Acc 12236/34 poem 366.
4 Fraser (1964), pp. 292–3.
5 Interview with Douglas Dunn (23 September 2003).
6 Copy in the author's possession.
7 McClure (2000), pp. 149–57.
8 NLS Acc 7538/2 (letter of 3 November 1965); Acc 7538/3.
9 NLS Acc 7440/1 (letter of 31 May 1965).
10 NLS Acc 7440/2 (notes, and letter of 28 May 1967).

11 McClure (2000), p. 156.
12 Interview with Alan Daiches (17 August 2004).
13 NLS Ms 9334/230–1 (letter of 3 July 1946).
14 Edinburgh University Special Collections: Maurice Lindsay Papers GEN 2030/31/145–60 (letter of 30 July 1947).
15 Crawford (2001), p. 1.
16 Interview with Douglas Dunn (23 September 2003).
17 Maurice Lindsay Papers MS 2030/30/151–3 (letter of 19 December 1970).
18 Maurice Lindsay Papers MS 2030/30/25–101 (letter of 19 September 1973) [misattributed to George Bruce].
19 Maurice Lindsay Papers GEN 2030/31/145–60 (letter of 30 July 1947).
20 NLS Acc 11535/3 (letter of 23 October 1977).

Notes to Chapter 10

1 Interview with Trevor Royle (8 January 2003).
2 Interviews with Roderick Lyall (24 January 2003) and Edwin Morgan (5 September 2002).
3 Interview with Ellie MacDonald (8 September 2003).
4 Interview with David Hewitt (16 June 2004).
5 Letter to the author (10 July 2003).
6 Interview with Bob Tait (22 September 2003).
7 Interviews with T. Douglas Gifford (11 September 2003), Crombie Scott (9 January 2003) and Catherine Scott (15 November 2002).
8 Interview with Donald Campbell (3 September 2004).
9 Interview with Crombie Scott (9 January 2003).

Bibliography

Selected List of Alexander Scott's Publications

Poetry

Robb, D. S. (ed.) (1994) *The Collected Poems of Alexander Scott*, Edinburgh: Mercat Press.

Scott, A. (1949) *The Latest in Elegies*, Glasgow: Caledonian Press.

Scott, A. (1950a) *Selected Poems*, Edinburgh and London: Oliver & Boyd.

Scott, A. (1954a) *Mouth Music: Poems and Diversions*, Edinburgh: M. MacDonald.

Scott, A. (1968) *Cantrips*, Preston: Akros Publications.

Scott, A. (1971) *Greek Fire: A Sequence of Poems*, Preston: Akros Publications.

Scott, A. (1972a) *Double Agent: Poems in English and Scots*, Preston: Akros Publications.

Scott, A. (1975) *Selected Poems 1943–1974*, Preston: Akros Publications.

Plays

Scott, A.(1948) *Prometheus 48*, Aberdeen: Aberdeen Journals Ltd.

Scott, A. (1950b) *Gift to the Queen*, published in *Scotlands*, Vol. 5, No. 2, 1998, pp. 15–33.

Scott, A. (1950c) *The Jerusalem Farers*, published as 'Killer Crusade: A Poem for Voices', *Akros* 16, April 1971, pp. 10–33.

Scott, A. (1951a) *The Last Time I Saw Paris*, published in a shorter form in *The Saltire Review*, 12, Autumn 1957, pp. 23–36.

Scott, A. (1952a) *Untrue Thomas: A Play in One Act, Being a Sequel to the Ballad of Thomas Rhymer*, Glasgow: Caledonian Press.

Scott, A. (1954b) *Shetland Yarn: A Comedy in One Act*, London: Hugh Quekett Ltd.

Other Major Publications

Scott, A.(1951b) (ed.) *Selected Poems of William Jeffrey*, Edinburgh: Serif Books.

Scott, A. (1952b) (ed.) *The Poems of Alexander Scott (c.1530–c.1584)*, Edinburgh: Oliver & Boyd.

Scott, A. (1958) *Still Life: William Soutar 1898–1943*, Edinburgh and London: W. & R. Chambers.

Scott, A. (1972b) *The MacDiarmid Makars 1923–1972*, Preston: Akros Publications.

Scott, A. (1954c) (ed.) *Diaries of a Dying Man by William Soutar*, Edinburgh and London: W. & R. Chambers.

Scott, A. (1978) (ed.) *Modern Scots Verse 1922–1977*, Preston: Akros Publications.

Scott, A. (1982) (ed.) *Scotch Passion: An Anthology of Scottish Erotic Poetry*, London: Robert Hale.

Scott, A. (1987) (ed.) *Voices of Our Kind: An Anthology of Modern Scottish Poetry from 1920 to the Present* (third edn), Edinburgh: W. & R. Chambers.

Scott, A. and Gifford, Douglas (eds) (1973) *Neil Gunn: The Man and the Writer*, Edinburgh and London: William Blackwood.

Scott, A. and Grieve, Michael (eds) (1972) *The Hugh MacDiarmid Anthology: Poems in Scots and English*, London, Henley and Boston: Routledge & Kegan Paul.

Scott, A. and Lindsay, Maurice (eds) (1989) *The Comic Poems of William Tennant*, Edinburgh: Scottish Academic Press.

Scott, A. and MacCaig, Norman (eds) (1970) *Contemporary Scottish Verse 1959–1969*, London: Calder & Boyars.

Recordings of Alexander Scott reading his own poetry and that of others are available from Scotsoun.

Criticism of Scott's Poetry

Annand, J. K. (1971) 'Alexander Scott: An Introduction', *Akros*, No. 16 (April), pp. 3–9.

Bruce, G. (1972) 'The Poetry of Alexander Scott', an appendix in Scott, A. (1972) *The MacDiarmid Makars 1923–1972*, Preston: Akros Publications, pp. 24–7.

Farrow, K. D. (2000) '"Waement the Deid": The Poetic Achievement of Alexander Scott (1920–89)', *Scottish Literary Journal*, Vol. 27, No. 1, pp. 39–64.

Lennox, R. (1977) 'The Poetry of Alexander Scott', *Akros*, No. 33 (April), pp. 60–8.

McClure, J. D. (2000) *Language, Poetry and Nationhood: Scots as a Poetic Language from 1878 to the Present*, East Linton: Tuckwell Press, pp. 149–57.

McCulloch, M. P. (2000) '"I'd Sing my Sang in Spite o Aa ...": The Significance of Song in the Early Poetry of Alexander Scott', *Scottish Literary Journal*, Vol. 27, No. 1, pp. 77–90.

Macintyre, L. (1974) 'Alexander Scott, Makar Extraordinary', *Akros*, No. 25 (August), pp. 71–8.

Robb, D. S. (1998) 'The Plays of Alexander Scott', *Scotlands*, Vol. 5, No. 2, pp. 1–14.

Robb, D. S. (1999) 'Granite's Secret Beauty: Alexander Scott's Other Poems on Aberdeen', *Studies in Scottish Literature*, Vol. 31, pp. 46–80.

Robb, D. S. (2000) '"A Teuch Toun": Alexander Scott's "Heart of Stone"', *Scottish Literary Journal*, Vol. 27, No. 1, pp. 65–76.

Simpson, W. L. (n.d.) *Apollo's Apprentice: Poet's Progress. Pioneer Appreciation of Alexander M. Scott*, Aberdeen: privately printed.

Sources and References

Aitken, W. R. (ed.) (1961) *Poems in Scots and English by William Soutar*, Edinburgh: Oliver & Boyd.

Bold, Alan (1983) *Modern Scottish Literature*, London: Longman.

Briggs, A. (1979) *Sound and Vision (The History of Broadcasting in the United Kingdom, Vol 4)*, Oxford, New York and Melbourne: Oxford University Press.

Butter, P. H. (1966) *Edwin Muir: Man and Poet*, Edinburgh: Oliver & Boyd.

Calder, J. (2001) *Pursuit: The Uncensored Memoirs of John Calder*, London: Calder Publications.

Campbell, D. (1996) *Playing for Scotland: A History of the Scottish Stage 1715–1965*, Edinburgh: Mercat Press.

Crawford, R. (2001) *The Modern Poet: Poetry, Academia, and Knowledge since the 1750s*, Oxford: Oxford University Press.

Crawford, R. (ed.) (1998) *The Scottish Invention of English Literature*, Cambridge: Cambridge University Press.

Dunn, D. (1992) *The Faber Book of Twentieth-Century Scottish Poetry*, London & Boston: Faber & Faber.

Findlay, B. (ed.) (1998) *A History of Scottish Theatre*, Edinburgh: Polygon.
Fraser, G. S. (1964) *The Modern Writer and His World*, rev edn, Harmondsworth: Penguin Books.
Glen, Duncan (1964) *Hugh MacDiarmid and the Scottish Renaissance*, Edinburgh and London: W. & R. Chambers.
Greig, A. (1983) 'Scottish identity: A white elephant in Anstruther', *The Scottish Review: Arts and Environment* No. 32 (November), pp. 3–8.
Hastings, M. (2004) *Armageddon: The Battle for Germany 1944–1945*, London: Macmillan.
Herdman, J. (1999) *Poets, Pubs, Polls & Pillar Boxes: Memoirs of an Era in Scottish Politics & Letters*, Kirkcaldy: Akros Publications.
Hook, A. (1998) 'Scottish academia and the invention of American Studies', in Crawford, R. (ed.) (1998) *The Scottish Invention of English Literature*, Cambridge: Cambridge University Press, pp. 164–79.
Lindsay, M. (1962) *Snow Warning and other poems*, Arundel: Linden Press.
Lindsay, M. (1983) *Thank You For Having Me: A Personal Memoir*, London: Robert Hale.
Lindsay, M. (2001) *Glasgow: Fabric of a City*, London: Robert Hale.
Lindsay, M. (ed.) (1979) *As I Remember: Ten Scottish Authors Recall How Writing Began for Them*, London: Robert Hale.
MacCallum, N. R. (1996) *Sing Frae the Hert:The Literary Criticism of Alexander Scott*, Edinburgh: Scottish Cultural Press.
McDowell, W. H. (1992) *The History of BBC Broadcasting in Scotland, 1923–1983*, Edinburgh: Edinburgh University Press.
MacQueen, J. (ed.) (1970) *Ballattis of Luve*, Edinburgh: Edinburgh University Press.
Moss, M., Munro, J. F. and Trainor, R. H. (2000) *University, City and State: The University of Glasgow since 1870* , Edinburgh: Edinburgh University Press.
Murray, I. (2000) *Jessie Kesson: Writing Her Life*, Edinburgh: Canongate.
Oliver, C. (1999) *Magic in the Gorbals: Cordelia Oliver's Personal Record of the Citizens Theatre*, Ellon: Northern Books.
Prüger, H. (2001) *Journey Without Ending: The Journals of William Soutar*, Salzburg and Oxford: Poetry Salzburg.
Rush, C. (1983) 'Elephants in Anstruther: In search of the Scottish identity', *The Scottish Review: Arts and Environment* No. 31 (August), pp. 43–8.
Scott, A. (1979) 'Growing up with granite', in Lindsay, M. (ed.) (1979) *As I Remember: Ten Scottish Authors Recall How Writing Began for Them*, London: Robert Hale, pp. 89–105.
Scott, A. (1984) 'Pink elephants in Anstruther: Scottish identity', *The Scottish Review: Arts and Environment*, No. 33 (February), pp. 3–8.
Scott, P. H. (2002) *A Twentieth Century Life*, Glendaruel: Argyll Publishing.
Smith, D. (1998) '1950 to 1995', in Findlay, B. (ed.) *A History of Scottish Theatre*, Edinburgh: Polygon, pp. 253–308.
Whitaker, D., and Whitaker, S. (2000) *Rhineland: The Battle to End the War*, 2nd edn, Toronto and New York: Stoddart.
Whyte, C. (2004) *Modern Scottish Poetry*, Edinburgh: Edinburgh University Press.
Wright, G. (1977) *MacDiarmid: An Illustrated Biography of Christopher Murray Grieve (Hugh MacDiarmid)*, Edinburgh: Gordon Wright Publishing.

Index

NOTE: The abbreviation "AS" is used for Alexander Scott. Subheadings under Scott, Alexander have been arranged thematically rather than alphabetically and highlighted in **bold** typeface.